MCSE Elective Study Guide

D1398705

Wave Technologies International, Inc.
MNT4-SGE1-7072A
Release 2

MCSE Elective Study Guide
MNT4-SGE1-7072A
Release 2
©1988-1998 Wave Technologies International, Inc.
All rights reserved.

Trademarks:

ISBN: 1-884486-16-9

10 9 8 7 6 5 4 3

STUDY GUIDE

Contents

Foreword

This Elective Study Guide manual is designed to help experienced candidates prepare for MCSE exams. Each module in the study guide is targeted to a specific MCSE elective requirement examination. The module title identifies the exam to which the module is written.

The material in the study guide focuses directly on the MCSE exam criteria. Background information, examples, and similar aids are not included in the study guide modules. The materials assume that you are already familiar with the materials and are using the study guide as a quick review before taking the MCSE exam.

While it can be used by itself as a preparation tool, the study guide is designed as part of a suite of training materials including self-study manuals, simulations, video segments, and practice exams. It is strongly suggested that less experienced learners make use of all of these materials when preparing for an MCSE examination. More experienced learners will find that their performance on the examinations will improve if they take advantage of all of the available materials.

As reinforcement and review for certification exams, the study guides are particularly effective with the *Challenge! Interactive*. The *Challenge!* contains approximately 200 sample test items for each exam. The sample tests are comprised of multiple choice, screen simulation, and scenario questions to better prepare you for the MCSE exams. It is a good idea to take the *Challenge!* test on a particular exam, read the study guide and then take the *Challenge!* test again. It is useful to take the *Challenge!* tests as frequently as possible because it is such an excellent reinforcement tool.

Module 1—Exam #70-059
Internetworking with Microsoft TCP/IP on Microsoft Windows NT 4.0

Microsoft Objectives

This study guide is designed to help you prepare for Exam #70-059, Internetworking with Microsoft TCP/IP on Microsoft Windows NT 4.0. The following criteria were obtained from Microsoft's Web site as of June 1998:

- Given a scenario, identify valid network configurations.

- Given a scenario, select the appropriate services to install when using Microsoft TCP/IP on a Microsoft Windows NT Server computer.

- On a Windows NT Server computer, configure Microsoft TCP/IP to support multiple network adapters.

- Configure scopes by using DHCP Manager.

- Install and configure a WINS server.

    Import LMHOSTS files to WINS.

    Run WINS on a multihomed computer.

    Configure WINS replication.

    Configure static mappings in the WINS database.

- Configure subnet masks.

- Configure a Windows NT Server computer to function as an IP router.

    Install and configure the DHCP Relay Agent.

- Install and configure the Microsoft DNS Server service on a Windows NT Server computer.

    Integrate DNS with other name servers.

    Connect a DNS server to a DNS root server.

    Configure DNS server roles.

- Configure HOSTS and LMHOSTS files.

- Configure a Windows NT Server computer to support TCP/IP printing.

- Configure SNMP.

- Given a scenario, identify which utility to use to connect to a TCP/IP-based UNIX host.

- Configure a RAS server and dial-up networking for use on a TCP/IP network.

- Configure and support browsing in a multiple-domain routed network.

- Given a scenario, identify which tool to use to monitor TCP/IP traffic.

- Diagnose and resolve IP addressing problems.

- Use Microsoft TCP/IP utilities to diagnose IP configuration problems.

    Identify which Microsoft TCP/IP utility to use to diagnose IP configuration problems.

- Diagnose and resolve name resolution problems.

Choosing the Right Protocol

Choosing a single protocol, even choosing a protocol as part of a set of protocols, is a decision that requires careful consideration. The decision will affect network planning, hardware purchases, system software and application selection, and future development tools.

Some issues to consider include:

- Routability

    This refers to the protocol's support of internetwork communications, passing packets between nodes on different subnets.

- Connectionless/Connection-Oriented

    These terms refer to whether or not communication is based on acknowledgment of data reception.

- Ports and Sockets

    These terms refer to protocol services supporting direct communications between systems within an application.

These activities are implemented at various points within the OSI Model. Your requirements may be different, depending on the applications you are supporting.

Routability

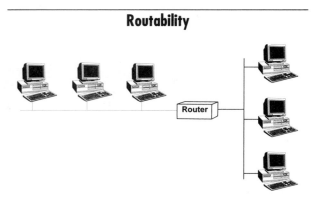

In a Local Area Network, data is sent between nodes using the hardware (MAC) address to identify the source and destination. This is a unique value identifying the machine, or more correctly, its network adapter. Assigned at the time of manufacture, no two machines will have the same address.

This works well on a small LAN but can lead to problems in an internetwork environment. All data packets would have to be propagated to all locations, searching for the destination. To get around this problem, routable protocols provide a secondary, internetwork address in addition to the MAC address. Each station has either a complete routing table or, at minimum, the address of a default router. Packets with a destination not listed in the routing table are passed to the default router. From the default router, the packets are forwarded toward their final destination.

Using Routing

When a station in an internetwork environment needs to communicate:

- The source and destination internetwork addresses are compared.

- If the internetwork addresses are the same, the MAC address is used.

- If the internetwork addresses are different, the packet is forwarded to the appropriate router in the chain. (If no router is specified, the packet will be forwarded to the default gateway.)

- Each router in the chain examines the internetwork address.

- Packets destined for a subnet attached to the router are sent to the destination MAC address.

- Packets not destined for an attached subnet are forwarded to the next router in the chain.

Intermediate routers will have tables of known networks and best routes. These tables can be static, predefined, or dynamic (able to build themselves as the router learns more about the network).

In most cases, you will want a protocol that can support both transmission types. This will help to provide reliable communications with a minimum of overhead traffic.

Connectionless/Connection-Oriented

This is often described as connectionless vs. connection-oriented communication. However, most network environments are best served by a protocol that provides both services.

- Connectionless

    A connectionless protocol is normally used when sending small packets of data, usually less than 1 KB. Reliability improvements in current networks mean that packets are infrequently dropped, and there is usually no need for the increased overhead of acknowledging each receipt.

- Connection-oriented

    Acknowledgment becomes more critical when sending a large amount of information, such as a large data file, that was divided into multiple packets for transmission. This is necessary because of the limits set on packet sizes by lower level protocols.

    In a large network, packets may end up taking different routes to the destination. Some may get lost in the process, or be delayed and arrive in the wrong order. A connection-oriented protocol uses packet sequence numbers to verify packet order and acknowledges the receipt of each packet. Lost or improperly delivered packets, those not acknowledged as a successful receipt, can be retransmitted.

Ports and Sockets

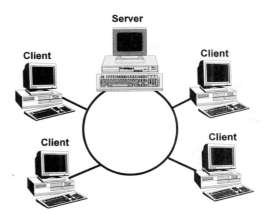

A common use of networks is the implementation of client/server applications. In these, the application is divided into two parts. The server performs background functions in response to client requests. The client provides an end-user interface and a means of communicating with the server. Internetwork addresses are used to direct service requests to the appropriate server and to return responses to the requesting client.

This process becomes more complicated when you consider that both the client and the server are likely to be running several simultaneous processes. Network packets need to contain not only the source and destination addresses, but the destination processes as well. These are indicated through the use of socket and port identifiers.

Using Ports and Sockets

Let's look at an example where ports and sockets become significant: working with file servers. When each user logs on, a session is started and a user connection assigned. Data transfers between the user and the server occur through that connection.

The process threatens to become more complicated when supporting multiple users. Packets must be associated with the proper user. How is this done?

The user is assigned a port or socket number when a service is requested. Packets to or from the user will include that port number as part of the address reference, ensuring that the packet remains associated with the correct user.

Port numbers are also used to identify application level processes. Each network application, such as file transfer and remote login session services, is assigned a different port number. Users specify that port number to attach to the correct process. The server is said to listen to the port, waiting for connections.

Port/socket address support is required for multitasking, multi-user environments.

Making the Choice

Considering that this is a TCP/IP course, it is obvious what we will suggest as the most likely selection as a single protocol. However, there are other protocols that also meet the proposed criteria. These include:

- SNA

  Developed by IBM, SNA has been widely used for communications between IBM systems and between otherwise incompatible systems. Most mainframe and minicomputer products incorporate the ability to communicate with IBM mainframes by design. Other products, such as Microsoft's SNA Server, provide a means for PCs to communicate in an SNA environment. SNA was developed to be a universal protocol. It is a well-documented protocol. Unfortunately, it is under total control of one manufacturer—IBM.

- IPX/SPX (XNS)

  The IPX/SPX protocol stack is the default protocol for Novell's NetWare. The stack is based on Xerox XNS, the original local area networking protocol. IPX/SPX is fast and flexible, meeting the criteria we've listed. However, the stack lacks some of the sophistication many applications and heterogeneous networks require. It has been unable to find acceptance among mainframe and minicomputer applications.

- DECnet

  Digital has also developed its own protocol meeting our criteria. DECnet is a prerequisite for all computer networks based on Digital equipment, however it has not found acceptance among other manufacturers.

- TCP/IP

  Currently the de facto standard for internetwork communications, TCP/IP is the most commonly implemented single protocol solution. Though not meeting all network communication requirements, it provides a good fit for most situations.

Most manufacturers have OSI-compliant stacks available, or at least theoretically compliant, since many have not been implemented to any great extent. Even those who provide OSI compliant stacks have only fully defined them at the lower levels.

TCP/IP Definition

Graduate students at the four pilot universities were asked to define the original ARPANET protocols. Convinced that a group of professionals would take over the project at any time, they were careful not to be too assertive in their early specifications, for fear of offending the professionals. With this in mind, the early documents were labeled RFC (Request for Comments) indicating that anybody could contribute anything and that nothing was official.

When it was obvious that no professional team was taking over, the RFCs became the defining documents that set the standards for the Internet protocol suite. TCP and IP are both defined by RFCs. RFCs are also used for information and guidance notes. There are even April Fool's RFCs created on a regular basis as Internet comic relief.

Unlike most documents defining protocol standards (for example, those created by the CCITT), RFCs are remarkably easy to read and understand. This is due to the fact that they were designed to provoke comments from the widest possible audience. RFCs can be obtained by FTP from a number of servers on the Internet. You may also request RFCs by standard mail from:

>DDN Network Information Center
>
>SRI International
>
>Room EJ291
>
>333 Ravenswood Avenue
>
>Menlo Park, CA 94024

It is RFCs, and the culture that underlies them, that are TCP/IP's real strength. When new enhancements or additions to TCP/IP are needed, someone will create a new RFC. After it has been published and any amendments or suggestions incorporated, it becomes an official protocol standard. This mechanism allows for easy change. Upgrades and improvements can be incorporated rapidly, allowing for quick adaptation to meet changing requirements.

Off the Internet

Because TCP/IP is not owned by any one organization or corporation, but accepted by almost all computer systems, it has value beyond the Internet. TCP/IP has become the obvious first choice for interconnectivity problems. The following is only a partial list of supported systems:

- MS-DOS PCs and compatibles
- Microsoft Windows-family PCs and compatibles (including NT)
- OS/2 PCs and compatibles
- Apple Macintosh
- Novell NetWare
- Banyan VINES
- DEC VAX VMS and ULTRIX
- IBM AS/400
- IBM VM or MVS mainframes
- UNIX-based systems

Though TCP/IP may not meet all networking needs, it fills the communication and connectivity requirements of most organizations.

Microsoft has been a primary driving force in putting TCP/IP on the desktop and into general use on Local Area Networks. Requirements for a powerful, flexible communications protocol will continue to grow as intelligent devices, including appliances, become the rule. It is likely that we will soon see home networks become as common as business networks are now.

TCP/IP and OSI

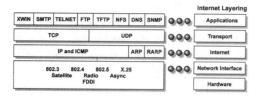

TCP/IP is based on a five-layer architectural model. This model has no equivalent to the OSI Presentation and Session layers. This is also referred to as the DoD (Department of Defense) reference model.

Hardware (Layer 1)

The Hardware Layer is equivalent to the OSI Physical Layer. This is where physical aspects of transmitting and receiving packets are defined.

Network Interface (Layer 2)

This layer describes the physical connection medium between hosts. It is responsible for packet frame content over different interfaces and low-level protocols. Protocols fall into two distinct categories, those associated with LANs and those associated with WANs. Common LAN protocols include Ethernet, Token Ring, and Token Bus. Common WAN protocols include Serial Line Internet Protocol (SLIP), Point-to-Point Protocol (PPP), X.25, Integrated Digital Services Network (ISDN), and Fast Packet Systems.

Internet (Layer 3)

This layer works like the OSI Network Layer and is responsible for routing packets between different hosts and networks. Protocols included in this layer are Internet Protocol (IP), the Internet Control Message Protocol (ICMP), Address Resolution Protocol (ARP), and the Reverse Address Resolution Protocol (RARP). Routing protocols also reside at this layer. Two of the significant ones are Routing Information Protocol (RIP) and Open Shortest Path First (OSPF).

Transport (Layer 4)

The Transport Layer is also called the Host-to-Host or Service layer. It is equivalent to the OSI Transport Layer, with some features of the Session Layer included. There are two protocols at this layer, Transmission Control Protocol (TCP) and User Datagram Protocol (UDP). They are responsible for end-to-end integrity of data packets transmitted across the network, supporting options for both connection-oriented and connectionless communication. They also provide communication with the higher-level application protocols.

Application (Layer 5)

The Application Layer, also called the Process Layer, is equivalent to OSI Model layers 5 through 7. An ever-increasing number of protocols have been defined at this layer. Each of these is designed to support a particular application requirement. Significant applications, which were part of the original design goals, include File Transfer Protocol (FTP), Terminal Network emulation (TELNET), and the Simple Mail Transfer Protocol (SMTP). Additional applications include Simple Network Management Protocol (SNMP), Domain Name Services (DNS), and the Network File Services (NFS).

TCP/IP applications usually conform to the client/server model. For that reason, they come in two parts, a client application and a server application, commonly known as a daemon. Application protocols define the communication format between the client and server processes.

TCP/IP Suite

All TCP/IP protocols are defined through RFCs, as mentioned earlier. The specification documents are part of the public domain. They may be acquired and reproduced free of charge.

Core protocols, utilities, and services associated with the TCP/IP suite include:

- IP (Internet Protocol)

    IP provides packet routing and delivery between computer systems. Since it is a connectionless protocol, there is no guarantee of proper sequencing or even arrival at the destination. Higher-level protocols are required to ensure data integrity and proper sequencing.

- TCP (Transmission Control Protocol)

    TCP provides acknowledged, connection-oriented communications. It includes fields for packet sequencing and acknowledgment, as well as source and destination socket identifiers to allow communications with higher-level protocols. Through these, TCP provides guaranteed delivery, proper sequencing, and data integrity checks. Should errors occur during transmission, TCP is responsible for re-transmitting the data.

- ICMP (Internet Control Message Protocol)

    ICMP is used to control and manage information transmitted using TCP/IP. It allows nodes to share status and error information. This information can be passed to higher-level protocols, informing transmitting stations of unreachable hosts and providing insight into the detection and resolution of transmission problems. ICMP also helps to re-route messages when a route is busy or has failed.

- ARP/RARP (Address Resolution Protocol/Reverse Address Resolution Protocol)

    ARP and RARP are maintenance protocols. They are used on Local Area Networks to enable hosts to translate IP addresses to the low-level MAC addresses that are needed to communicate at the Data Link level.

    ARP is used to request a station's MAC address when only its IP address is known. Once obtained, this information is stored in the requesting system's ARP cache for later use. Since the information can be broadcast, it can also be used to update other systems. RARP is used when the MAC address is known, but not the IP address. Updated information, when received, is also cached.

- UDP (User Datagram Protocol)

    UDP is designed for connectionless, unacknowledged communications. Using IP as its underlying protocol carrier, UDP adds information about the source and destination socket identifiers. UDP also supports optional checksums for verifying header and data integrity.

- TELNET

    TELNET may be more accurately described as a connectivity utility. It is a simple remote terminal emulation application, allowing one host to connect to and run a session on another. Variants have been implemented to handle different terminal data streams. For example, there are 3270 and 5250 variants for communications with IBM mainframe and minicomputers. TELNET uses TCP for acknowledged communications.

- FTP (File Transfer Protocol)

    FTP supports file transport between dissimilar systems. TELNET is used for initial user authentication. FTP supports interactive use. Assuming sufficient rights, directory searches and file operations are supported, as well as file format and character conversion.

- SMTP (Simple Mail Transfer Protocol)

    SMTP provides a mechanism for the exchange of mail information between systems. It is not concerned with the mail format, just the means by which it is transferred. SMTP is the most widely used service on the Internet.

- SNMP (Simple Network Management Protocol)

    SNMP uses UDP to send control and management information between TCP/IP hosts. SNMP can collect management statistics and trap error events from a wide selection of devices on a TCP/IP network. An SNMP management station gives you the capabilities of remote device control and parameter management.

- DNS (Domain Name System)

    Through DNS, a common naming convention is provided throughout the Internet. It is implemented as a distributed database supporting a hierarchical naming system. DNS requires a static name-to-IP address mapping.

- NFS (Network File Services)

    NFS is the industry standard for UNIX environment distributed file systems. It provides a common, transparent environment in which users can share files, regardless of their hardware platform.

TCP/IP at the Desktop

TCP/IP is accepted as the standard for internetwork communications. Its popularity at the desktop continues to grow. However, TCP/IP was not designed for use with PCs. In fact, PCs didn't exist when TCP/IP was developed. This has led to some potential problems.

- Population size

    TCP/IP was designed for use with a limited population, mainframes and minicomputers. The large number of PCs in modern networks leads to problems, allocating unique IP addresses and may eventually create an address shortage.

- Portability

    PCs, by design, are portable. They can move easily between different physical locations. This means that they can be moved between logical subnets. This, in turn, requires reconfigured IP addresses, or the need for dynamic address management.

- End users

   The average PC user lacks the sophistication required to fully understand IP address and subnetting concerns. This can sometimes lead to errors in address and configuration parameters.

Manufacturers, including Microsoft, have developed products and procedures to help work around these problems and simplify TCP/IP management.

Microsoft Implementations

Microsoft supplies full support for TCP/IP in its Windows-family products. Features supported by Windows NT include:

Core TCP/IP protocols
   This includes support for TCP, IP, UDP, ARP, and ICMP.

Application interface support
   Support is provided for Windows Sockets 1.1, RPC, NetBIOS, and Network DDE. These interfaces make it easy to *plug in* third-party TCP/IP products and utilities.

Connectivity utilities
   A full set of connectivity utilities are supported, including finger, ftp, lpr, rexec, rsh, telnet, and tftp.

Diagnostic tools
   Available diagnostic tools include: ARP, HOSTNAME, IPCONFIG, LPQ, NBTSTAT, PING, ROUTE, and TRACERT.

Network services
   Service support and administrative tools are provided for Windows Internet Name Service (WINS), Dynamic Host Configuration Protocol (DHCP), Domain Name System (DNS), and TCP/IP printing services.

SNMP   Windows NT stations can be managed through SNMP management tools.

TCP/IP support is also bundled with Windows 95 and available for Windows for Workgroups 3.x.

Terms and Concepts

Let's start with some basic terms and concepts.

Packet

Information being sent across the network is referred to as a packet. A message will often contain several packets, which must be delivered in order with the data intact. Upper-level protocols, TCP and UDP, are used to help ensure proper delivery and sequencing.

Protocol

A protocol is a set of rules defining how two processes communicate. The TCP/IP suite contains multiple protocols, each with its own packet type.

Host

Also referred to as an end node, the term host refers to the devices configured as part of the network. It acts as the destination for an IP packet. Hosts can include mainframes, minicomputers, workstations, file servers, and even intelligent peripheral devices such as printers.

Address

Each node must have a unique address to communicate via TCP/IP. The address must follow the IP address format. The four-octet IP address identifies the host and the network on which that host resides. Each host will also have a six-byte MAC (Media Access Control) address, which is encoded on the network adapter.

Names

Each host will also have a unique name. A common method for managing names is Domain Name System (DNS). DNS servers map IP addresses to DNS names. Microsoft networks also use a NetBIOS-based naming convention, with support provided through a name file or dynamically through the Windows Internet Naming Service (WINS).

Routers

Routers connect networks together, using the network portion of the IP address to identify the appropriate subnet. Once located by passing the packet to a router directly connected to the network, the packet is delivered using the host address.

Binary Numbers and IP Addresses

IP addresses are based on 32-bit addresses which are written in dotted decimal notation. The Windows calculator performs decimal-to-binary and binary-to-decimal conversions. However, you might not always have a calculator handy to perform the conversion for you. This appendix steps you through some of the basics of working with binary numbers.

A binary number is made up of a series of bits, binary digits. Each bit can be set to either 0 or 1. Bit values are based on powers of 2 and based on the digit position. Since IP addresses are grouped in octets, sets of eight bits, let's look at the position values for an octet.

Position	8	7	6	5	4	3	2	1
Power of 2	2^7	2^6	2^5	2^4	2^3	2^2	2^1	2^0
Decimal Value	128	64	32	16	8	4	2	1
	MSB							LSB

The left-most bit is considered the most significant bit (MSB). The right-most is considered the least significant bit (LSB).

It may be easier to see how this works looking at a more familiar numbering system:

104	103	102	101	100
10,000	1000	100	10	1

Decimal numbers are managed in the same fashion, with the right-most digit representing 1s, the next 10s, the next 100s, and so on.

Combinations

Before moving into conversions, we need to mention number combinations. This is an important consideration when determining IP address and subnet requirements. The number of unique combinations you can create depends on the number of bits you have available. With one bit, you can have 0 or 1; two combinations. Two bits allows 00, 01, 10, and 11; a total of four combinations.

# of bits	1	2	3	4	5	6	7
# of combinations	2	4	8	16	32	64	128

This is the total number of possible combinations. When figuring available addresses, however, you have to remember that values with all zeros or all ones are not allowed.

# of bits	1	2	3	4	5	6	7	8
# of address combinations	0	2	8	14	30	62	126	254

Refer to the addressing and subnetting information in the training manual for additional information on IP addresses.

Binary to Decimal

To convert binary to decimal, determine the decimal value for each of the bits. Add up the bit values and you have the decimal number. Let's look at some examples:

11000000	11011010	10011101	00000011	11111111

1	1	0	0	0	0	0	0
128	64	32	16	8	4	2	1
128	64	0	0	0	0	0	0

The decimal value is 128+64, or 192.

1	1	0	1	1	0	1	0
128	64	32	16	8	4	2	1
128	64	0	16	8	0	2	0

The decimal value is 128+64+16+8+2, or 218.

1	0	0	1	1	1	0	1
128	64	32	16	8	4	2	1
128	0	0	16	8	4	0	1

The decimal value is 128+16+8+4+1, or 157.

0	0	0	0	0	0	1	1
128	64	32	16	8	4	2	1
0	0	0	0	0	0	2	1

The decimal value is 2+1, or 3.

1	1	1	1	1	1	1	1
128	64	32	16	8	4	2	1
128	64	32	16	8	4	2	1

The decimal value is 128+64+32+16+8+4+2+1, or 255.

Decimal to Binary

There are different methods you can use to convert decimal into binary. One is to set up a table similar to the one shown below.

128	goes into	_____	___	times, leaving	_____
64	goes into	_____	___	times, leaving	_____
32	goes into	_____	___	times, leaving	_____
16	goes into	_____	___	times, leaving	_____
8	goes into	_____	___	times, leaving	_____
4	goes into	_____	___	times, leaving	_____
2	goes into	_____	___	times, leaving	_____
1	goes into	_____	___	times, leaving	_____

The fourth column provides bit values, with the MSB on top. Let's look at one of our earlier examples, 157:

128	goes into	157	1	times, leaving	29
64	goes into	29	0	times, leaving	29
32	goes into	29	0	times, leaving	29
16	goes into	29	1	times, leaving	13
8	goes into	13	1	times, leaving	5
4	goes into	5	1	times, leaving	1
2	goes into	1	0	times, leaving	1
1	goes into	1	1	times, leaving	0

This gives a value, reading top to bottom of 10011101, which agrees with the earlier example.

AND

Another concept you need to understand is logical AND. In a logical AND, you compare two values. The following are your possible results:

0 AND 0 = 0	0 AND 1 = 0
1 AND 0 = 0	1 AND 1 = 1

Logical AND is used to find the subnet address value from an IP address. Let's look at the last octet of the address, for simplicity's sake. You have an IP address of 199.121.30.67 and a subnet mask of 255.255.255.192. Looking at the last octet:

192	1	1	0	0	0	0	0	0
67	0	1	1	0	0	0	1	1
	0	1	0	0	0	0	0	0

This give you a value of 64, or a full subnet address of 199.121.30.64.

IP Address Fundamentals

Each host is assigned a unique IP address for each network connection (installed network adapter). The IP address is used to identify a packet's source and destination hosts.

An IP address is a 32-bit address, written as four octets (bytes) separated by periods. For example:

195.143.67.2

This way of representing an IP address is also known as dotted decimal notation. Each address will also have an associated subnet mask, dividing the address into its network prefix and host suffix. For example, you might have the following defined as a subnet mask:

255.255.255.0

The subnet mask is used to identify the network and host portions of the address.

Network	Host

As stated earlier, the network portion identifies where the host is located, and the host portion identifies the device connected to that network.

IP Address Coordination

Address assignments on the Internet must be carefully coordinated. With millions of hosts operating on thousands of networks, the potential for duplicate addresses is significant. The job of coordinating IP addresses is given to the Network Information Center.

If you are connected to the Internet, your network address will be assigned to you through the Internet Network Information Center (InterNIC). An assigned address is only required if your network is connecting to the Internet.

To get your own address, contact InterNIC at:

InterNIC Registration Services

c/o Network Solutions, Inc.

505 Huntmar Park Drive

Herndon, Virginia 22070

(703) 742-4777

hostmaster@internic.net

An organization is assigned a network address. The organization can further divide this into its own subnets and assign host addresses.

Rather than going to InterNIC, an organization will more likely work through a local provider for address assignment. The organization will then subdivide the address, if necessary, and assign host addresses. There are five classes, or levels, of IP addresses defined.

Why Subnets?

Why divide a network into subnets?

The primary reason relates to network performance and available bandwidth. Without separate networks, each transmission would be broadcast across the internetwork, waiting for the destination system to respond. As the network grows, traffic increases until it exceeds the available bandwidth.

When a network is divided into subnets, all members of that subnet will have the same network prefix. Routers divide the networks and provide communications between the networks. Packets bound for a destination within the local network are kept local. Only packets bound for other networks are propagated across the network, moving from router to router. Overall traffic levels are reduced.

Organizing Addresses

Before looking at how IP addresses are implemented, let's take a look at some theoretical limits. Keep in mind, these are theoretical maximums only. In practical applications, the values are significantly reduced. The following section will focus on these practical values.

If all the available bits in an address were used for host addresses, 32 address bits would support some four billion hosts.

    hhhhhhhh.hhhhhhhh.hhhhhhhh.hhhhhhhh

The problem is, all of the systems would be on a single network. This would result in a situation similar to four billion people trying to talk at the same time.

As already mentioned, TCP/IP gets around this through subnetting. If the first octet were given to network addresses, you could, in theory, support 256 networks and about 16 million hosts on each.

    nnnnnnnn.hhhhhhh.hhhhhhhh.hhhhhhh

This would result in some obvious problems. One, you still have a very limited number of networks, and you still have a very large number of hosts on each network.

The size of each network can be decreased further by dedicating two octets to the network address and two octets to the host address. You could then support 65,536 networks with 65,536 hosts each.

    nnnnnnnn.nnnnnnnn.hhhhhhhh.hhhhhhhh

Large organizations would likely find this a more appropriate solution, but for most businesses, this affords far more host addresses than required.

Taking the process one more step, the first three octets could be dedicated to the network address.

    nnnnnnnn.nnnnnnnn.nnnnnnnn.hhhhhhhh

Potentially, this would support up to 16 million networks with 256 hosts on each.

Remember that these are theoretical maximums. Real-world values are smaller.

Obviously, no one solution meets every organization's needs. IP addresses have been set up to support different levels of addressing called address classes.

Address Classes

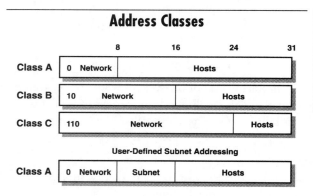

IP Addresses

This section introduces IP address classes and the concept of subnet masks. The following topics will be covered in this section:

- IP Address Classes
- Class A Network
- Class B Network
- Class C Network
- Special Addressing
- Private Internets

It is important that you understand how IP addresses are organized. You will need this information when implementing and troubleshooting TCP/IP.

IP Address Classes

Five address classes are supported (A-E). Only Classes A, B, and C are assigned to the general user community. Class D addresses are reserved for multicasting and Class E addresses are reserved for experimental purposes. A value of 127 in the first octet is reserved for loopback testing.

Class	Opening Bits	Default Subnets Mask	Network Range	# of Networks	# of Hosts per Network
A	0	255.0.0.0	1-126	126	16,777,214
B	10	255.255.0.0	128.0-191.255	16,384	65,534
C	110	255.255.255.0	192.0.0-223.255.255	2,097,152	254
D	1110	N/A	224-239	N/A	N/A

Your subnet mask is restricted by your choice of network ID. With a Class A network, your subnet mask must be at least 8 bits long. A Class B subnet mask must be at least 16 bits long and a Class C address must be at least 24 bits long.

All Class A addresses are already allocated, and Class B addresses are difficult to obtain. New connections to the Internet are assigned Class C addresses. If this does not meet an organization's needs, multiple Class C addresses are assigned.

Even if you are not planning to connect to the Internet, you must select an IP address from the appropriate class to provide the host address range required. This decision should not be made lightly. You may decide you need to connect to the Internet at a later date. A Class B address is flexible, but conversion to multiple Class C addresses in the future, if necessary, will likely be difficult.

Class A Network

In a Class A network, the first octet defines the network portion of the address. The last three octets are used for subnet masking and host addresses.

In the first octet, the first (also called the most significant or high order) bit must be set to zero. Only the seven least significant bits are used for addressing, and may be set to either zero or one. This defines 128 Class A networks with network addresses ranging from 0 to 127. Out of these, only 126 are useable. Addresses 0 and 127 are reserved.

A default subnet mask of 255.0.0.0 is assigned for a Class A network. This means that you may not change the value of any number positioned in the first octet, the assigned network address. The octet is masked since this number cannot be changed, once assigned.

Class A networks support up to 16,777,214 (2^{24}-2) hosts. You cannot use .0.0.0 or .255.255.255 as the host portion of the address. A host address of all 0s means "this network" and a host address of all 1s means "broadcast to all nodes."

Class B Network

In a Class B network, the first two octets are used for the network address. The last two octets are used for subnetting and host addresses.

The most significant bit of the first octet must be set to one. The second most significant bit must be set to zero. The next fourteen bits are used for addressing purposes. This gives us 16,384 Class B networks, ranging from 128.0 to 191.255.

A default subnet mask of 255.255.0.0 is assigned for a Class B network. This says that we may not change the value of any number positioned in the first two octets.

Class B networks support 65,534 (2^{16}-2) hosts. The values of all 0s or all 1s cannot be used as address values. A host address of all 0s means "this network" and a host address of all 1s means "broadcast to all nodes."

A Class B address is often used when setting up a moderate- to large-sized network. You can do this as long as you are not connecting to the Internet, are connecting through a firewall or some other means of isolating your network, or already have a Class B address assigned by InterNIC.

Class C Network

In a Class C network, the first three octets are used for the network address. The last octet is used for subnetting and host addresses.

The first two bits of the first octet must be set to one, and the following bit must be set to zero. The following five bits in the first octet, plus the following sixteen bits from the next two octets are used to determine the network address. This provides 2,097,152 Class C networks, ranging from 192.0.0 to 223.255.255.0.

A default mask of 255.255.255.0 is assigned to a Class C network. This means that the value of any number positioned in the first three octets cannot be changed.

Class C networks support 254 (2^8-2) hosts. This number is derived from the value of 2^8 which is 256. The values 0 and 255 cannot be used as address values in the last octet. The number 0 means "this network" and the number 255 means "broadcast to all nodes."

Special Addressing

There are several special addressing structures of which you should be aware. These fall under the guidelines of generally accepted principles. These conventions are documented and used on the Internet and are part of the Internet Protocol.

Destination	Network	Host
Host on this Net	All Zeros	Host ID
Local Broadcast	All Ones	All Ones
Directed Broadcast	Network ID	All Ones
Loopback	127	Anything

Since these addresses are defined as having a special use, they are not available as host addresses. Other invalid addresses include:

- Inappropriate subnet mask
- Class D address
- Class E address
- Duplicate address
- Two systems, separated by a router, with the same network address
- Two systems on the same physical network with different network addresses

A valid address will be unique, have a network address falling in the defined class range, and have an appropriate subnet mask.

Private Internets

A *private internet* is one that will not be connecting directly to the Internet. The term *intranet* is commonly being used to refer to internetwork environments of this type. The two most common intranet examples are:

- Networks with no need to connect to the Internet.
- Networks connecting to the Internet through an application gateway (such as Microsoft's Proxy Server) that remaps IP addresses.

The Internet Assigned Numbers Authority (IANA) has set aside three sets of addresses for use on intranets:

```
10.0.0.0 - 10.255.255.255
172.16.0.0 - 172.31.255.255
192.168.0.0 - 192.168.255.255
```

There are some obvious disadvantages to using these addresses, the foremost being that it will be impossible to connect directly to the Internet or reference these addresses from the Internet. They have no meaning in the global Internet community. Routers connecting to the Internet should filter out any reference to these addresses.

Subnetting Fundamentals

Before jumping into subnetting, let's review addressing and network configurations:

- Each network must have its own network address.
- Networks are linked by routers.
- The subnet mask identifies the network and host addresses.
- An assigned address class, using the default subnet mask, provides a single network address.

If you were limited to the subnet mask definitions provided with the address classes, you would have to place all of your hosts on a single network. While you may do this with some Class C configurations, it is very unlikely with Class A or B. Realistically, many organizations find it necessary to subdivide a Class C license into two or more subnets.

You can use the subnet mask to identify your own subnetwork addresses within the network address you have been assigned. This is done by adding additional bits to the default subnet mask, which are then used to identify the physical subnet.

Why Subnet

Why is it necessary to define additional subnets on an internetwork? Through proper use of subnets, you can improve network efficiency and better design your internetwork to meet your particular requirements.

- Keep local traffic local.

    By setting up subnets and keeping systems that need to share information together, you can cut the overall traffic levels on the network.

- Accurately locate remote hosts.

    In a well-organized network it is much easier to set up and manage routers.

- Make the best use of assigned addresses.

    You can organize the network to best meet your business requirements.

Any time you want to communicate with a remote host in an internetwork environment, you need three pieces of information:

- IP address

    This uniquely identifies the host.

- Subnet mask

    This identifies the network or subnetwork on which the host is located.

- Default gateway

    This is the path to be used if you are communicating with a host on a different subnetwork and a route is not specifically identified.

Only the IP address and subnet mask are needed when locating a host on the local subnet.

Subnetting Example

Let's begin by looking at a simple subnetting example. Assume that you have been assigned a Class B address of 155.110.0.0, which has a default subnet mask of 255.255.0.0. This gives you the potential for 65,534 hosts, but all of the hosts must be connected to the same physical network.

What if you needed more networks with fewer clients per network? You can do this by specifying a subnet mask with the mask set beyond the limits of the default. For example, you might use the following:

```
255.255.255.0
```

This would give you 254 available subnets, each capable of supporting up to 254 host systems. Remember that all 0s and all 1s (255) are not legal address values. Using a subnet mask to divide an assigned address is common with Class A and Class B addresses, and is becoming more common on Class C networks.

When using subnetting, it might be helpful to think of the address in this fashion:

Network Address	Physical Subnets	Host Suffix

The original (default) subnet mask identifies the network address portion of the IP address. The portion of the mask you've added identifies the subnet. The unmasked portion is used for host addresses. This type of addressing is sometimes referred to as hierarchical addressing.

Class B Subnetting

With a Class B address, the following combinations are available for defining subnets:

Max. Subnets	Max. Host/ Subnets	Subnet Mask	Subnet ID Length in Bits	Host ID Length in Bits
2	16382	255.255.192.0	2	14
6	8190	255.255.224.0	3	13
14	4094	255.255.240.0	4	12
30	2046	255.255.248.0	5	11
62	1022	255.255.252.0	6	10
126	510	255.255.254.0	7	9
254	254	255.255.255.0	8	8
510	126	255.255.255.128	9	7
1022	62	255.255.255.192	10	6
2046	30	255.255.255.224	11	5
4094	14	255.255.255.240	12	4
8190	6	255.255.255.248	13	3
16382	2	255.255.255.252	14	2

As you can see by our table, either the third octet or the third and fourth octets can be used for defining subnets. As the number of subnets increases, there is a proportionate decrease in the number of host addresses available.

Class C Subnetting

Should the need arise, it is possible to subnet a Class C address. The following combinations are supported:

Max. Subnets	Max. Host/ Subnet	Subnet Mask	Subnet ID Length in Bits	Host ID Length in Bits
2	62	255.255.255.192	2	6
6	30	255.255.255.224	3	5
14	14	255.255.255.240	4	4
30	6	255.255.255.248	5	3
62	2	255.255.255.252	6	2

As with our Class B example, the number of available host addresses decreases as the number of subnets increases.

Defining Subnets

There are a few points you should keep in mind when defining subnets:

- The subnet mask must be equal to or greater than the default subnet mask.

- A subnet is defined by adding contiguous bits to the subnet mask, starting at the most significant bit following the default subnet mask.

- The additional network address bits beyond the default subnet mask cannot be all 1s or all 0s.

Your address class is only limited if you are connecting to the Internet. In that case, you must apply for a valid address, or set of addresses, if necessary. If you are not, and have no intention of connecting to the Internet, you are free to use any valid address you wish.

Because of this, it might be tempting to set up your network with either a Class A or Class B address. While this is possible, it may cause problems should you want to connect to the Internet in the future.

Address applications are being filled with Class C addresses only at this time. It would likely be easier to convert a network already based on Class C addresses to assigned addresses.

IP Addressing

One of the most challenging jobs with any new TCP/IP-based network is address definition and management. Planning is a vital part of the process. You should:

- Determine network address requirements.

    You must determine the maximum number of networks and the maximum number of hosts you must support per network. Leave room for growth, both planned and unplanned. Be sure to include: workstation adapter cards, router interfaces, network printers, and all other managed network equipment.

- Determine your class address(es).

    If connecting directly to the Internet, you must apply for an appropriate range of addresses. If not, you can invent an address range to use, keeping in mind the future possibility of Internet connection.

- Define your subnet mask.

    Define a subnet mask that meets your addressing requirements. It is possible to have different-sized subnet masks on your network, but this is not suggested. It can lead to confusion and make the management process more difficult.

- Determine the valid IP address ranges on each subnet.

    These are the addresses that can be assigned to the hosts. Review your addresses carefully to ensure you have not included any invalid addresses.

During this planning process, you may want to refer back to the tables provided in the IP Addressing chapter (previous chapter) for information on subnet masks and address maximums.

Determining your requirements is a simple case of counting what you have and what you plan to add. For now let's move past that step and look at how you create your subnet mask.

Subnet Mask

How do you determine your subnet mask requirements? An easy way is to look at the tables provided in this manual. Unfortunately, this method only works if you have the tables available. It's relatively easy, however, to calculate your requirements.

Once you have determined your maximum number of subnets and hosts, convert each of these values to binary. This will give you the minimum number of bits required for your subnet mask. From that, you can determine the class of address you need.

Remember that Class A and Class B addresses have all been assigned. If you find you need a Class A or Class B address and you need to connect to the Internet, you will need to find a way to make Class C addresses work. If you are not connecting to the Internet, or have a way to isolate your network from the Internet, you can select an address class to meet your needs.

Determining Subnet Requirements

Suppose you have determined that you need five subnets with up to 20 hosts on each. Convert these values to binary:

```
5=101 (3 bits)
20=10100 (5 bits)
```

You need a total of eight bits to define the subnet and host addresses. Since a Class C address provides you with eight bits for addressing, you can use a Class C address value.

What if you have a larger network? Let's assume you have 21 networks with 240 hosts on each. We start by converting these to binary:

```
21=10101 (5 bits)

240=11110000 (8 bits)
```

You need a total of 13 bits to define the subnet and host addresses. A Class B address will more than meet your needs. Realistically, if you were connecting to the Internet, you would need to apply for 21 Class C licenses, one for each subnet.

For our last example, let's assume that you are not connecting to the Internet, and can choose any class address you wish. You need to support 20 subnets, with 300 hosts on each. Convert these to binary:

```
20=10100 (5 bits)

300=100101100 (9 bits)
```

In this case, you need 14 bits to meet your address requirements. Since you are not limited to an assigned address, you can select a Class B license, which gives you 16 bits for subnet and host addresses. Notice in this case that you cannot use a series of Class C addresses, since a Class C address can only support 254 hosts.

There is one exception to this method. Consider this example. You have a network address of 200.200.200.0. You need to support seven subnets and up to twelve hosts per subnet. If this example worked the same as the ones we've seen:

```
7 = 111 (3 bits)

12 = 1100 (4 bits)
```

But this won't work. Three bit positions for the subnetwork address only supports six subnets. Remember that all 0s and all 1s are not allowed. When the binary value for the number of networks or number of hosts is all 1s, you must add an additional binary digit. The correct way to look at this example is:

```
7 = 0111 (4 bits)

12 = 1100 (4 bits)
```

You need four bits in both the subnet and host portions of the address for a total of eight, so you can be supported under a Class C address.

A Class C Example

Going back to the first example, let's put some numbers together. You need to support five subnets with up to 20 hosts on each. You already determined that you can use a Class C license to meet your needs, so let's give you a license:

```
198.214.7.0
```

Your default subnet mask is:

```
255.255.255.0
```

You need to change your subnet mask to support five subnets. To do this, you need three bits for the subnet address. In binary, this would look like:

```
11111111.11111111.11111111.11100000
```

Converting this back into decimal, you get:

```
255.255.255.224
```

This gives you 6 (2^3-2) possible subnet addresses and 30 (2^5-2) host addresses. Remember that neither address can contain all 0s or all 1s.

Another Class C Example

If you assume that you are either connecting to the Internet, or will likely connect to the Internet at some future time, the second example is less complicated than the first. In this case, you'd need a set of Class C licenses. Let's assume you are able to get those in series:

```
192.121.72.0 - 192.121.93.0
```

For each of these, the default subnet mask is:

```
255.255.255.0
```

In this example, you will leave the subnet mask at default and assign a different Class C address to each network. If you tried to break each of these down into subnets, you would not have enough host addresses on the subnet to meet your needs. Using the default subnet mask, you have 254 (2^8-2) host addresses available.

A Class B Example

For the last example, remember that you are neither connecting to the Internet nor do you have any future connection plans (for the purpose of these examples). Because of this, you are free to select an address that meets your needs without worrying about its availability for assignment.

In an earlier example, you needed to support 20 subnets with up to 300 hosts on each. This could be done using a Class B address, so select one:

```
131.142.0.0
```

The default subnet mask for this address is:

```
255.255.0.0
```

You have 16 bits available for defining subnet and host addresses. You need a minimum of 14, leaving you two additional bits to use as you please. This means you have some flexibility in setting up the subnet mask.

To maximize available expansion for hosts, you would select the minimum bits possible for the subnet mask. The binary and decimal values are given below:

```
11111111.11111111.11111000.00000000
255.255.248.0
```

This gives you a 21-bit subnet mask total. It supports up to 30 (2^5-2) subnets and up to 2046 (2^{11}-2) hosts.

You have the option of splitting the difference evenly between them, as shown below:

```
11111111.11111111.11111100.00000000
255.255.252.0
```

This gives you up to 62 (2^6-2) subnets and 1022 (2^{10}-2) host addresses.

Finally, you can select to maximize the growth potential of subnets on your networks.

```
11111111.11111111.11111110.00000000
255.255.254.0
```

This supports 126 (2^7-2) subnets and 510 (2^9-2) hosts.

Address Ranges

Now that you have determined your subnet mask, you have to determine your valid address ranges. This is the range of addresses that may be assigned to hosts on each of your networks. When using the default subnet mask, the range is easy to calculate. The full range of addresses is available, except for all 0s and all 1s. For example, the host address range on a Class C address using the default subnet mask is 00000001 to 11111110 binary, or 1 to 254.

The process becomes slightly more complicated when working with a subnet mask you have defined. You must take both the valid subnet address values and valid host values when calculating the range for each subnet.

To determine the address range for each subnet, use the values:

```
Subnet_address +
    minimum_valid_address
                to
Subnet_address +
    maximum_valid_address
```

The subnet address is the address value with all of the host address bits set to zero.

Each subnetwork will also have a Subnetwork Broadcast Value. To calculate this:

```
255 - Subnet_mask +
    subnetwork_address = Subnetwork_
    Broadcast_Address
```

Working in binary math, you can determine the Subnetwork Broadcast Address by setting all of the host address bits to 1. It would probably be best to go through some examples of this.

Class C Example

Suppose you have a Class C address of 193.25.141.0 and a subnet mask of 255.255.255.192. Since only the last octet will change in a Class C address, you only need to calculate that portion of the address.

First let's determine the valid subnetwork addresses by setting the host address bits to 0. We get:

```
01000000 or 64 decimal and 10000000
    or 128 decimal
```

The table below gives us our valid host address values for the network:

	Minimum Host Address	Maximum Host Address	Starting Address (decimal)	Ending Address (decimal)
Subnetwork 64	01000001	01111110	65	126
Subnet 128	10000001	10111110	129	190

You also need to calculate the Subnetwork Broadcast Address for each of these. Remember, a host address of all 1s is the Subnetwork Broadcast Address. This means that a subnetwork's broadcast address will always be calculated as:

```
Subnetwork_Broadcast_Address =
    Maximum_Host_Address + 1
```

In the case of these two subnetworks, the broadcast address would be 127 and 191, respectively.

Your full address ranges for each subnet would be 193.25.141.65 through 193.25.141.126 for subnet 64, and 193.25.141.129 through 193.25.141.190 for subnet 128.

Class B Example

When designing a network that will not be connected to the Internet, you may encounter a situation where you need to determine valid addresses for a Class B network. Going back to the earlier example of 20 subnets with up to 300 hosts on each, you have selected an address of 131.142.0.0 and a subnet mask of 255.255.252.0. This subnet mask supports up to 62 networks. Let's look at the first three subnetworks. You only need to look at the last two octets, since they are the only ones that will change.

Since all 0s is not a valid address, your first three subnetworks are:

```
00000100.00000000    .4.0
00001000.00000000    .8.0
00001100.00000000    .12.0
```

From this, you can determine your first three sets of address ranges:

Subnetwork	Minimum Host Address	Maximum Host Address	Starting Address (decimal)	Ending Address (decimal)
4.0	00000100.00000001	00000111.11111110	4.1	7.254
8.0	00001000.00000001	00001011.11111110	8.1	11.254
12.0	00001100.00000001	00001111.11111110	12.1	15.254

As with the subnet address, host addresses of all 0s or all 1s are not allowed. You could continue this process until you get to the last valid subnet.

To determine the Subnetwork Broadcast Address for each of these, add 1 to the maximum host address The Subnetwork Broadcast Addresses would be .7.255, .11.255, and .15.255, respectively.

Another Method

Let's take a look at an alternate method for determining valid address ranges. Assume that you have the Class C address 200.200.201.0 and have determined that your most appropriate subnet mask is 255.255.255.224. In binary the last octet is:

```
11100000
```

Three bits, the number in the subnet mask, support up to 32 different values. Do not worry about invalid addresses yet. To determine the subnetwork address ranges, simply count up by 32s, starting at zero.

0-31	128-159
32-63	160-191
64-95	192-223

96-127	224-255

The first and last ranges must be dropped, because they are invalid. In the first, the subnet value is all 0s, and in the last, the subnet value is all 1s. This leaves:

```
32-63
64-95
96-127
128-159
160-191
192-223
```

Unfortunately, these still contain invalid values. The first is the network address, with the host address all 0s. The last is the network broadcast address, with the host address set to all 1s. Our final valid ranges are:

Address Range	Network Address	Broadcast
33 - 62	32	63
65 - 94	64	95
97 - 126	96	127
129 - 158	128	159
161 - 190	160	191
193 - 222	192	223

Let's try another one. Assume that you have the Class C address 220.136.17.0 and have determined that your most appropriate subnet mask is 255.255.255.240. In binary the last octet is:

```
11110000
```

Four bits, the number in the subnet mask, support up to sixteen different values. To determine the subnetwork address ranges (don't worry about the invalid ones for now), we simply count up by 16s, starting at zero.

0-15	128-143
16-31	144-159

32-47	160-175
48-63	176-191
64-79	192-207
80-95	208-223
96-111	224-239
112-127	240-255

Address Range	Network Address	Broadcast
193-206	192	207
209-222	208	223
225-238	224	239

The first and last ranges are dropped because they are invalid. In the first, the subnet value is all 0s, and in the last, the subnet value is all 1s. This leaves:

16-31	128-143
32-47	144-159
48-63	60-175
64-79	176-191
80-95	192-207
96-111	208-223
112-127	224-239

Remember, these still contain invalid values. The first is the network address, with the host address all 0s. The last is the network broadcast address, with the host address set to all 1s. Our final valid ranges are:

Address Range	Network Address	Broadcast
17-30	16	31
33-46	32	47
49-62	48	63
65-78	64	79
81-94	80	95
97-110	96	111
113-126	112	127
129-142	128	143
145-158	144	159
161-174	160	175
177-190	176	191

Combining Addresses

Up to now, the chapter has concentrated on breaking up an address into subnetworks. The process also works in the other direction. You have the ability to combine consecutive addresses through the use of the subnet mask.

It's not uncommon to have more hosts than you can support with a single Class C address, but far too few to justify a Class B address. One solution is to combine two or more Class C addresses into a single subnetwork. To do this, you need two or more consecutive Class C addresses. For example:

```
200.23.217.0
200.23.218.0
200.23.219.0
```

The first step is to convert the third octet to binary for each of the addresses:

```
217 = 11011001
218 = 11011010
219 = 11011011
```

Look for the portion of the address that does not change. This becomes your subnet mask. In the example, the six most significant bits do not change, giving you a subnet mask for the third octet of:

```
11111100
```

This converts to a decimal value of:

```
252
```

Your full subnet mask would be:

```
255.255.252.0
```

It is important to remember that, even though we are treating them like subnets in a class B address for the purpose of defining a subnetwork, these are still Class C addresses. You still have only the fourth octet available for defining host addresses.

Address Resolution

The IP address operates at the Internet Layer of the TCP/IP architectural diagram. However, the physical passing of data occurs at the Hardware Layer. Because of this, it is necessary to know the host's IP address and MAC (hardware) address. If the initiating host does not have this information, it must have a way of learning the missing address. The TCP/IP protocol suite provides two protocols supporting this process.

- Address Resolution Protocol (ARP)

    ARP is used when the host IP address, but not its MAC address, is known. This information, once collected, is stored in an ARP table, sometimes called the ARP cache.

- Reverse Address Resolution Protocol (RARP)

    This is the counterpart to ARP, which is used when the MAC address is known, but not the IP address. As with ARP, when this information is received, it is recorded in the ARP table.

Both processes are transparent to users.

ARP

The process used by ARP is very similar, whether the destination host is on the local subnet or a remote subnet. The initiating station can determine this by looking at the remote host's IP address and subnet mask. In either case, the process is very similar. If looking for a local host, the ARP packet is broadcast on the local subnet only. If on a remote subnet, the packet is transferred through routers until it arrives at the proper subnet, where it is sent on to its destination.

- ARP request sent

    The ARP request contains the destination host's IP address, as well as the sending host's IP and MAC addresses. This information is either broadcast on the local subnet or passed to its eventual destination through routers.

- ARP request received

    Each host receiving the ARP request will compare the packet destination with its own IP address. If they match, the host will generate and transmit an ARP reply. It will also cache the IP address and MAC address of the transmitting station.

- ARP reply sent

    The ARP reply contains the destination host's IP address and MAC (NIC hardware) address. When the original sending host receives this information, it is stored in the ARP cache.

RARP works in a similar fashion except that it sends a packet with the NIC address, rather than the IP address, of the destination.

Routers

By now, the importance of routers in TCP/IP networking should be obvious. Any time you must communicate between subnetworks, a router is used.

Some key points about routers include:

- A router connects two or more subnetworks.
- A router may be configured to support a single protocol or multiple protocols.
- A router will only process packets specifically addressing it as a destination.
- Packets destined for a locally connected subnetwork are passed to that network.
- Packets destined for a remote subnetwork are passed to the next router in the path.

Routers are intelligent devices. Many can dynamically determine the best route to a destination subnetwork. They can also inform the originating host if any problems occur during transmission.

Routers can be either static, where the routing table is built manually, or dynamic, capable of automatically building the router table. In modern networks, dynamic routers are the most common type. Windows NT 4.0 now supports dynamic routing. Windows NT 3.5 and 3.51 only supported static routing.

Routing Tables

Both static and dynamic routers use routing tables to pass packets on to remote subnetworks. The only difference is whether the table is created manually or automatically. In either case, the routing table will contain the same information:

- The destination network IP address
- The destination network subnet mask

- The router interface used to get to the network
- The IP address of the next router in the path to the destination
- The number of hops to the destination

The number of hops refers to the number of intermediate networks (other routers) that must be crossed to reach the destination. Each packet will have a Time to Live (TTL) value that is decremented with each hop. When TTL reaches zero, the packet is dropped.

An IP address of 0.0.0.0 refers to a default router. A default router intercepts all packets destined for networks not specifically designated in the routing table. Routing table contents are described in more detail later in this manual.

Routing Examples

Let's look at how some specific situations are handled:

- Local destination

    The packet will be addressed for the destination host. Any other systems, including routers, will ignore the packet.

- Remote destination, next hop known

    The source host will place the IP address for the next router as the immediate destination. That router will then pass the packet on to the following hop, if known. If not known, the router will pass the packet to its default gateway.

- Remote destination, next hop unknown

    The source host will place the IP address for the default gateway as the immediate destination. That router will then pass the packet on to the following hop, if known. If not known, the router will pass the packet to its default gateway.

If a packet reaches a point where no routing is available to the next hop, the packet is destroyed and an ICMP message returned. If the TTL value reaches zero, indicating that the packet is likely lost and being bounced between default gateways, the packet is destroyed and an ICMP message generated.

ICMP (Internet Control Message Protocol) provides error reporting during datagram processing. This is a means by which dynamic routers can update their routing tables.

Static Routers

While still used in some situations, most static routers have been replaced by dynamic routers. Static routers are more difficult to manage and less efficient than their dynamic counterparts, for several reasons:

- Manual configuration

    Each entry in the routing table must be made manually. In a large network, this can be a time consuming process.

- Manual updates

    If there are changes to the network, such as subnets added or removed or other router configurations changed, these must be entered into the routing table manually. The more dynamic the network, the more time that must be spent configuring routers.

- Changing environments

    A static router cannot compensate for a failed route or high levels of traffic on a primary route. This means that data may be lost, or may be delayed over an inefficient route.

Static routers may provide an inexpensive solution on small networks, but it can become difficult to manage them efficiently on a larger network. Use of default routers is also critical, to avoid losing packets whose destination has not been configured on the router.

Dynamic Routers

Dynamic routers use an Interior Gateway Protocol (IGP) to communicate with each other. The two most common such protocols are:

- Routing Information Protocol (RIP)

    Routers use RIP to keep each other informed about routing destinations. It is based on a Distance Vector algorithm, which normally uses the fewest hops (router transversals) to determine the best path.

- Open Shortest Path First (OSPF)

    OSPF uses a Link State algorithm which provides for configuration of hierarchical topologies and allows quick response to changing network conditions.

In a network connected to the Internet, it would clearly be impossible for any routing table to contain a list of all the available networks. Only information about networks on the network's own side of the Internet gateway is exchanged using the IGP.

Gateway-to-Gateway Protocol is used to update the massive routing tables maintained on routers within the Internet. To access the Internet, routers are configured with a default gateway (or smart gateway). Any requests for networks to which a route is not known are forwarded to the default gateway.

In Windows NT 4.0, routing is RIP-based.

RIP

When a router comes on line, it broadcasts a request for routing table information from all other routers it can see. The information passed through RIP includes a destination, routing metric, and hop count for each known route. The information received is used by the router to determine the shortest path to each destination. The route information is then entered into the local routing table. Once the table is built, the router sends a RIP broadcast every 30 seconds, containing its known destinations and the cost (in hops) to get to each.

While effective, RIP is not without its drawbacks:

- Maximum fifteen hops

    This path limit is too restrictive to support some larger internetworks.

- Routing loops

    Because of time delays in the transmission of updated routing table information, routing loops may occur in very large internetworks.

- Network conditions

    Fixed metrics are used to determine routing paths. Because of this, there is no allowance for dynamic conditions such as changes in traffic load or transmission delays.

RIP assumes that all devices keep a routing table.

OSPF

Rather than a separate protocol, OSPF packets are carried within IP datagrams. Its Link State algorithm provides several enhancements over RIP, including:

- Hierarchical topology configuration
- Support for very large internetworks
- Adaptation to changing conditions

- Traffic balancing over multiple paths
- Authentication of router table information exchange

RIP remains the most common implementation of dynamic router support, but OSPF is gaining popularity.

ICMP

Internet Control Message Protocol (ICMP) is a module of IP that provides error reporting during datagram processing. A common use is passing error information between host and router. This error data allows for dynamic routing table updates.

ICMP messages are generated when:

- A packet cannot reach its destination.
- A packet's Time to Live (TTL) expires.
- An error is detected in IP header parameter data.
- A router cannot buffer an incoming packet.
- A router cannot keep up with an incoming stream of packets.
- A router sends a message to a host advising of a shorter route to a destination.
- A host sends an echo packet to determine if another host is alive.
- A host needs to determine to which network it is attached.

ICMP helps to keep the network running smoothly when hard errors, such as a router going offline, occur.

Network Naming

Addresses work well when computers need to communicate. If a user needs to locate a system, however, it is much easier when recognizable names are used. This chapter discusses two naming systems:

- Domain Name System (DNS)

  In a DNS environment, each system will have a Fully Qualified Domain Name (FQDN), uniquely defining it on the network. DNS uses a distributed, hierarchical naming system. For example, www.wavetech.com

- NetBIOS

  NetBIOS compatibility is essential in all Microsoft Networking engine-based network operating systems. NetBIOS is a common interface for creating network applications. Under NetBIOS, each device must have a unique name.

It is likely that you will encounter networks where it is necessary to manage both DNS and NetBIOS names for network devices.

DNS

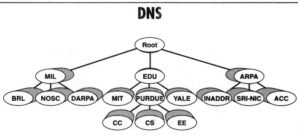

Domain Name Space Extract

DNS is a hierarchical naming system for identifying hosts on the Internet in the format somewhere.domain, for example, wavetech.com. The format is sometimes described as *host.subnet.domain*. DNS requires a static DNS name to IP address mapping.

The hierarchical structure identifying domain names is called the domain name space. Each domain can be divided into subdomains, and these into host names, with a period acting as delimiter between each portion of the name.

Domains are the root level of the DNS identifiers and include organization types and countries. Each domain name is unique. This root is managed by the Internet Network Information Center. Each domain is managed by a different organization which administers its own subdomain. Each subdomain must be unique to the domain, and administration of that subdomain is normally assigned to the organization it represents.

DNS Domains

The following are some DNS domains you may encounter.

Organizational domains:

com	Usually a company, commercial institution, or an organization. For example, the DNS name for Wave Technologies International is wavetech.com.
edu	This identifies educational institutions. For example, mit.edu is the name of Massachusetts Institute of Technology.
gov	These are government organizations, such as nasa.gov for the National Aeronautic and Space Administration.
mil	This represents a military site, such as af.mil for the United States Air Force.
net	This is used for Internet gateways and administrative hosts.

org   This identifies non-commercial organizations or organizations that don't fit easily into other domain classes. For example, the address for National Public Radio is npr.org.

Example country domains include:

us   United States

au   Australia

ca   Canada

fr   France

uk   The United Kingdom

Country domains also support subdomains. For example, the United States has a subdomain for each of the 50 states. The United Kingdom supports subdomains, such as co.uk for commercial organizations and ac.uk for educational institutions.

Name Resolution Basics

DNS names are maintained and managed through DNS servers. Each top-level domain, such as com, will have one or more DNS servers. It contains information about all of the domains that it supports. DNS servers are also supported at the subdomain level, which will contain the host name information. Subdomains can be further divided into logical zones, with a server managing all of the hosts for that zone.

When name resolution is required, the request is handled through name servers. A name server interprets the FQDN it receives to determine its specific address. If the local name server does not contain the requested information, the request is passed on to other name servers that are likely to contain the information. The query continues until the name and IP address are located.

Name servers will locally cache domain name space information learned during the query process. The information then becomes locally available to the local hosts. The Windows NT 4.0 implementation of DNS is discussed later in the course.

NetBIOS

NetBIOS is an application layer (OSI model Session Layer) interface between the network operating system and lower-level functions. It is implemented across most popular network protocols, including TCP/IP. The NetBIOS implementation that operates over TCP/IP is called NBT. NetBIOS support is provided with Microsoft LAN Manager-based network operating systems including:

- Microsoft LAN Manager
- Windows NT
- Windows for Workgroups
- Windows 95
- IBM PC LAN and LAN Server
- DEC Pathworks
- HP LM/X

In addition to these, NetBIOS support is included with most other popular network operating systems, including Novell NetWare and Banyan VINES.

NetBIOS is also popular with application programmers. It is an easy interface to use. It is easy to write to when creating applications. Since it is supported across different protocols, it provides an easy means of producing protocol independent applications.

NetBIOS Names

As previously stated, NetBIOS is a relatively easy to use interface. A full range of session-based, datagram, and broadcast services is provided, identifying destinations through NetBIOS names. This is done with eighteen simple commands.

All NetBIOS activity is based on NetBIOS names. Each network device supporting NetBIOS communications must have a unique NetBIOS name, up to 15 characters long. Each client or server process running at the station will have its own NetBIOS name. The 16th character position identifies the service a NetBIOS object is running.

NetBIOS devices can be divided into a virtual network through the use of a Scope ID. This is assigned to a group of devices and has the effect of isolating them from other NetBIOS calls. This keeps NetBIOS traffic from being propagated across the full network. When in use, the name with scope ID is stored in the following format:

```
scope_id.device/service
```

NetBIOS Name Resolution

Traditionally, NetBIOS name registration and resolution was supported through broadcasts. Each workstation maintained a cache of resolved NetBIOS names for future reference. NetBIOS has no concept of and no support for routing.

Because of the size of some TCP/IP networks, as well as the need to support routing, traditional NetBIOS management procedures do not always work well. The routing problem is handled by encapsulating NetBIOS packets inside of a TCP or UDP packet when routing is required. Name resolution is normally managed through one of the alternate name resolution proposals.

- B-Node (Broadcast Node)

  B-node supports resolution of NetBIOS names and IP addresses on small LANs with no routers.

- P-Node (Point-to-Point Node)

  P-node resolution uses a NetBIOS Name Server (NBNS) to manage NetBIOS names and IP addresses and supports larger networks.

- M-Node (Mixed Node)

  M-node is a combination of B-node and P-node resolution.

- H-Node (Hybrid Node)

  H-node is a new method supporting a dynamic NBNS in combination with B-node and P-node broadcasts.

B-node, P-node, and M-node are the subject of RFCs 1001 and 1002.

Supported Features

Microsoft Windows NT provides a wide base of support for TCP/IP features, including:

- Core TCP/IP protocols

  This includes support for TCP, IP, UDP, ARP, and ICMP. Dial-up access support is provided through Point-to-Point Protocol (PPP) and Serial-Line IP (SLIP). In addition, Windows NT 4.0 now supports Point-to-Point Tunneling Protocol (PPTP).

- Application interface support

  Support is provided for Windows Sockets 1.1, Remote Procedure Call (RPC), NetBIOS, and Network Dynamic Data Exchange (Network DDE).

- Connectivity utilities

    Connectivity utilities allow communications with non-Microsoft hosts. Supported basic connectivity utilities include FINGER, FTP, LPR, RCP, REXEC, RSH, TELNET, and TFTP.

- Diagnostic tools

    Tools provided to help diagnose and resolve TCP/IP networking problems include ARP, HOSTNAME, IPCONFIG, LPQ, NBTSTAT, NETSTAT, PING, ROUTE, and TRACERT.

- Administrative services and tools

    These tools and services include FTP Server services, Dynamic Host Configuration Protocol (DHCP), Windows Internet Naming Service (WINS), and TCP/IP Printing.

- Simple Network Management Protocol (SNMP) support

    The SNMP agent allows for remote monitoring and administration of TCP/IP protocols.

- Path MTU Discovery

    Path MTU Discovery supports the ability to determine datagram size for routers between NT computers and other systems.

Support for these protocols and services is integrated into Windows NT.

TCP/IP Benefits

Windows NT ships with integrated protocol options including NetBEUI, NWLink (Microsoft's implementation of IPX/SPX), and TCP/IP. Why select TCP/IP?

- Standard protocol

    TCP/IP is the de facto standard for enterprise networking. All modern operating systems provide TCP/IP support, either integrated into the operating system or available as an option.

- WAN support

    TCP/IP has the most complete set of protocols and utilities for using and managing Wide Area Networks. It is fully routable with the ability to configure subnetworks as needed.

- Connectivity

    TCP/IP provides connectivity between dissimilar hardware and software platforms. Utilities allow for easy access and managed file transfer.

- Client/server environment

    Windows Sockets 1.1, supported under TCP/IP on Windows NT, is a popular interface for developing client/server applications. Windows NT's implementation of Windows Sockets 1.1 is compatible with other vendor's Windows Sockets-compliant stacks.

- Internet connectivity

    TCP/IP, PPP support, and Windows Sockets provide a powerful and flexible platform for Internet connectivity.

One of the main reasons for installing TCP/IP is that you are adding Windows NT to an existing TCP/IP network.

About DHCP and WINS

Two additional services are referenced during this chapter, DCHP and WINS. These are covered in detail in later chapters, but some mention should be made as to what they provide on your NT system.

- DHCP (Dynamic Host Configuration Protocol)

    DHCP provides an automated means of managing host IP addresses. The DHCP server is configured with IP address information, including a range of valid addresses and a lease period for addresses. DHCP clients can query the server for an IP address when they start up.

- WINS (Windows Internet Name Service)

    WINS is an automated Windows name resolution service. This provides an easy way of managing name resolution in a Windows network. As you will see in later chapters, Windows NT 4.0 provides WINS and DNS integration.

These services will be mentioned as available for installation.

TCP/IP Installation

The TCP/IP protocol is installed through the Control Panel Network utility. All of the necessary software ships with the Windows NT (Server and Workstation) installation software set.

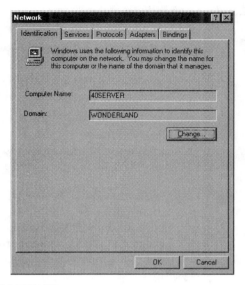

To add TCP/IP support:

1. Launch the Control Panel.

2. Launch the Network utility.

3. Select the **Protocols** tab.

4. Click on **Add**.

5. Select TCP/IP protocol and click on **OK**.

6. You will be prompted for the path to the installation files. This can be a local or UNC pathname.

TCP/IP Components

To add Additional TCP/IP components:

1. Select the **Services** tab of the Control Panel Network utility.

2. Click on **Add**.

3. Select the service you want to install and click on **OK**. You will be prompted for a path to the installation files.

Additional services include:

SNMP Service

Use this selection to install SNMP service. Installation of this service also lets you monitor TCP/IP performance statistics through the Performance Monitor.

Microsoft TCP/IP Printing

Installation of this service lets you use TCP/ IP to print over the network. With this service installed, you can print to UNIX print queues, print to printers directly connected to the network, and allow UNIX computers to print to Windows NT printers.

Simple TCP/IP Services

With this service installed, your computer can respond to requests from other computers supporting these services, which include CHARGEN (Character Generator), DAYTIME, DISCARD, and QUOTE (Quote of the Day).

Microsoft DHCP Server

This option installs the services necessary for your system to act as a Dynamic Host Configuration Protocol server. IP address information must still be manually configured for this machine.

Windows Internet Name Service

This option lets you set up your system as a primary or secondary WINS server.

Microsoft DNS Server

This option enables a Windows NT Server to function as a Domain Name System (DNS) name server.

DHCP Relay Agent

Allows the computer to act as a DHCP BOOTP relay agent.

NOTE: *These services are discussed in more detail later in the course.*

TCP/IP Configuration

The Control Panel Network utility lets you configure TCP/IP or change your configuration information whenever necessary. Select TCP/IP Protocol from the **Protocols** tab and click on **Properties**. This will display the TCP/IP Properties sheet.

TCP/IP Properties Sheet

The TCP/IP Properties sheet has several tabs that allow you to configure TCP/IP and any utillities that have been installed. The following tabs are available:

- IP Address

    This tab allows you to assign an IP address, subnet mask, and default gateway to a particular adapter card. If the station is configured as a DHCP client, this information will be configured automatically.

NOTE: *It is only necessary to define a default gateway if your network is supporting multiple subnets or if your server is connected to the Internet.*

- DNS

    This tab allows you to configure the Domain Name System (DNS) to which the server subscribes.

- WINS Address

    This tab allows you to configure the Windows Internet Name Service to which the server subscribes.

- DHCP Relay

  This allows the server to relay DHCP and BOOTP broadcasts.

- Routing

  IP routing is enabled through this tab, enabling the system to act as a router.

Online Help

The Windows NT online help system supplies help for TCP/IP commands and utilities.

To access online help:

1. Launch **Help** from the **Start** menu.
2. Select the Index tab and type:

   ```
   TCP/IP
   ```

3. Click on **Display**.
4. When the Topics Found box appears, select TCP/IP Procedures Help and click on **Display**.

Use the **Contents** tab for information about general TCP/IP topics, or choose the **Index** tab to search for a specific topic. The **Find** tab allows you to search the help files for a word or phrase.

PING

The PING utility is commonly used to test for the presence of other systems. To test for a particular system, type **ping** followed by the host's IP address at the command line.

```
ping 150.4.5.21
```

A successful response would look something like this:

```
Reply from
  150.4.5.21:bytes=32time=101ms
  TTL=243
```

```
Reply from
  150.4.5.21:bytes=32time=100ms
  TTL=243
```

```
Reply from
  150.4.5.21:bytes=32time=120ms
  TTL=243
```

```
Reply from
  150.4.5.21:bytes=32time=120ms
  TTL=243
```

This example shows that four replies were received, each 32 bytes long, and each taking just over 100 ms to return the information.

The following list offers several ways to use PING:

- Ping yourself with the loopback address (127.0.0.1) to determine if you have a working TCP/IP stack.

- Ping yourself with your IP address to see if it is configured properly and to see if the address is duplicated on the network.

- Ping another system on the local network to test network integrity.

- Ping another system on a different subnetwork to verify that default gateways are operational and that network components are working properly.

- Ping each intermediate router between you and a remote host to test the route.

PING Options

PING supports the following command-line options:

-t	The command will ping the specified host until interrupted.
-a	This option is used to resolve addresses to host names.

-n *count*   This will send the number of ECHO packets you specify in the count, defaulting to four.

-l *length*   This is used to set the size of ECHO packets. According to the documentation, the size defaults to 64 bytes. However, in actuality the default size is 32 bytes. You can specify a packet size of up to 8192 bytes.

-f   Use this option to send a Do Not Fragment flag in the packet, so that it will not be fragmented by gateways on the route.

-i *ttl*   This is used to set the Time to Live field to a specified value.

-v *tos*   Use this to set the Type of Service field to a specified value.

-r *count*   The option records the outgoing and returning packet routes in the Record Route field. You must specify a host count value between one and nine.

-s *count*   This is used to specify the timestamp for the number of hops set in the count value.

-j *computer_list*
               This is used to route packets via the hosts in the computer-list, up to a maximum of nine. Intermediate gateways may separate consecutive hosts.

-k *computer_list*
               This is used to route packets via the hosts in the computer-list, up to a maximum of nine. Intermediate gateways may not separate consecutive hosts.

-w *timeout*   This sets the timeout value. The timeout value is in milliseconds.

destination_list
               As the final command line parameter, lists the hosts to ping.

IPCONFIG

The IPCONFIG utility displays current network configuration values. When IPCONFIG is executed with no option switches, the following information about each network adapter is returned:

- IP Address
- Subnet Mask
- Default Gateway

When IPCONFIG is executed with the **/all** option switch, the following information about each network adapter is returned:

- Description of the network adapter
- Physical Address
- DCHP Enabled
- IP Address
- Subnet Mask
- Default Gateway

IPCONFIG also returns the following information about the machine itself.

- Host Name
- DNS Servers used by the host
- Node Type
- NetBIOS Scope ID
- IP Routing Enabled
- WINS Proxy Enabled
- NetBIOS Resolution Uses DNS

The information IPCONFIG offers is especially helpful when working with DHCP clients. Because IP addresses are assigned automatically for DHCP clients, IPCONFIG gives you an easy way to view the IP address assigned.

The following IPCONFIG parameters are supported:

/all   This option displays all configuration information for all installed adapters. Without this switch, IPCONFIG displays only IP Address, Subnet Mask, and Default Gateway information for all installed adapters.

/renew [*adapter*]
This option is only available on DHCP clients. It renews the DHCP configuration parameters.

/release [*adapter*]
This option is only available on DHCP clients. It releases the current DHCP configuration, disabling TCP/IP support on the specified adapter. If an adapter is not specified, TCP/IP is disabled on the system.

NOTE: DHCP client and server configuration and support are discussed in detail later in the course.

TELNET

TELNET provides access, through terminal emulation, to any host running a TELNET daemon service. This includes most UNIX hosts, as well as DEC and IBM mainframes running TCP/IP. It is also commonly used for remote configuration of hubs and routers. You cannot logon interactively to Windows NT through TELNET.

There are several variants of TELNET. This allows for versions configured in a manner appropriate to the host with which it is designed to communicate. Some versions have special terminal facilities, such as VT220 or VT320 support. Others have the ability to handle special data streams, such as providing 3270 or 5350 support for communication with IBM mainframes and minicomputers.

TELNET is also a powerful diagnostic tool. TELNET provides a way of sending commands directly to a server process and viewing the results when higher-level protocols or applications appear to be failing.

When launching a TELNET session, you specify both an IP address and a port/socket address. The port address defaults to 23 for the TELNET daemon process.

TELNET Utility

When you install TCP/IP on a Windows NT station, TELNET is added to the Accessories program group. This is a basic TELNET utility providing VT52, VT100, and TTY terminal emulation. None of these terminal emulation utilities provide a TELNET daemon.

To connect to a remote host, run **Connect** from the **Connect** menu. You are prompted to identify the destination host, either by host name or IP address. You can also specify the terminal emulation type, defaulting to VT100, and port ID, defaulting to telnetd even though NT does not have a telnetd process. There are additional port options supported, matching the simple TCP/IP services provided with Windows NT. You can connect to any service port by manually entering the port number. You can connect to a Simple TCP/IP Services service port on a Windows NT station through TELNET.

Simple TCP/IP Services

Simple TCP/IP services are accessed through TELNET. The following services are installed when you install Simple TCP/IP services on Windows NT.

ECHO (Port 7)
> The echo service echoes back everything that it receives.

CHARGEN (Port 19)
> This is a character generator that creates endless strings of characters until the connection is broken.

QOTD (Port 17)
> The Quote of the Day returns a random quote of up to 512 characters without regard to input. As soon as the quote is returned, the connection is broken. Windows NT provides a standard quote file or you can create your own. The quote file is stored under:

\systemroot\SYSTEM32\DRIVERS\ETC
> Where *systemroot* represents the WINNT installation directory.

DAYTIME (Port 13)
> The daytime service returns the date and time. Once returned, the connection is broken.

FTP Client

The FTP command uses File Transfer Protocol to transfer text and binary files between systems, including dissimilar platforms. If necessary, it will perform a format and type conversion on the file. FTP can be used interactively at the command prompt or in a script (batch) file. The source host must be running the FTP server service (daemon).

The syntax for FTP is:

```
ftp [-v] [-d] [-i] [-n] [-g]
    [-s:filename] [-a] [-w:windowsize]
```

FTP uses TCP to manage communications between hosts and ensure delivery.

FTP supports the following command-line options:

-v
> This option suppresses the display of remote server responses to the command.

-n
> Use this option to suppress auto-login at initial connection.

-i
> When performing multiple file transfers, this option can be used to disable interactive prompting.

-d
> This is used to enable debugging. When enabled, all FTP commands passed between the client and server are displayed.

-g
> This option disables filename globbing. When globbing is enabled (the default setting), wildcard characters are supported in local path and file names.

-s:*filename*
> This is used to execute a series of FTP commands. Replace filename with the name of a text file containing FTP command strings. When FTP starts, the commands in the file will be run automatically.

-a
> Any local interface can be used during data connection binding.

-w:*windowsize*
> Will override the default transfer buffer size.

FTP Commands

FTP supports a wide range of commands. There are 42 in Microsoft's implementation of the utility. This includes a mix of DOS and UNIX commands. For example, you can use either **dir** or **ls** to list the contents of the current working directory on the remote host. Type **help** at the FTP interactive mode prompt, FTP>, to display a list of supported commands. You can also view the command list and additional help through the Windows NT help system. Commands must be entered in lowercase.

Commonly used commands include:

help [*command*]Typing **help** without additional input displays a command list. Type help followed by a command's name to receive help information specific to that command.

quit or

bye   Running either **quit** or **bye** exits FTP interactive mode.

ascii   This converts the file transfer type to ASCII. This is the default setting. A carriage return is added after each line feed found in the file.

binary   This converts the file transfer type to binary.

get   Use the **get** command to transfer a file from a remote FTP server.

put   Use the **put** command to transfer a file to a remote FTP server.

Additionally, it is important to use the appropriate file transfer type. Text files frequently require CR (carriage return) codes appended to the end of each line. In a binary file, there may be values equal to the line feed character. Appending carriage returns would cause file corruption.

TFTP

Trivial File Transfer Protocol, the TFTP utility, supports the transfer of small files. However, it is a connectionless transfer and there is no session established with the host. This means that the user transferring the file is not authenticated. Because of this, Windows NT does not provide a TFTP server. It does include a TFTP client for connectivity to UNIX hosts. It transfers 512-byte packets using unacknowledged UDP services. With larger files, the receipt of each packet must be acknowledged by the destination host before the next can be sent. One application of TFTP, working with the BOOTP protocol, is passing bootstrap code and supporting initial server communications for diskless workstations. However, since Windows NT does not provide a TFTP server service, a third-party TFTP server must be used.

The syntax for TFTP is:

```
tftp [-i]host[get|put]
    source[destination]
```

TFTP supports the following command-line options:

-i   This option is used to transfer the file in binary mode, byte by byte. If not specified, ASCII mode transfer is used.

host   This required parameter specifies the local or remote host.

get   Specifying a **get** transfers a
            destination file on the remote host
            to the specified source file name on
            the local host.

put   Specifying a **put** transfers a source
            file on the local host to a specified
            destination file name on the remote
            host.

source   This is the file you want to transfer.

destination This is the location where the file
            will be stored.

FINGER

The FINGER utility displays information about a user,
or all users, on a specified host system. The remote host
must be running the FINGER service. The
information supplied is somewhat system (remote host)
specific.

The syntax for the command is:

```
finger [-l][user]@host
```

The following command-line parameters are supported:

-l   This specifies that a detailed listing,
            known as long list format, will be
            generated.

user   You have the option of entering a
            username, or specifying the host
            only. If only one user is specified,
            then only information about that
            user is displayed. If you do not
            specify a username, information
            about all users on that host is
            displayed.

host   This is the remote system from
            which you want to receive user
            information.

You can name a single user or host, or list multiple users
and hosts on the command line.

REXEC

The Remote Execution utility lets you pass commands
to a remote host for execution. REXEC requires
username and password authentication for execution.
After authentication, the command is immediately
executed and control is returned to the workstation.

The syntax for this command is:

```
rexec host [-l username][-n]command
```

host   This identifies the host on which
              the command is executed.

-l *username*   Use this command to specify the
              username for authentication. The
              remote host will prompt for the
              password.

              If a username is not specified, the
              current username is used. You are
              still prompted for a password.
              Passwords are not encrypted for
              transmission.

-n   If the **-n** option is used, command
              results are redirected to NULL and
              are not displayed.

command   Replace the parameter with the
              command name and any
              command-line parameters.

Any command-line parameters are passed with the
command. Redirects are also supported. You cannot
use REXEC to run interactive commands remotely.

Remote Shell Command

The next two commands can be used between a
Windows NT computer and a UNIX system running
the remote shell service, RSHD. The RSHD server
service is only available on UNIX-based systems.
Windows NT systems can issue commands, but cannot
act as the destination for the commands.

rsh   This command is used to initiate a command on a remote host that is running the RSHD service.

rcp   This command supports file transfer between a Windows NT system and an RSHD server, or between two RSHD servers from a command issued by an NT system.

To use either command, the following conditions must be met:

- The NT system responsible for username validation must be available.

- The .rhosts file in the user's home directory on the remote host must contain the user and host names for the user issuing the command.

- The hostname and IP address of the station issuing the command must be present in the HOSTS file.

The .rhosts file must be defined in advance of using either command.

.rhosts

The .rhosts file is used to identify remote users or systems that are given local account access through RSH or RCP. The file must exist in the user's home directory on the remote host. There is no provision for a password.

The .rhosts file is an ASCII text file with each entry recorded as a separate line, in a format similar to that shown below:

```
sta23 gwalls #This system in a
   floor 2, cubicle 15
```

Separate the local host and usernames with a space or tab. The pound (#) symbol is used to identify the start of a comment line. Comments are optional.

RSH

The Remote Shell is similar to REXEC and uses the same command-line parameters.

```
rsh host[-l username][-n]command
```

host   This identifies the host on which the command is to execute.

-l username Use this command to specify the username for authentication. If a username is not specified, the current username is used.

-n   If the **-n** option is used, command results are redirected to NULL and not displayed.

command   Replace the parameter with the command name and any command-line parameters.

The RSH command uses .rhosts for authentication.

RCP

The RCP utility copies files between local and remote hosts using .rhosts for user authentication. The command can also be used to copy files between two UNIX RSHD servers.

The syntax of the command is:

```
rcp [-a|-b][-h][-r] source1 source2
   ... destination
```

The following command options are supported:

-a   This specifies for the transfer to use ASCII transfer mode. This is the default transfer mode.

-b   Files are transferred using binary transfer mode.

-h	This option is required to transfer files with the hidden attribute set on a Windows NT system. Otherwise, any hidden files are ignored.
-r	This option performs a recursive copy, copying subdirectories and files under the source directory.
source	This identifies the source file for transfer. Multiple sources may be specified.
destination	This specifies the destination for file transfer. If multiple sources are specified, the destination must be a directory name.

Care must be taken that the source(s) and destination are entered in the proper format.

RCP Source/Destination

Source and destination entries both follow the same format under the RCP command:

```
[host[.user]:]filename
```

If the host is not specified, the local host is assumed. If the host is specified, but the user is not specified, the current Windows NT user account name is assumed. Because a period is used as a delimiter between the host and the user, you must explicitly define the user when using a specifying a host using the fully qualified domain name (FQDN). Otherwise, the last portion of the hostname is interpreted as the username.

You must also be careful when specifying the filename. The file is assumed to be in the current working directory unless the filename begins with a forward slash (/) for a UNIX host file or a reverse slash (\) for a Windows NT host file. A period (.) is used to identify the current directory in path. Wildcards may be used, if identified by escape characters (\, ", or ').

Microsoft Internet Explorer

Windows NT 4.0 ships with Microsoft Internet Explorer. This Web browser utilizes TCP/IP support. Once TCP/IP has been installed on the server, Internet Explorer can be used to:

- Browse local Web pages

    Type the name of the Web server on your local network to browse local Web pages.

- Connect to an Internet Service Provider

    Use a modem or ISDN connection to connect to the Internet. By installing Remote Access Service (RAS) in addition to TCP/IP, you can access the Internet through an Internet Service Provider.

- Access the Internet through your corporate network

    Connect to the Internet through your network proxy server (if available).

IP Address Configuration

Earlier you learned how to configure Windows NT to support a single IP address for a network adapter. Windows NT is also capable of supporting multiple addresses on the same adapter. You can also configure the system to use multiple default gateways. This may be necessary if, for example, you are supporting multiple logical subnets on the same physical network.

To configure support for multiple addresses, launch the Control Panel Network utility. Select the **Protocols** tab, select TCP/IP Protocol, and click on **Properties**. When the **IP Address** tab of the TCP/IP Properties page appears, click on **Advanced**.

An adapter with more than one configured address is called a multihomed adapter. At current levels, DHCP support is provided for the adapter's primary address, the one on the basic configuration screen only.

Advanced IP Addressing

The Advanced Microsoft TCP/IP Configuration dialog is used to manage multiple IP addresses, subnet masks, and default gateways. If you have multiple adapters installed, each is configured separately. Any changes you make will not take effect until you restart your system.

The Advanced IP addressing sheet allows you to set the following options:

- Adapter

    This is for selecting the adapter to which you will assign an additional IP address.

- IP Addresses

    To add an IP address to the list, click on **Add** and type the IP address and subnet mask in the appropriate fields. To edit an existing address, select the address and click on **Edit**. To remove an address, select the address and click on **Remove**.

- Gateways

    The default gateway values work in the same fashion. Click on **Add** and type the IP address of the default gateway. To edit an existing gateway, select the address and click on **Edit**. To remove a gateway, select it and click on **Remove**.

- Enable PPTP Filtering

    Check here to enable Point-to-Point Tunneling Protocol (PPTP) filtering. PPTP supports multi-protocol Virtual Private Networks (VPNs). This allows remote users to securely access corporate networks across the Internet. When checked, only PPTP packets are accepted, effectively disabling the adapter from accepting all other protocols.

- Enable Security

    This provides control over the type of TCP/IP network traffic that comes through the Windows NT server. This security is typically used on an Internet/intranet server.

TCP/IP Security Sheet

When you check **Enable Security** on the Advanced IP Addressing sheet, the **Configure** button becomes active. Click on **Configure** to display the TCP/IP Security Sheet.

- Adapter

    Select the adapter for which you are configuring TCP/IP security.

- Permit All

    The TCP Ports, UDP Ports, and IP Protocols are all set to **Permit All** by default.

- Permit Only

    The **Permit Only** option allows you to select only the TCP Ports, UDP Ports, and IP Protocols.

TCP Ports   Transmission Control Protocol (TCP) is the major transport protocol in the Internet suite of protocols, providing reliable, connection-oriented, full-duplex streams. It uses IP for delivery.

UDP Ports   User Datagram Protocol (UDP) is the connectionless transport protocol in the Internet suite of protocols. UDP, like TCP, uses IP for delivery. However, unlike TCP, UDP provides for exchange of datagrams without acknowledgments or guaranteed delivery.

IP Protocols   Internet Protocol (IP) is the layer 3 (routed) protocol used to transmit packets on a TCP/IP network.

Set security options as appropriate for your network requirements.

Configuration Parameters

The example below shows the information displayed by IPCONFIG for a sample configuration.

```
Windows NT IP Configuration


Token Ring adapter IbmTok1:

IP Address. . . . . . . . . :
    193.121.63.67
```

```
Subnet Mask . . . . . . . . :
    255.255.255.192
IP Address. . . . . . . . . :
    197.142.6.105
Subnet Mask . . . . . . . . :
    255.255.255.0
IP Address. . . . . . . . . :
    199.20.51.19
Subnet Mask . . . . . . . . :
    255.255.255.0
Default Gateway . . . . . . :
    193.121.63.65


Ethernet adapter Elnkii2:

IP Address. . . . . . . . . :
    193.131.216.97
Subnet Mask . . . . . . . . :
    255.255.255.192
Default Gateway . . . . . . :
    193.131.216.195
```

As you can see in the example, the Token Ring adapter in this system is configured to support three IP addresses. The Ethernet adapter is set up to support a single address.

MAC/IP Address Resolution

This section will provide a brief overview of address resolution relating to MAC addressing using the ARP utility. The following topics will be covered in this section:

- Address Resolution
- ARP Utility

While it is not commonly needed, there are situations where ARP can be a helpful support and troubleshooting tool.

Address Resolution

Address resolution remains a critical issue in a Windows NT environment. This is especially true when you consider the potentially volatile nature of IP addresses under DHCP. As previously discussed, Address Resolution Protocol (ARP) broadcasts are used to map IP addresses to MAC addresses.

If a system wishes to send a packet and only knows the receiving system's IP address:

- The host wishing to transmit a packet sends an ARP request.

- The ARP request is forwarded to every host on the local subnet.

- The host recognizing its IP address will record the sending system's IP and MAC addresses and transmit an ARP reply.

- The original sending system receives the reply and caches the destination system's IP and MAC addresses.

Relevant IP addresses and MAC addresses are kept in the local ARP cache for up to 10 minutes, at default configuration values. If the cache becomes full, the oldest entries are removed to make room for new entries.

ARP Utility

The ARP utility lets you manually view and manage the ARP cache. You can display current entries, add permanent entries, and delete entries.

The command is controlled through a set of options. Running ARP without any options displays the options list.

arp **-a** [*inet_addr*]
> The **-a** option queries TCP/IP and displays current ARP cache contents. Include *inet_addr* to display the IP and MAC addresses for the specified computer only.

arp **-N** [*if_addr*]
> The **-N** option can be used in combination with the **-a** option. It limits the display to the network adapter specified by *if_addr*.

arp **-d** *in_addr* [*if_addr*]
> The **-d** option deletes the ARP entry for the IP address specified as *in_addr*. You must include an IP address with this option. If a MAC address is supplied, only the entry for that network adapter is deleted.

arp **-s** *in_addr ether_addr* [*if_addr*]
> The **-s** option creates a permanent entry, mapping the IP address (*in_addr*) to the MAC address (*ether_addr*) specified. If a local adapter address is provided (*if_addr*), the entry is changed for that adapter only.

By making permanent entries for common destinations, you can reduce the broadcast traffic on your network. The ARP utility can also be helpful in diagnosing and correcting communications failures.

Routing

While discussing address concerns, we need to consider routing in a Windows NT environment. Any multihomed Windows NT Workstation or NT Server can act as a router. A multihomed host is a system with multiple IP addresses. Under NT, this can include:

- A single network adapter with multiple IP addresses.

    This situation occurs when you have multiple logical subnets communicating on the same physical network.

- Multiple adapters, each with its own IP address(es).

    This is used when you have multiple physical subnets.

In either case, you will first configure the TCP/IP protocol support for any installed adapters through the Control Panel Network utility. Points to remember include:

- Give each adapter a different IP address and the appropriate subnet mask.

- Each adapter can support up to five IP addresses and subnet masks.

- Routing can occur between different subnets on the same adapter and between the adapters.

A Windows NT 4.0 system can function as a RIP-based multiprotocol router.

Router Configuration

Configuring a multihomed system as a router is a simple case of enabling IP routing.

To enable IP routing:

1. Launch the Control Panel Network utility.

2. Select the **Protocols** tab, highlight TCP/IP Protocol, and click on **Properties**.

3. When the TCP/IP Properties sheet appears, select the **Routing** tab.

4. Click to set the **Enable IP Forwarding** checkbox.

This is a global setting affecting all network adapters. In other words, routing is either enabled for all installed adapters or it is disabled for all installed adapters.

Multiple Nets/Single Cable

The idea of multiple subnets on a single physical cable may initially seem a little confusing. In reality, it's relatively easy to understand.

The first thing to realize is that subnets are sometimes drawn as separate physical entities as a matter of convenience. It is easier to visualize them as being different subnets if they are physically shown as such. Subnets are, however, logical entities based on an IP address and subnet mask.

Systems with different IP addresses and subnet masks will not respond to each other's packets. This is true whether the packets are following a path between routers toward an eventual remote destination, or if the packet is addressed to a destination on the same cable. Packet delivery is based on the logical IP addressing, not physical proximity.

Since hosts on different subnets are unable to directly communicate, effectively ignoring each other, you can have any number of autonomous subnets configured on the same physical path. Communication between the hosts is only possible if facilitated by a router.

There are exceptions in this scenario. General protocol-based broadcasts, such as DHCP Discover packets, will be seen by all hosts, no matter what the logical subnet.

Router Example

When looking at a router and its router table, it is important that you have all the information you need at hand. For example, to quickly evaluate a system's router table, you need to know how its network adapter or adapters are configured. If you don't already have that information on hand, run **ipconfig /all** to list the installed adapters and configuration of each.

```
Windows NT IP Configuration

    Host Name. . . . . . . . . . . .
    :  UK-RTR01.wave.co.uk

    DNS Servers. . . . . . . . . . .
    :

    NetBIOS Scope ID . . . . . . . .
    :

    IP Routing Enabled . . . . . . .
    :  Yes

WINS Proxy Enabled . . . . . . . .
    :  No

    NetBIOS Resolution Uses ENS . . .
    :  No


Ethernet adapter NE2000:

    Description. . . . . . . . . . .
    :  Novell 200 Adapter

    Physical Address . . . . . . . .
    :  08-00-17-09-90-F0

    DHCP Enabled . . . . . . . . . .
    :  No

    IP Address . . . . . . . . . . .
    :  150.200.200.250

    Subnet Mask. . . . . . . . . . .
    :  255.255.255.0
```

```
    IP Address . . . . . . . . . . .
    :  150.200.100.250

    Subnet Mask. . . . . . . . . . .
    :  255.255.255.0

    Default Gateway. . . . . . . . .
    :  150.200.200.251

    Primary WINS Server. . . . . . .
    :  150.200.200.1


Token Ring adapter IbmTok2

    Description. . . . . . . . . . .
    :  IBM Token Ring Adapter

    Physical Address . . . . . . . .
    :  00-20-AF-0E-93-12

    DHCP Enabled . . . . . . . . . .
    :  No

    IP Address . . . . . . . . . . .
    :  150.200.201.250

    Subnet Mask. . . . . . . . . . .
    :  255.255.255.0

    Default Gateway. . . . . . . . .
    :

    Primary WINS Server. . . . . . .
    :  150.200.200.1
```

You can see that this machine, named UK-RTR01.wave.co.uk, has two network adapters installed.

The NE2000 Ethernet adapter (the first adapter listed) has two configured addresses. These are 150.200.200.250 and 150.200.100.250, both with a subnet mask of 255.255.255.0. That means this is a multihomed adapter. The default gateway for this adapter is 150.200.200.251.

The Token Ring adapter has a single IP address assigned, 150.200.201.250, with a subnet mask of 255.255.255.0. Its default gateway is blank, indicating that a default gateway has not been defined for this adapter.

With this information in hand, you are ready to take a look at the example netstat -r printout.

NETSTAT

The NETSTAT utility displays protocol statistics and current TCP/IP connections.

The following is the syntax for the **netstat** command:

```
netstat [-a] [-e] [-n] [-s] [-p
    protocol] [-r] [interval]
```

The following command-line parameters are supported:

-a   This will display all connections and listening ports.

-e   This option limits the display to Ethernet statistics. It can be combined with the -s option.

-n   Rather than attempting name look-ups, addresses and port numbers are displayed numerically.

-s   This option lets you display statistics per protocol. Default statistics include TCP, UDP, ICMP, and IP. Use the -p option to specify a selection from the default protocols.

-p *protocol*   This option lets you select the protocol to view, either TCP or UDP. If used in combination with the -s option, you may specify TCP, UDP, ICMP, or IP.

-r   This option displays the contents of the routing table.

interval   This parameter sets a period, in seconds, for redisplay of statistics. If not specified, the information is displayed once.

For our purposes, the coverage of **netstat** will be limited to using it to display router table information.

```
C:\>netstat -r

Route Table
```

Network Address	Netmask	Gateway Address	Interface	Metric
0.0.0.0	0.0.0.0	150.200.200.251	150.200.100.250	1
127.0.0.0	255.0.0.0	127.0.0.1	127.0.0.1	1
150.200.50.0	255.255.255.0	150.200.200.252	150.200.100.250	1
150.200.100.0	255.255.255.0	150.200.100.250	150.200.100.250	1
150.200.100.250	255.255.255.255	127.0.0.1	127.0.0.1	1
150.200.200.0	255.255.255.0	150.200.200.250	150.200.100.250	1
150.200.201.250	255.255.255.255	127.0.0.1	127.0.0.1	1
150.200.255.255	255.255.255.255	150.200.200.250	150.200.100.250	1
244.0.0.0	244.0.0.0	150.200.201.250	150.200.201.250	1
224.0.0.0	224.0.0.0	150.200.200.250	150.200.100.250	1
255.255.255.255	255.255.255.255	150.200.200.250	150.200.100.250	1

```
Active Connections
```

Proto	Local Address	Foreign Address	State
TCP	UK-RTR01:1025	150.200.100.2:nbsession	ESTABLISHED
TCP	UK-RTR01:1027	150.200.200.1:nbsession	ESTABLISHED
TCP	UK-RTR01:1029	150.200.100.2:nbsession	ESTABLISHED
TCP	UK-RTR01:nbsession	150.200.100.2:1048	ESTABLISHED

The first two entries do not refer to destination locations. 0.0.0.0 is a default gateway entry. Anything requiring routing and not covered elsewhere in this table is sent to the default gateway at 150.200.200.251, via the interface address 150.200.100.250. If you refer back to the IPCONFIG printout, you will see that both this default gateway and adapter address are defined on the first adapter. 127.0.0.0 refers to the local loopback.

The next address, 150.200.50.0 (subnet mask 255.255.255.0), is a network address identifying the route for all host addresses on that network. This is a remote subnetwork. You can tell because any transmissions for this are sent to a router at 150.200.200.252, via the network adapter addressed 150.200.100.250 (NE2000 adapter).

The remaining entries are all generated automatically, starting with a locally connected subnet, 150.200.100.0 (subnet mask 255.255.255.0). The entry tells you that packets are not being routed to another subnet, but being kept local. You can tell this because the Gateway Address and Interface entries are the same.

The address 150.200.100.250 is for the local machine. You can identify entries for a local host because they have a subnet mask of 255.255.255.255. The Gateway Address and Interface entries are both set to local loopback.

The next two entries follow the same pattern, a local network address (150.200.200.0) and a local machine address (150.200.201.250).

The 244.0.0.0 and 224.0.0.0 entries are used internally. These are Class D (multicast) addresses. The final table entry is the local broadcast address.

Close examination of this table indicates what might look like an inconsistency. On some routes, you have packets going out through 150.200.100.250, but going to either 150.200.200.250 or 150.20.200.252, a different network. This is possible because the NE2000 adapter is a multihomed adapter. Both 150.200.100.250 and 150.200.200.250 are physically attached to the same network, the same network as the destination routers.

ROUTE Command

The **route** command is primarily used to enter static routing information at static routers. Although Windows NT 4.0 supports dynamic routing, the **route** command can still be used to view, modify, or add routing table information. The syntax for the command is:

```
route [-f] [command[destination][mask
    subnet_mask][gateway]]
```

The following parameters are supported:

-f	This option clears all gateway entries from the routing tables. If used with an additional command, the tables are cleared before executing the command.
-p	Makes a route persistent (preserved when the system is rebooted) when used with the **add** command. Use with the **print** command to display a list of persistent routes.
command	Four optional commands are supported:
print	This command prints a route.
add	Use this command to add a route to the routing table.
delete	This command is used to delete a route.
change	This command lets you modify an existing route.
destination	This identifies the destination host or network for the route and command execution.

mask subnet_mask

> This is used to specify a subnet mask value to be associated with the route entry. A default value of 255.255.255.255 is used if nothing is entered.

gateway   The gateway is the next router on the way to the destination.

Symbolic names may be used for the destination and gateway values.

Changes are only remembered as long as the router is up and running. After shutdown, any route additions must be made again. This does not apply to routes that were added with the **-p** parameter.

TRACERT

The **tracert** command will report information about the route that is used between you and a remote host. For example:

```
C:\WINDOWS>tracert www.microsoft.com

Tracing route to www.microsoft.com
  [207.68.156.16]

1  236ms 216ms 228ms border3-serial2-
   2.KansasCity.mci.net
   [204.70.42.17]

2  260ms 273ms 258ms core1-fddi-
   0.KansasCity.mci.net [204.70.2.65]

3  254ms 308ms 236ms
   KansasCity.mci.net [204.70.4.249]

4  288ms 235ms 280ms core2-hssi-
   2.Denver.mci.net [204.70.1.157]

5  286ms 284ms 261ms borderx1-fddi-
   1.Seattle.mci.net [204.70.203.52]

6  268ms 278ms 285ms borderx1-fddi-
   1.Seattle.mci.net [204.70.203.52]
```

```
7  338ms 319ms 308ms
   microsoft.Seattle.mci.net
   [204.70.203.106]

8  260ms 294ms 282ms 207.68.145.54

9  286ms 478ms 278ms www.microsoft.com
   [207.68.156.16]

Trace complete.
```

Tracert uses a series of packets to discover the route. The first is sent with a TTL of one. The TTL is increased by one on each packet until the destination is found.

Each router will decrement the TTL by (at least) one before forwarding to the next router in the path. When the TTL on a packet goes to zero, the router should send back an ICMP time exceeded to the source. These are intercepted by **tracert** and used to build the route.

It should be noted that some routers drop expired packets without generating an error message. These routers will be invisible to **tracert**.

TRACERT Options

The **tracert** command uses the following syntax:

```
tracert [-d] [-h max_hops] [-j
   host_list] [-w timeout] target_name
```

The following options are supported:

-d   This specifies that IP addresses should not be resolved to hostnames.

-h *max_hops*   This sets a limit on the number of hops that will be attempted when trying to reach the target, defaulting to 30.

-j *host_list*   This is used to specify an informal source routing along the hosts listed.

-w *timeout*   The timeout value sets the maximum time that the command will wait for a reply on an Echo packet it has sent out.

target_name   This identifies the name of the target host.

Unless otherwise specified, an attempt will be made to resolve the host name for any returned IP addresses.

DHCP Assignment

Let's take a quick look at the process used for assigning client addresses.

- DHCP client IP address is set to 0.0.0.0 and the Discover packet is sent.

    The Discover packet (DHCP request) is used to locate a DHCP server.

- Discover packet received and Offer packet sent.

    Any DHCP server receiving the Discover packet and having an available IP address responds with an Offer packet. The Offer packet includes the proposed IP address, subnet mask, and lease time.

- Offer received and Request sent.

    The client will select an Offer packet, usually the first one it receives. It will broadcast a Request packet that includes the IP address of the offering DHCP server. Any DHCP servers whose offer was not accepted will return the offered IP address to the available address pool.

- Request received and ACK sent.

    When the offering DHCP server receives the Request, it responds with an ACK. The ACK packet will include the client IP address and subnet mask, the DHCP server IP address and subnet mask, lease time, T1 and T2 times, and any other requested parameters for which the server is configured.

After the client has received its address, it is considered to be in the bound state. Once assigned, the client will continue to use this address until released or until the lease period expires.

DHCP Renewal

Along with its lease time, a DHCP client receives two additional times:

T1   This is 50% of the lease time. After this time period passes, the client will begin attempting to renew its lease from the issuing server.

T2   This is 87.5% of the lease time. After this time period passes, the client will attempt to renew its lease from any server.

At the T1 time, the client moves into the renewal state. The client will issue a Request containing its current IP address. The issuing DHCP server should respond with an ACK containing configuration parameters, including any changed parameters, such as the revised lease time.

If the client is unable to renew its address, it enters the rebinding state at the T2 time. The client will broadcast its Request and wait for response from any server. It is unlikely that any DHCP server will be able to respond with verification of the IP address. The client will continue to use its current address until the lease expires, at which time it will issue a Discover packet and bid for a new address.

DHCP Client

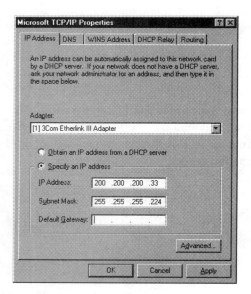

You can select to configure a system as a DHCP client during installation or through the Control Panel Network utility. To configure from the Network utility:

1. Launch the Control Panel Network utility.

2. Select the **Protocols** tab, highlight TCP/IP Protocol, and click on **Properties**.

3. Select the **Obtain an IP address from a DHCP server** option button. You will receive a message verifying that you want to enable DHCP.

4. Click on **Yes**.

5. Click on **OK** to close the TCP/IP Properties sheet.

6. Click on **OK** to exit the Network utility. You will be prompted to restart the system.

The DHCP server can be configured to supply all additional configuration parameters for your client, minimizing the time and effort required for client administration.

Normally, only workstations are configured using DHCP. Servers and routers should be configured manually. This will help ensure the reliability of these devices should a DHCP server fail.

IPCONFIG will display the IP address and other configuration information, as shown in earlier examples. You can run **ipconfig /renew** to force renewal of the current IP address, or to bid for an address if one doesn't exist for the client. Run **ipconfig /release** to release the current IP address. This will leave the client without an address.

DHCP Server

To set up a system as a DHCP Server, you must install the DHCP Server service. To do so:

1. Launch the Control Panel Network utility.

2. Select the **Services** tab and click on **Add**.

3. When the Select Network Service dialog box appears, select Microsoft DHCP Server and click on **OK**.

4. Enter the path to the installation source files and click on **Continue**.

5. When returned to the Network Services page, click on **Close**.

6. When prompted, select to restart your system.

Installation adds the DHCP Manager utility to the Administrative Tools (Common) program group. After Windows NT restarts, use DHCP Manager to configure the DHCP Server service.

DHCP Manager

DHCP Manager is used to configure DHCP parameters for DHCP servers. Each DHCP server will have a DHCP scope, the IP addresses available for assignment, excluded addresses, and the lease duration. You can also define a name and textual comment field to further identify the DHCP server.

DHCP Manager also supports a number of additional options, letting it automatically configure client parameters such as:

*   Router information
*   DNS Servers
*   WINS Servers

This, as well any other configuration information you've defined, is passed to the DHCP clients with the IP address acknowledgment (ACK packet).

DHCP Scope

To create a scope definition, select the DHCP server's IP address from the list on the initial DHCP Manager screen and run **Create** from the **Scope** menu. Type the Start Address and End Address under the IP Address Pool to define the range of addresses supported. You must also identify any excluded addresses, such as addresses within the range that are assigned to non-DHCP clients.

Define the lease period as a period of days, hours, and minutes. This will be used to calculate the T1 and T2 times for renewal and rebinding. You may also select to set the lease period as unlimited, in which case client IP addresses never expire.

The Name and Comment fields are both optional.

When you click on **OK**, you will be prompted with the option of activating the scope immediately. You will normally not enable the scope until all other configuration parameters have been defined.

Defining Scopes

Before defining the DHCP server's scope:

*   Determine the valid IP address range to be supported.
*   Determine the appropriate subnet mask value.
*   Identify any addresses to be excluded.
*   Do not define overlapping scope values.

The procedures for determining an appropriate subnet mask and calculating the valid IP address range were discussed earlier in the course.

It is possible to define multiple scopes on the same DHCP server. If you select to do this, it is strongly suggested that you enter appropriate text strings in the Name and Comment fields. This will help you identify the scopes and how they are meant to be used.

By defining multiple scopes for a DHCP server, you enable it to support multiple subnetworks. It is generally suggested that this be limited to subnetworks connected by high-speed links.

About Leases

The lease period defines how long a client may use an assigned IP address without having to renew or having the address expire. As described earlier, the client will attempt to renew the IP address with the issuing DHCP server, and if unable, will attempt to renew the address with any available server. If the client does not renew the address (for example, if the client has been removed from the network) its IP address becomes available for reassignment after lease expiration.

The default lease time is three days. This value may be too short for some businesses, since it does not account for systems that may be turned off over holidays or long weekends. As systems come back online and have to bid for new addresses, there will be an increase in broadcast traffic.

Use a short lease period when there is a regular need to reassign IP addresses, for example:

- When the number of hosts is near or exceeds the available IP address range, but hosts are used infrequently.

- When supporting a mobile user population, such as a number of Notebook PCs.

Use a longer lease period when there is seldom a need to reassign IP addresses. For example:

- When there is sufficient capacity on the subnet to meet IP addressing requirements.

- When supporting a stable user population that seldom moves or goes offline.

A lease period of nine days is generally suggested as a good compromise for most situations.

DHCP Options

Windows NT, Windows for Workgroups, and Windows 95 clients require parameters, in addition to the IP address and subnet mask, such as the default router, DNS server, and WINS server. This information may be configured at the client, at the DHCP server for a particular scope, or globally for all scopes defined on the DHCP server.

- Locally configured parameters take precedence over those defined at the DHCP server.

- Parameters defined for a particular scope take precedence over those defined globally for the DHCP server.

- Global configuration values are only used for parameters not defined locally or for the scope.

The DHCP Manager's **DHCP Options** menu lets you set the Scope and Global configuration options, as well as defined default option values.

Supported Options

Windows and Windows NT clients will only request the following configuration parameters in addition to the IP address, subnet mask, and T1 and T2 renewal values.

- Router [03]

    If one router IP address is entered, it is assumed to be the default gateway. If multiple addresses are entered, the DHCP client will query each in turn when communicating with a remote host.

- DNS Server [06]

    This allows you to identify one or more DNS servers. The servers are queried for DNS name resolution in the order entered.

- Domain Name [15]

    This allows you to specify the name of the domain that the client should use for host name resolution.

- WINS/NBNS Servers [44]

    One or more WINS/NBNS servers may be identified. They will be queried for name resolution in the order entered.

- WINS/NBT Node Type [46]

    This allows you to enter the node type as B-Node, P-Node, M-Node, or H-Node. When using WINS, select H-Node.

- NetBIOS Scope ID [47]

    This option lets you configure a NetBIOS scope ID, if required.

Several additional parameters can be configured under the DHCP Manager. This is to allow the DHCP server to remain compliant with all possible DHCP client types, rather than limiting support to Windows-family clients only.

Options Configuration

Run **Scope** or **Global** from the **DHCP Options** menu to configure optional parameters. Active options are listed on the right. Unused options, those listed on the left, are options you have not defined. The **Value** button displays the option's value, by expanding the lower part of the dialog.

Click on **Edit Array** to add, modify, or remove option values. The edit screen will be somewhat specific to the type of value being edited.

You will need to activate the scope after all configuration option values have been entered. Once activated, the DHCP server can begin issuing client IP addresses.

Client Reservations

Microsoft DHCP Server offers a way to reserve an IP address for a specific client computer. This feature will ensure that the client receives the same IP address each time it is started on the network. Some of the clients that may require reserved addresses include:

- Domain controllers (if the network uses LMHOSTS files to specify the IP addresses of the domain controllers).

- Windows NT servers that are used as routers.

- DNS servers.

- WINS servers.

NOTE: If your network uses more than one DHCP server to assign IP addresses in the same scope, the client reservations should be the same on each DHCP server. That way, you can be assured that the client will receive the proper IP address regardless of which DHCP server assigns the address.

To create a client reservation, launch the **DHCP Manager**, and select **Add Reservations** from the **Scope** menu.

When the Add Reserved Clients dialog box appears, enter the following information:

- IP Address

  Enter the address to be reserved for the client.

- Unique Identifier

  Enter the MAC address of the client's network adapter card. The MAC, or physical, address can be found by typing **ipconfig /all** at the client machine.

- Client Name

  Enter the name of the client computer.

- Client Comment

  Use this field for any optional comments.

Ongoing Management

Once configured, DHCP servers require little ongoing management. After activation, the server will begin leasing addresses to requesting clients. The **Active Leases** selection in the **Scope** menu lets you view the current leases.

Active leases are shown in our example, along with each machine's NetBIOS name.

You can select properties for any client, which displays the:

- IP address
- MAC address
- Client name
- Comment
- Lease expiration date/time

You can also use IPCONFIG to identify the address assignment at the client end.

DHCP Support on Large Networks

On a large network, it is unlikely that you would place a DHCP server on each subnet. One DHCP server can support multiple subnets, through the use of multiple scopes, providing that the client can communicate with the server.

This is accomplished through RFC 1541 and 1542 BOOTP specification-compliant routers. Routers meeting these specifications have the ability to forward DHCP broadcasts. Here's how the process works:

- The router receives the Discover packet from the client.
- The router forwards the packet, attaching its IP address in the giaddr (Relay IP Address) field.
- The DHCP server examines the giaddr field value and checks for matching scopes.

At that point, the lease process continues normally with the issue of an Offer, a Request, and an ACK.

By using DHCP Relay agents to forward packets between clients and preconfigured DHCP servers, it would be possible for one DHCP server to support an entire network. This is not suggested, since it creates a potential single point of failure for the entire network. However, it may be necessary in situations where you do not have an RFC-1542 compliant BOOTP router.

You have the option of managing remote access server (RAS) clients through a static pool configured through the RAS server service. Any addresses included in this pool should be excluded from your DHCP scopes.

DHCP Relay Agent

In order for a Windows NT 4.0 machine to function as a DHCP relay agent, you must install the DHCP Relay Agent service.

To install the DHCP Relay Agent service:

1. Access the **Services** tab of the Control Panel Network utility and click on **Add**.

2. Select DHCP Relay Agent and press *ENTER*. Provide the path to the installation files and click on **Continue**.

3. Click on **OK** to close the Network utility.

4. You will be prompted to restart your system after installation.

You must also identify the DHCP servers being supported. DHCP messages will be forwarded to the server(s) listed. You will be prompted for this information during installation. However, you may add or change the settings later. DHCP relay parameters are set through the **DHCP Relay** tab of the TCP/IP Properties sheet.

Disaster Planning

When planning a network, you must always look ahead to "What if?" situations. For example, what if one of your DHCP servers fails? Clients with valid leases will continue to operate until their leases expire, but will be unable to renew. New clients coming online will be unable to receive an IP address.

Unfortunately, Microsoft's implementation of DHCP does not support replication between multiple servers. Each DHCP server must be configured with unique IP address scopes. There is still a way, however, to set up backup DHCP servers.

Rather than assigning all available addresses on the primary DHCP server, the address scope should only contain about 80% of the addresses. Normally, the primary DHCP server will be the one nearest the supported subnet.

The remaining 20% should be configured on the backup DHCP server. If the primary server fails, the backup server will be able to provide IP addresses for clients whose addresses expire or for new clients coming on the network. It will also provide client addresses should the primary DHCP server exhaust all of the addresses in its scope.

DHCP Configuration Files

Before leaving the subject of DHCP support, some mention should be made of the configuration file locations. On the client side, the client IP address as well as that of the DHCP server is stored in the registry. For Windows NT, it is stored at:

```
HKEY_LOCAL_MACHINE\SYSTEM
    \CurrentControlSet\Services
    \adapter_ID\Parameters\Tcpip
```

Each adapter installed in the system will have a different adapter ID.

The DHCP database and related information is stored under the following directory:

```
systemroot\SYSTEM32\DHCP
```

The *systemroot* placeholder refers to the Windows NT destination directory during installation. DHCP information will include the following files:

- DHCP.MDB

  This is the DHCP database containing DHCP information such as active leases.

- J50.LOG and J50#####.LOG

  These contain a log of all database transactions and can be used by the database to recover data.

- J50.CHK

  This is a database checkpoint file.

- DHCP.TMP

  This is a temporary file used as a swap file by the DHCP database.

These files appear similar to Microsoft Access files, but cannot be read if opened under Access. By default, the DHCP database is backed up every 15 minutes. That interval can be changed by editing the BackupInterval parameter of the following Registry key:

```
HKEY_LOCAL_MACHINE\SYSTEM
    \CurrentControlSet\Services
    \DHCPServer\Parameters
```

DHCP Configuration Scenario

Read through the scenario and determine how you would meet all of the configuration requirements. A sample solution in provided in Appendix A at the end of the manual.

You have three LANs, each with its own assigned Class C address, connected by 56-Kbps links. Each LAN currently has no more than 100 nodes and is expected to grow to no more than 150 nodes. The routers connecting the LANs are BOOTP-compliant.

Currently, static address assignments are being used. This causes a problem with managing field sales personnel who travel between the offices. You have been tasked with setting up DHCP for the LANs. Traffic between LANs should be kept to a minimum, but you want to build in a level of fault tolerance so that addresses are available should a server be taken down for maintenance.

How would you set up DHCP support?

HOSTS Names

HOSTS name resolution uses a locally stored ASCII text file. The file is named HOSTS and is stored in the *systemroot*\SYSTEM32\DRIVERS\ETC directory. Since this is an ASCII text file, it can be edited using any ASCII text editor.

Each HOSTS file entry will contain an IP address, a *TAB* or space, and one or more symbolic name(s). A *TAB* is the preferred delimiter.

```
193.121.98.65     mainserver
193.121.98.78     wavesite WAVESITE
                  wbase WBASE
```

Each IP address should appear only once in the HOSTS file. Any number of aliases, each separated by a *TAB*, may be included on the line. Host names are case-sensitive, so host names are often entered as both lower and upper case. If you decide to use HOSTS name resolution, edit the sample HOSTS file that was created when you installed TCP/IP. Include the IP addresses and host names with which you need to communicate.

If a HOSTS file exists, it will be parsed by TCP/IP when a command is issued with a symbolic name. Depending on how your system is configured, other methods may first be consulted for name resolution.

HOSTS name resolution does not support **net use**, or other Microsoft network-style commands. These must be managed through NetBIOS name resolution.

DNS Resolution

DNS was discussed earlier in the course. It is the global name system used by TCP/IP hosts on the Internet. It is also sometimes used for name management on large private internetworks. A hierarchy of DNS servers respond to names requests from TCP/IP hosts.

Under DNS, millions of host names can be configured and managed. The database(s) containing the host names can be centrally managed.

Windows NT 4.0 includes a DNS Server service and graphic interface for managing DNS entries. You can configure windows clients to query DNS running on NT or DNS servers on other platforms. One or more DNS servers can be specified for name resolution.

Domain Name System (DNS)

The Domain Name System, or DNS, allows users to locate systems and access information from UNIX-based systems, across the Internet, and in corporate intranets. Administrators can easily configure and manage name-to-IP address mapping through a graphical administration tool. Before the GUI utility, administrators would manually edit an ASCII file to resolve IP addresses. This process was tedious and error-prone.

A DNS name server is a subtree of a DNS database that is administered as a single separate entity also called a zone. A zone can consist of a single domain or a domain with subdomains. One or more name servers can be set up for the zone.

Under Windows NT Server 4.0, the DNS server is RFC-compliant. DNS server supports RFCs 1033, 1034, 1035, 1101, 1123, 1183, and 1536. It is also compatible with BIND (Berkeley Internet Name Domain) implementation. Since DNS server is RFC-compliant, it creates and uses standard DNS database files and record types. These are also known as resource record types.

Microsoft goes beyond the standard features of RFCs by having a graphical user interface (DNS Manager) to aid administration. It also supports tight integration with WINS. Integration of DNS and WINS services allow interoperability between non-Microsoft and Microsoft Windows-based TCP/IP clients and provides the ability to resolve host names for Windows-based computers using DHCP IP addressing and NetBIOS computer names.

DNS as Primary and Secondary Servers

Microsoft's DNS server is not limited to being only a primary server. It can be a secondary server to another Microsoft DNS server or a DNS server that is running under another operating system.

- A primary name server pulls from the local DNS database file(s) to get the data for its zones.

- A secondary name server receives its zone data file from the primary DNS server that is authoritative for that zone.

When a DNS server receives a DNS name query, it tries to resolve the information by retrieving data from its local zone files. If it is unable to resolve the information, the server will communicate with the other DNS servers to resolve the request.

Caching-only Servers

DNS servers that only perform queries, cache the answers, and return the results are called caching-only servers. Caching-only servers will only store data that has been cached while resolving queries and they are not authoritative to any domain(s). In other words, they do not store host name and address information for any domain.

Caching-only servers initially start with no cached information and build up the information as they service requests over time. With that in mind, a caching-only server does not generate zone transfer over the network traffic.

To set up a server as a caching-only server, do not configure it as the primary server for any domain.

DNS Installation

The Control Panel Network utility is used to install DNS on an NT Server. To add the Microsoft DNS Server service:

1. Launch the Control Panel Network utility.

2. Select the **Services** tab.

3. Click on **Add**.

4. Select Microsoft DNS Server from the Network Service list, and click on **OK**.

5. The system prompts for the location of the installation source media. This can be either a drive path or a UNC name and path. After verifying that the path is correct, the system will transfer the files necessary for your selected options.

6. When you return to the Network Settings dialog, click on **Close** to complete the installation.

7. Restart the system when prompted. You must restart the system for the changes to take effect.

DNS Manager

When you install DNS, the DNS Manager is installed and added to the **Start** menu's **Administrative Tools** submenu. Through DNS Manager, you can:

- Add a new server.

    Run **New Server** from the **DNS** menu to add a DNS server. You will be prompted for the name or IP address of the DNS server. The server must be running and accessible. An icon with the name or the IP address will appear under the Server List. You can also add a new server by clicking with mouse button two on the Server list, then running **New Server** from the pop-up menu.

    NOTE: If a red X is drawn through the icon, it indicates that the DNS Manager was unable to connect to the specified server.

    Three reverse lookup zones are added by default: 0.in-addr.arpa, 127.in-addr.arpa, and 255.in-addr.arpa. These are added for performance reasons. The administrator does not need to do anything with them.

- Add a new zone.

    A primary zone has a Start of Authority (SOA) resource record associated with it and is also known as the zone root domain. A world icon in the DNS Manager Server List represents the primary zone(s). A secondary zone is a read-only copy of an existing zone.

Adding a Server

After you launch the DNS Manager for the first time, you will need to add the DNS Server to the list of those being managed. Run **New Server** from the **DNS** menu. Type in the server name or IP address and click on **OK**.

The only entry below the server name after initial creation is for cached entries.

Adding a Zone

When installing a new DNS Server and setting up your network, one of the first things you will likely want to do is add a zone. To add a new zone, highlight the DNS Server List icon. Run **New Zone** from the **DNS** menu or right-click on the DNS Server List icon and choose **New Zone** from the pop-up menu. Choose **Primary** or **Secondary** from the Zone Type area. Click on **Next**.

Enter a name for the zone in the Zone Name field. When you click in the Zone File field, the system will put the zone name in by default. You may change this name to something that is easier to remember. Click on **Next**, then click on **Finish**.

This will add the zone folder icon with the zone name.

Adding Host Records

You can add host records to either a zone or domain. Select the zone or domain and run **New Host** from the **DNS** menu. Alternately, you can right-click on the zone or domain and run **New Host** from the pop-up menu.

You will be prompted for the host's name and IP address. Click on **Add Host** after entering the information. Click on **Done** after entering all of your host records.

While this is a somewhat manual procedure, it is still an improvement over many earlier implementations of DNS servers on other platforms. Often, adding a host entry required manually editing multiple files.

Additional DNS Manager Procedures

You can also perform the following procedures through the DNS Manager:

- Pause Zone

    To pause a zone, highlight the zone, then either open the **DNS** menu or right-click the highlighted zone, and choose **Pause Zone**. This effectively takes the zone offline. The zone's icon will have two bars across it showing that it has been paused.

- New Domain

    To add a new domain to the zone, highlight the zone, then either open the **DNS** menu or right-click the appropriate zone and choose **New Domain**. In the Domain Name box enter a name for the new domain in that zone, then click on **OK**.

- New record

    A New Record can be added to either a zone or a domain. There are several different records that may be added. A listing is provided in Appendix C.

- Delete

    Delete is used to remove any item that the administrator may have added. To delete an item, highlight the item and choose **Delete** from the **DNS** menu or press *Y*. You will be prompted to verify your action.

- Update Server Data Files

    Choosing to update server data files from the DNS menu will broadcast any updated or new information about the DNS server to secondary DNS name servers the authoritative DNS server has been configured to notify.

- Properties

    Properties allow the administrator to update any item listed. To view the properties of an item, highlight the item and choose **Properties** from the **DNS** menu.

- Split

    This option allows the administrator to re-proportion the panes of the DNS Manager window. To activate Split, choose **Split** from the **View** menu or click on and drag the splitbar.

- Refresh

    Refresh causes the DNS Server to recheck all connections. To activate Refresh either choose **Refresh** from the **View** menu or press *F5*.

- Preferences

    This allows the administrator to set up a timed auto refresh. To set up auto refresh, run **Preferences** from the **Options** menu.

DNS Client Configuration

The **DNS** tab of the Control Panel Network utility allows you to configure the computer to use the DNS to resolve the names of Internet or UNIX computer(s).

- Host Name

    This is used to identify your computer on the network. By default, this is the Windows NT computer's machine name.

- Domain

    This is used to enter the domain name to which your computer belongs.

- DNS Service Search Order

  This provides name resolution by allowing you to specify the IP addresses of the DNS servers. The query is done in the order in which the server's IP addresses are listed.

- Domain Suffix Search Order

  This allows you to append DNS domain suffixes to host names during name resolution. There can be up to six domain suffixes and they will append in the order listed. A domain suffix is a name that identifies your computer on the Internet.

Using Domain Names

It is not always necessary to use the FQDN when communicating with a remote host. You can use only the host name if:

- The host is part of your local DNS domain.

- The host domain is listed in your Domain Suffix Search Order.

The domain suffix is automatically appended to the host name for name resolution, starting with the local domain suffix and working through the search order list. If attempting to communicate with a host that is not part of the local DNS domain and whose domain is not listed in the Domain Suffix Search Order, you must provide the FQDN.

Domain names, host names, and associated IP addresses are stored in hierarchical domain databases, as described earlier in the course. These are managed and queried through the DNS server. DNS databases and DNS server support are beyond the scope of this course.

DNS and WINS Integration

A DNS zone will change when a host is moved to a different subnet or when a new host is added. Because DNS is not dynamic, the administrator must manually change the DNS database file so that the zone will reflect the new configuration. This can cause a lot of administrative overhead if zones change frequently. To help eliminate the overhead, WINS and DNS have been integrated in Windows NT Server 4.0. Microsoft has used the strong points of each product to make, for a lack of a better term, a dynamic DNS. When DNS needs to resolve a name at the lower level of a DNS tree zone, it will query WINS. Because all of this is transparent, it appears as though DNS is handling the entire process. Let's look at an example of DNS and WINS integration.

The Scenario

In this example there is a local DNS name server and a MAIN DNS server. A user, at a client workstation, enters a URL to access the accounting folder on the intranet. Before a connection can be established, DNS and WINS must resolve the IP address for the FQDN. The URL that is being used is //company.WAVETECH.MAIN.com/accounting. No data is being cached on the name server for this procedure.

How It Works

The DNS client will send a resolution request to the local DNS name server. The local DNS name server will forward the request to the DNS root server. (DNS root servers are used to resolve such things as com, edu, org, etc.) The DNS root server will find the com at the MAIN DNS server and will send a packet to the local name server instructing it to go to the MAIN server for further resolution. At this point the local DNS name server will send its original request to the MAIN DNS server. The MAIN DNS server will respond with a referral packet for the WAVETECH name server. The local DNS name server will now send its original request to the WAVETECH name server. The WAVETECH name server is configured to use WINS to resolve the host name. Upon receiving the request, the WAVETECH name server will contact its WINS server to resolve the company part of the DNS name. The WINS server will send an IP address for company to the WAVETECH name server. The local DNS name server will then receive an IP address for the FQDN from the WAVETECH name server. The local DNS name server will send the IP address to the client system. The client system will establish a connection with company.WAVETECH.MAIN.com and the user will be able to access the accounting folder.

> *NOTE: If DNS caching had been enabled, the number of requests would have been reduced.*

In the previous example, the WAVETECH name server was the only component that was integrated with WINS. Because the integration is transparent, it appears as though the name was resolved through DNS. If the IP address changes for company.WAVETECH.MAIN.com, WINS will be automatically updated. Therefore, no changes will be needed on the DNS servers.

DNS and Third-Party DNS Servers

When using a third-party DNS server with Microsoft's DNS Server, you must manually add an A-type resource record to the zone data file for each virtual server IP Address/DNS domain name pair.

NetBIOS Names

Microsoft networks, including workgroups and Windows NT Server domains, always use NetBIOS names to identify workstations and servers. Machines recognize each other through unique machine names. Shared resources, files, and printers are accessed using NetBIOS names. For example, resources are identified by their Universal Naming Convention (UNC) name, in the format:

```
\\servername\share_name
```

In a UNC name, *servername* is the NetBIOS name of the machine where the resource is physically located and *share_name* is the name uniquely identifying the resource.

In an internetwork TCP/IP environment, it is necessary to support resolution between NetBIOS names and IP addresses. Microsoft provides two methods of supporting this name resolution:

- LMHOSTS

    Name resolution is based on a locally stored ASCII text file.

- WINS (Windows Internet Naming Service)

    Name resolution is based on WINS servers.

When designing your network, you will need to select the most appropriate method for your organizational requirements.

NetBIOS

Before looking at NetBIOS name resolution, let's take a closer look at NetBIOS names and their use. Microsoft NetBIOS names may contain up to fifteen characters and are used to identify entities to NetBIOS. These include: computers, domain names, workgroup names, and users.

The NetBIOS interface supports several easy-to-use commands to provide datagram and broadcast services.

All of these commands use NetBIOS names to identify the source and destination.

NetBIOS Commands

The NetBIOS command set is usually divided into four command categories:

- Name service

  These include commands to register a unique NetBIOS name, register a group (non-unique) name, such as domain name, and to release a name so it can be used by another system.

- Session service

  Session commands include those used to initiate, manage, and terminate a session.

- Datagram service

  These include commands for sending and receiving datagrams. Separate commands are provided for directly addressed and broadcast datagrams.

- Miscellaneous functions

  Included are commands for initializing a network adapter, aborting a pending command, and returning network adapter status.

NetBIOS is supported over most desktop communications protocols.

NetBIOS Name Resolution

RFCs 1001 and 1002 proposed NetBIOS name resolution methods for NetBIOS over TCP/IP implementations. These are:

- B-Node

  Broadcast node (B-node) is generally used on small IP networks with no routing requirements.

- P-Node

  Point-to-Point node (P-node) uses a NetBIOS Name Server (NBNS) to manage name resolution.

- M-Node

  Mixed node (M-node) is a combination of B-node and P-node. It is used when not all of the systems in the network can support P-node.

There are also two other variants not covered under the original RFCs. They are:

- H-Node

  Hybrid mode (H-node) is a new variant supporting dynamic NBNS. WINS is implemented as H-node.

- Enhanced B-node

  LMHOSTS name resolution uses a modified B-node.

B-Node

B-node is based on two broadcast types:

- Name registration requests

    A name registration request broadcasts a NetBIOS name and waits for a response. If none is received, the system assumes the name to be unique. If there is a duplicate of the name, the system with the duplicate name issues a negate name registration broadcast.

- Name query requests

    These are used to determine IP addresses. The information received is cached for future use.

Since many routers will not forward broadcasts, these are normally sent across the local subnet only. Routers that will forward broadcasts are not necessarily an improvement.

Forwarding all NetBIOS broadcasts increases network traffic and may cause performance problems.

P-Node

Under P-node, NetBIOS names and IP addresses are stored on an NBNS server. The server responds to all name query requests it receives and queries the database for the IP address associated with the NetBIOS name. Each host using P-node name resolution must be configured with the NBNS server's IP address.

While generally seen as an improvement over B-node where it can be implemented, P-node is not without its potential drawbacks:

- Server management

    In a large network, NBNS table maintenance can result in a significant amount of management overhead.

- Mixed environment

    In a mixed system environment, different operating systems will have different ways of handling NetBIOS. Not all of these environments will support NBNS access and will have to use B-node broadcasts.

Despite these potential problems, P-node can help to reduce network broadcast traffic and allow for efficient communications and name resolution across routers.

M-Node

M-node uses a mixture of B-node and P-node implementations. Stations will first attempt address resolution with a B-node broadcast. If this is unsuccessful, an attempt is made to contact an NBNS.

This method is relatively flexible and helps to reduce management overhead. Local address resolution is handled through broadcasts. The NBNS table will only need to contain entries for key remote hosts.

H-Node

H-node was developed to support dynamic NBNS servers. A current example of this is Microsoft WINS servers.

Each system registers itself with the WINS server during startup. This helps to ensure that the database will contain all systems with which you are likely to communicate. P-node is used first, in this case, to attempt address resolution using the WINS server's database. If this fails, B-node is used. Since most systems will be in the WINS server database, broadcast traffic is kept to a minimum.

LMHOSTS

LMHOSTS address resolution is a modified B-node resolution method. It uses a combination of B-node name querry broadcasts and the contents of one or more LMHOSTS files.

During address resolution with LMHOSTS support installed:

- The name is checked to see if it is a local name (assigned at the local computer).
- The local LMHOSTS cache is checked.
- A name query broadcast is issued.
- All LMHOSTS files are checked for the name.

If these methods fail, an error is returned that the network name was not found.

LMHOSTS File

The LMHOSTS file is stored in the \systemroot\SYSTEM32\DRIVERS\ETC directory, the same as the HOSTS file discussed earlier. A sample file named LMHOSTS.SAM is placed in that directory during installation. The actual file should be renamed LMHOSTS without the .SAM extension. The LMHOSTS file can contain both local and remote subnet entries. Below is a sample LMHOSTS file:

```
#This is the standard LMHOSTSfile for
   WAVE Technologies UK Ltd.

150.200.100.2  STL-DC01 #DOM:STLOUIS
   #Admin Server  & BBS

150.200.101.1  RST-DC01 #DOM:RESTON
   #Development Server

150.200.101.56 RST-WEB1 #WWW Server
   in Reston

#INCLUDE \\UK-DC-01\PUBLIC\LMHOST
   #Standard UK LMHOSTS file
```

```
#BEGIN_ALTERNATE

#INCLUDE \\EUR-DC01\PUBLIC\LMHOST
   #European LMHOSTS file

#INCLUDE \\USA-DC01\PUBLIC\LMHOSTS
   #US LMHOSTS file

#END_ALTERNATE

150.200.200.1  EUR-DC01 #DOM:EUROPE
   #PRE

150.200.200.2  UK-DC-01 #DOM:UK #PRE

150.200.100.1  USA-DC01 #DOM:USA #PRE
```

As you can see, the file format is similar to that used with the HOSTS file. It does, however, support some special keyword values.

LMHOSTS Example

Using the previous LMHOSTS file as an example, we can look at how name resolution occurs.

When the system initially launches, all #PRE entries are added to the LMHOSTS cache as permanent entries. Next, the system issues a broadcast name query.

When name resolution is attempted, and the name isn't local or in the cache, the LMHOSTS file is checked. Entries in the file are parsed in order. That is why the #PRE entries are the last entries in the file, so they aren't encountered every time the file is checked.

The IP address entries are checked first. Since the #DOM keyword is used to identify a domain controller, older types of systems, such as IBM LAN Server, will ignore the #DOM in the entry, treating it as a remark.

Next, any #INCLUDE entries are checked. Notice in our example that the IP address for the #INCLUDE entry is in the LMHOSTS file so that the system can be located. If still unable to locate the name and address, any entries between #BEGIN_ALTERNATE and #END_ALTERNATE are checked. LMHOST file entries, unlike their HOST file counterparts, are not case sensitive. Also, alias entries are not supported.

LMHOSTS Keywords

Some entries in the LMHOSTS file are preceded by a pound sign (#): In most cases, this indicates a comment line. In some cases, it is used to identify special keywords.

#PRE This is an entry that should be preloaded into the cache at system startup. Place these entries near the end of the file. They are only used during TCP/IP initialization.

#DOM:domain

This is used to identify domain controller entries. The entry is the domain controller for the specified domain.

#INCLUDE:filename

An #INCLUDE statement lets you use a remote, centrally managed LMHOSTS file. The file is treated as if it were a local LMHOSTS file. Use the #PRE statement to preload the servers containing LMHOSTS files into the cache.

#BEGIN_ALTERNATE...

#END_ALTERNATE

A list of LMHOSTS files will be bracketed between these statements. They are used to identify alternate LMHOSTS files. Alternate files are only read if the entry is not found in the cache or any of the preceding entries.

Your station must be configured for LMHOSTS support if using LMHOSTS files for address resolution.

LMHOSTS Configuration

The Control Panel Network utility is used to configure LMHOSTS support. After launching the Network utility, access the TCP/IP Properties sheet and select the **WINS Address** tab.

Enable LMHOSTS Lookup

When checked, LMHOSTS support is enabled. This is the default selection.

Import LMHOSTS

Click on the **Import LMHOSTS** button to specify the directory path to the LMHOSTS file you want to use.

Scope ID If using scope IDs, you must enter the appropriate value in this prompt.

As with other configuration parameters, you must restart the machine for any of the changes to take effect.

NBTSTAT

The **nbtstat** command is a diagnostic utility that lets you view and manage NetBIOS name cache information. The syntax for this command is:

```
nbtstat [-a remote] [-A IP_address]
   [-c] [-n] [-R] [-r] [-S]
   [-s] [interval]
```

The following command-line parameters are supported:

-a *remote*	This option lets you specify a remote computer's name and list its name table.
-A *IP_address*	This option lets you specify a remote computer by its IP address and lists the computer's name table.
-c	This option lists the contents of the NetBIOS name cache. The listing includes the IP address for each name.
-n	This option lists the local NetBIOS names and whether registered by B-Node broadcast or WINS.
-R	This option purges all names from the NetBIOS name cache and reloads the LMHOSTS file.
-r	Name resolution statistics are listed by this option.
-S	This option lists client and server sessions. Remote hosts are listed by IP address.
-s	This option lists client and server sessions. When possible, the HOSTS file is used to convert remote IP addresses to names.
interval	If specified, this sets the interval, in seconds, for repeating the information. If not specified, the information is printed once.

NBTSTAT Example

```
C:\>nbtstat -n

Node IpAddress:  [200.200.200.19]
   Scope Id: []

NetBIOS Local Name Table
```

Name	Type		Status
40SERVER	<20>	UNIQUE	Registered
40SERVER	<00>	UNIQUE	Registered
WONDERLAND	<00>	GROUP	Registered
WONDERLAND	<1C>	GROUP	Registered
WONDERLAND	<1B>	UNIQUE	Registered
40SERVER	<03>	UNIQUE	Registered
NTADMIN	<03>	UNIQUE	Registered
WONDERLAND	<1E>	GROUP	Registered

Looking at a sample **nbtstat -n**, you can see that a Windows system tracks several NetBIOS names. In this example, this includes the computer name 40SERVER and a domain name of WONDERLAND. There is also a user named NTAdmin logged on at the server. Along with each of these there is a hexadecimal value indicating a process running on the computer and attached to that NetBIOS name.

The hexadecimal values following the names are NetBIOS service IDs. The definition of each of these is related to the type of name with which it is associated. For example, a value of 03h following a computer name indicates that the messenger service is running on that computer. The same value following a username indicates that the user is registered to receive messages.

With its reliance on NetBIOS names, it is easy to see why it is necessary to find the IP address for NetBIOS names when working in a TCP/IP environment. When you also consider the size of many TCP/IP internetworks, you can see why management through broadcast only can be difficult.

Service IDs

In the previous example, each of the NetBIOS names had a service value attached. This is managed on Microsoft networking products by adding a sixteenth character to the NetBIOS name. Common extensions include:

computer	[00]	This indicates the workstation service process.
computer	[03]	This indicates that the messenger service is running at this computer.
computer	[BE]	This entry is listed if the Network Monitoring Agent is started.
computer	[1F]	This entry is listed if the Network DDE service is running.
computer	[20]	This identifies that the computer is running the server service.
domain	[00]	This is used to indicate domain membership so that the system can receive browser broadcasts.
domain	[1B]	This indicates that the machine is a domain controller, typically the primary domain controller.
domain	[1C]	This indicates the group name for domain controllers.
domain	[1D]	This indicates that the master browser is running on this machine.
domain	[1E]	This identifies the group name used by browsers.
username	[03]	This indicates that the current username is registered. This allows the user to receive messages from the **net send** command, the Alerter service, and any Print Job messages.
—__MSBROWSE__—	[01]	This is a special name used by the Browser service.

All values are given in hexadecimal.

WINS

Windows Internet Name Service, or WINS, is an automated way of supporting NetBIOS address resolution. It is a modification to NBNS, using dynamic name registration. As each WINS client system starts up, it registers itself with a WINS server.

WINS uses H-node for address resolution. When a client issues a command to a NetBIOS name, the client will try the following:

- Check to see if the name is on the local machine.
- Check the local cache of remote NetBIOS names.
- Query the WINS server for address resolution.
- Issue a local name query broadcast.

- Parse the LMHOSTS file, if LMHOSTS support is configured at the client.

- Parse the HOSTS file, if one exists.

- Query DNS, if supported.

Each of the above will be attempted until address resolution occurs.

WINS Client Configuration

Use the Control Panel Network utility to configure a station as a WINS client. After launching the Network utility, select the **Protocols** tab, highlight TCP/IP Protocol, and click on **Properties**. When the TCP/IP Properties sheet appears, select the **WINS Address** tab. Enter the IP address of the primary WINS server. You may also enter a secondary WINS server that will be used if the station is unable to contact the primary server.

If you wish, a station may also be configured to support DNS and LMHOSTS with WINS.

WINS Client

As each WINS client starts, it registers itself with the WINS server. As you can see in the example WINS database, this includes the LAN Manager service IDs, the special values in byte sixteen of the NetBIOS name.

When a name is registered with a WINS server, the server returns an acknowledgment. Included in this is a Time-To-Live (TTL) value. This indicates when the name must be renewed. It is the client's responsibility to renew the name before the TTL expires. The client will start attempting renewal after half of the TTL time period has expired. After expiration, the name is removed from the WINS database.

A situation may occur where a client attempts to register a name that already exists in the database. When this happens, the WINS server sends a challenge to the original entry's owner. If a response is received from the original owner, the client is sent a negative name registration response. If no response is received from the original owner, the name is registered.

WINS Server Installation

To install WINS from the Control Panel Network utility:

1. Launch the Control Panel Network utility.

2. Select the **Services** tab and click on **Add**.

3. Highlight Windows Internet Name Service and click on **OK**.

4. Enter the path to the installation source files and click on **Continue**.

5. When returned to the **Services** tab, click on **Close**.

6. When prompted, select to restart your system.

This process installs the WINS server service and adds the WINS Manager to the Administrative Tools (Common) program group. You will need to provide the client systems with the WINS Server's IP address. For small networks, this is normally all that is required.

WINS Server Management

The WINS Manager (WINSADMN) is used to manage WINS servers. It can be used to configure both local and remote WINS servers.

WINS Manager lets you:

- Add or delete WINS servers.

- View or modify configuration parameters.

- Identify replication partners.

- View the WINS database.

- Add static mappings to the database.
- Set WINS options.

There is also a version of WINS Manager that lets you manage WINS servers from remote clients. This is set up through the Network Client Administrator, part of the Network Administration program group.

WINS Manager

When you first launch WINS Manager, it will list managed servers, defaulting to any local servers. It will also display statistics for the default server, which includes the number of registrations, releases, and queries.

Run **Add WINS Server** from the **Server** menu to add servers to the list.

When prompted, enter the additional WINS server you wish to manage from this location. You can identify the WINS server by either its IP address or NetBIOS name.

WINS Configuration

Most configuration options are managed through the **Configuration** command in the **Server** menu.

Renewal Interval

This sets the TTL time period, which determines how often a client must register its name. The default period is six days. The client will attempt renewal after half this time has passed, defaulting to three days. If the entry is not renewed, it is marked as released.

Extinction Interval

This sets the time between an entry being released (not renewed by the client) and the entry being marked as extinct. The default is six days.

Extinction Timeout

This sets the interval between an entry being marked as extinct and it being scavenged from the database. This defaults to the same time as the renewal period, six days.

Verify Interval

This sets the time period after which the WINS server will verify the existence of names that it does not own. This would include, for example, names received from other WINS servers. This defaults to 24 days.

Pull Parameters

The Pull Parameters determine if the current WINS server will pull replicas from other known partners. Set **Initial Replication** to have this occur if a replication-related parameter is modified and if the system is initialized. The retry count sets the number of times the server will attempt to connect with a partner. The replication retry interval is set separately.

Push Parameters

The Push Parameters control how replicas are sent to other servers. If **Initial Replication** is enabled, the server will inform partners of its database status when the system is initialized. Enable **Replicate on Address Change** to have the server inform all servers of database status if an address mapping changes.

Advanced Configuration Options

Click on **Advanced** to display the advanced configuration parameters.

Logging Enabled
> When set to on, database changes are logged to the J50.LOG file.

Log Detailed Events
> This parameter determines the format for event logging. Set to on, verbose logging is used. Verbose logging requires considerable system resources and may impair system performance.

Replicate Only With Partners
> When set to on, replication occurs with push and pull partners only. If not set, an administrator can force push or pull with a non-listed WINS server.

Backup On Termination
> When set to on, the database is backed up automatically when the WINS server service is stopped.

Migrate On/Off
> This option should be checked when upgrading a non-Windows NT system to Windows NT. It specifies that static unique or multihomed records are treated as dynamic if conflicts occur with either new registrations or replica. If no longer valid, the entries are overwritten with the new data.

Starting Version Count
> This sets the version ID for the database, starting at zero. Increment this value if the database becomes corrupted and must be recreated. The value should be set to a number higher than any version numbers appearing in replication records on WINS server remote partners.

Database Backup Path
> This sets the destination path for database backups. You may enter a path or use the Browse button to locate a path. Do not specify a network drive as the backup destination.

WINS Preferences

Additional configuration parameters are available through the Preferences dialog. To edit preferences, run **Preferences** from the **Options** menu.

Address Display
> Set the format for displaying addresses. You can display computer name only, IP address only, both with the computer name listed first, or both with the IP address listed first.

Server Statistics
> Set Auto Refresh on to automatically refresh the database mapping display. You can also set the refresh frequency.

Computer Names
> This determines whether fifteen-character LAN Manager names are used (default), or sixteen-character NetBIOS names.

Miscellaneous Settings

These settings determine if the list of servers is queried for available servers at startup and if verification is required when deleting static mappings.

Click on **Partners >>** to display new partner default configuration parameters, including the replication start time and interval for pull partners, and the number of registrations and changes to trigger updates from a push partner.

Show Database

To view the current server's database, run **Show Database** from the **Mappings** menu. Each mapping entry includes:

- An icon identifying the entry as a unique or group NetBIOS name.
- The NetBIOS name and attached service ID.
- The IP Address.
- Active/Static entry identification.
- The name expiration date.
- The version ID number assigned by the WINS server.

Items with a check in the A column are Active entries. Those with a check in the S column are Static, or manual, entries.

Options at the top of the screen let you determine the mappings to be shown and the mapping sort order. Entries can be sorted by IP address, computer name (default), expiration date, version ID, and type.

Database Updates

WINS clients will automatically update the WINS database with their names. You may, however, need to add static mappings to the database. For example, if you are using an NT system as an IP router, you will have to configure it as a multihomed static mapping. Static mappings are also required to if you need to resolve the NetBIOS name of systems that do not register with WINS servers.

Run **Static Mappings** from the **Mappings** menu to display a list of static mappings. From this dialog, you can add, edit, or delete mappings. You can also import mappings from any text file using the LMHOSTS file format.

When you add a static mapping, you must provide the name, IP addresses, and static mapping type.

Static Mapping Types

The following static mapping types are supported:

Unique

This identifies a unique name, one with only one address attached to the name. Duplicates of this name will not be allowed in the database.

Group

This identifies a normal group name. Groups are used, for example, when a client broadcasts name packets.

Domain Name

A Domain Name group can store up to 25 member addresses. New entries exceeding the limit of 25 will overwrite a replica address, if one is available, or the oldest entry.

Internet Group

An Internet Group can store up to 25 member addresses and is typically used to identify NT Server domain controllers. New entries exceeding the limit of 25 will overwrite a replica address, if one is available, or the oldest entry.

Multihomed

This is used to identify a unique name that can have more than one address. Up to 25 IP addresses can be defined for a multihomed name. WINS will only register one address automatically.

This allows you to select a name type appropriate to your needs.

Database Backup

The WINS database is stored in the *\systemroot*\SYSTEM32\WINS directory. These files are:

J50.LOG	If logging is enabled, database entries are logged to this file. It is used as a transaction log in case of failure.
J50.CHK	This is a database checkpoint file.
WINS.MDB	This is the WINS database.
WINSTMP.MDB	This is a temporary file used as a swap file by the WINS Server service.

These files may appear to be Microsoft Access files, but they cannot be opened using Access.

The WINS Server Configuration dialog lets you set up automated backup. To do so, choose **Backup Database** from the **WINS Manager Mappings** menu. When the Select Backup Directory dialog box appears, provide the directory name and path. Once this information has been provided, WINS will back up the database every three hours.

Supporting Large Networks

Supporting WINS over medium- to large-sized networks carries its own special problems. You will often need to support multiple WINS servers to provide redundancy, reliability, and performance.

Some special concerns include:

• Replication

When supporting multiple WINS servers, replication provides a way of passing names between servers, so that a name registered on one server can be queried on another.

• Browsing and trusts

In a large network with multiple subnets and multiple domains, maintaining browse lists and trust relationships can be a significant concern.

Let's take a closer look at each of these.

Replication

Database replication is necessary when supporting multiple WINS servers. This allows a name registered on one server to be queried on another server. Replication is configured through WINS Manager.

Replication is managed through replication partners. There are two types of partners:

- Push Partner

    Push partners provide the current WINS server with updates.

- Pull Partner

    Pull partners request and receive updates from the current WINS server.

A WINS server can be a partner with one or more other servers. Each can act as a push partner, a pull partner, or both.

Replication Partners

Run **Replication Partners** from the **Server** menu to define WINS servers that will act as partners with the current server. You can select to list push partners, pull partners, or both. This dialog lets you configure replication options for replication partners. Default options are set through the Preferences dialog.

You can also force replication information to be sent to selected push and pull partners. If you select to push with propagation, any destination server will propagate the trigger to its pull partners.

Replication Partner Options

You can set the update count for each push partner separately. When the number of new registrations and database changes reaches the update count, replication will occur.

For pull partners, you can set the start time and replication interval. Any changes made through this dialog override the default settings configured through the Preferences dialog.

Replication Triggers

A number of events can trigger replication, depending on how the WINS servers are configured:

- A pull partner will automatically request all updates having a higher version number than previously received at startup time.

- A pull partner will start replication at the specified start time and poll its partner(s) at a specified interval.

- A push partner will notify all pull partners that replication may be necessary when a defined update count is reached.

- Replication can be initiated with push or pull partners through the Replication Partner dialog by sending a replication trigger.

- Immediate replication can be initiated with push or pull partners through the Replication Partner dialog by clicking on **Replicate Now**.

Replication parameters should be set for frequent replication between primary and secondary WINS servers. Replication intervals should be lengthened for partners connected through slower wide area links.

By setting the replication on the push count to a high value, you can control replication through the pull partner's configuration settings. This makes it easy for you to specify the times for replication. This can be important when working with international remote hosts.

WINS Proxy Agents

Not all systems running NetBIOS over TCP/IP can be configured to use WINS servers. They can, however, be given access to WINS server databases through the use of proxy agents.

Windows NT, Windows for Workgroups, and Windows 95 stations can be configured as a WINS proxy. Existing WINS servers are an exception. If a system is configured as a WINS server, it cannot also act as a WINS proxy agent.

A computer can be configured as a WINS proxy by editing the system's registry. Change the EnableProxy parameter to 1 in the following key:

```
HKEY_LOCAL_MACHINE\SYSTEM
    \CurrentControlSet
    \Services\NetBT\Parameters
```

How it Works

WINS proxy agents provide indirect access to the WINS database. When a system broadcasts a name query:

- A WINS proxy agent intercepts the broadcast.
- The broadcast is answered, if possible, from the local cache or a WINS server query.

There is a possibility of a strain being placed on the WINS proxy agent, depending on the number of name query broadcasts occurring. Only a limited number of WINS proxy agents should be defined on each domain, preferably on systems that are not already supporting resource-intensive tasks.

Trust Relationships

You may encounter additional management overhead when primary domain controllers are located on different subdomains. When using LMHOSTS for address resolution, both primary domain controllers must have a #DOM entry for the other domain controller in the LMHOSTS file. Even when using WINS, it is often suggested that you do this for domain controllers to ensure that they will be able to properly locate and communicate with each other.

The procedure for managing this with WINS depends on how you've configured WINS support. If all primary domain controllers involved are configured to use the same WINS server, there will be no problem in establishing or maintaining trust relationships. If any two primary domain controllers involved are managed on different WINS servers, you must configure database entry replication between the servers.

Browsing

The Browser is a service that maintains the list of available NT Server domains, servers, and resources. In this usage, a server refers to any system running the server service and able to share resources to the network. Each domain has a Master Browser, usually the primary domain controller. It maintains the Browser tables which list available resources.

- Each Master Browser announces the existence of its domain through broadcasts.
- The Master Browser collects server and domain announcements from servers and other Master Browsers.
- Collected announcements are used to update the Browser table.
- Tables are propagated to Backup Browsers, other domain controllers, and workstations through broadcasts.

This model works fine unless you are supporting a network with multiple subnets. A Master Browser on one subnet won't see announcements from another subnet. Domains on the remote subnets would be invisible to domain workstations.

Supporting Browsing

Let's look at some particular support situations in a network with multiple subnets.

- NT workgroup

  It is normally not possible to split a workgroup across subnetworks.

- NT Server domain on one subnet

  Domain browsing is handled normally. The domain will not appear in browse lists for domains on other subnets. The Master Browser will not include domains on other subnets.

- NT Server domain on multiple subnets

  Each subnet will have its own Master Browser. The primary domain controller acts as the Domain Master Browser, collecting and propagating information from the Master Browsers.

If all of the systems are using the same WINS server and database or a shared WINS database, the Domain Master Browser will supplement its list of known domains with those it finds in the database. This can lead to another problem, however. It can take days for a domain or workgroup that no longer exists to be removed from the WINS database, and therefore, from the browse list.

WINS and DNS

Windows NT Server was designed to have WINS and DNS support each other. When configuring a WINS client, there is an option button to use DNS to resolve NetBIOS names. However, the ability of WINS to support DNS is more significant.

DNS servers are static by design, and assume that all host addresses tend to be static. This can be a problem in PC networking environments because of the portability of the machines. Problems can also arise from the use of DHCP, since it is possible for a host's address to change.

WINS support for DNS is configured at the Zone level. Right-click on the zone and run **Properties**, or select the zone and run **Properties** from the **DNS** menu. Select **Use WINS Resolution**.

If unable to resolve the host name from available databases, the DNS server will query the specified WINS server for the host name. Since the data in the WINS database updates automatically, automatic updates are provided for DNS support.

Print Services

Windows NT also supports UNIX print services. You can configure support for:

- Printing to UNIX print queues.

- Printing to printers directly attached to the network.

- Provide Print services to UNIX hosts.

You must install Microsoft TCP/IP Printing as part of your installed components to access or provide print services. As with other services, this is installed through the **Services** tab of the Control Panel Network utility.

Once you have configured an NT system to print to a UNIX or network destination, you can share that as a printer resource to other Microsoft network workstations, whether or not they are running TCP/IP. The NT system acts as a print server, passing the print jobs to their eventual destination.

Printing to the Network

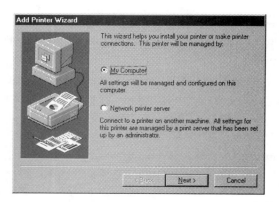

Setting up network printer support is similar to setting up a local printer. You need to provide a printer name, select the appropriate driver, and designate a printer destination. You can select to share the printer, making it available to other network clients, whether or not they are running the TCP/IP protocol.

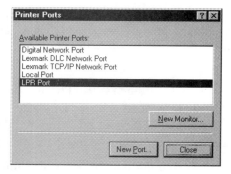

When configuring a UNIX or network printer, select Add Port, choose LPR Port, and click on **New Port**. You can then select the appropriate network printer destination, or LPR Port if printing to a UNIX printer.

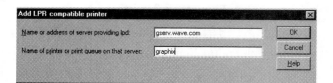

You will need to provide the DNS name or IP address of the direct-connected printer or UNIX host. You must also enter the printer name.

Supporting UNIX Clients

You must have the Lpdsvc service running at your NT station to support printing for UNIX clients. It enables the NT system to accept UNIX client print requests. The Lpdsvc can be started through the Control Panel Services utility or by running the following at an NT command prompt:

```
net start lpdsvc
```

You must also make a registry change to allow access to printers shared under a UNC name. You will need to designate the shared printer as a null share. Use the Registry Editor to modify the following Registry key:

```
HKEY_LOCAL_MACHINE\SYSTEM
    \CurrentControlSet
        \Services\LanmanServer\Parameters
```

Modify the NullSessionShares keyword value, entering the printer's UNC name.

Print Utilities

Windows NT printer objects can be configured to send print jobs to UNIX- and network-connected printers. Microsoft TCP/IP also supports command-line print utilities.

LPR

LPR can be used to send a print job to a printer on a TCP/IP host running the LPD (Line Printer Daemon) service. This includes NT systems running Lpdsvc and directly connected printers with devices such as the HP JetDirect card. The syntax for the command is:

```
lpr -Sserver -Pprinter [-Cclass]
    [-JJobname] [-Ooption] filename
```

You must specify the host (server) and printer names, along with the file to be printed. This is used to specify the class banner. The jobname gives the print job a name. These are both optional parameters. All parameters are case-sensitive.

LPQ

The LPQ utility returns print queue status for the selected host and printer. The syntax for this command is:

```
lpq -Sserver -Pprinter [-l]
```

The host (server) and printer names are required parameters, and are case-sensitive. The **-l** option provides a detailed listing.

Remote Access Service (RAS) Server

Remote Access Service (RAS) is installed through the Services tab of the Control Panel Network utility. During RAS installation you are prompted to specify the network protocol. This gives you the opportunity not only to install TCP/IP support, but to identify address support and security for clients.

Keep in mind there is a distinction between RAS and remote-control solutions. RAS is a multiprotocol router that is software-based. A remote-control solution works by sharing control of the mouse, keyboard and screen over a WAN connection. A RAS server is dedicated to communications, not running applications, while remote-control solution clients share resources.

RAS and IP Addressing

As RAS clients call in, the RAS server manages IP address assignment. It locally manages a pool of leased addresses that are obtained from the DHCP server, then clients are configured by RAS using the TCP/IP configuration parameters obtained by DHCP. If a lease needs to be renewed or if more addresses are needed, the RAS server will contact the DHCP server. However, the DHCP server is not checked each time a RAS client starts.

Acting like a proxy for TCP/IP clients, RAS uses proxy ARPs to the ARP requests made by the RAS clients, also setting up the network host routes to each client. The RAS server can obtain configuration parameters by using PPP IPCP (Internet Protocol Control Protocol) as defined in RFC 1332 to dynamically configure clients parameters through a DHCP server.

New Features of RAS in Windows NT 4.0

A number of improvements and enhancements were made to RAS for Windows NT 4.0. These include:

- PPP Multilink

    By using RAS Multilink you can increase your access and throughput bandwidth by combining two or more physical communications links. Analog lines, ISDN lines, and even a mix of analog and digital links are easily combined. This allows a higher speed connection for the Internet or to an intranet. This cuts down on the long delay times, making RAS more time and cost effective. RAS Multilink is based on the IETF standard RFC 1717.

- Point-to-Point Tunneling Protocol (PPTP) support

    PPTP allows you to use the Internet for low-cost, secure remote access to your private corporate network. PPTP allows a company to use local Internet Service Providers to connect to (via the Internet) the corporate network with a secure remote access. Being an open industry standard, PPTP can support most network protocols (IP, IPX and NetBEUI). At present, using PPTP on a RAS server is only supported on Windows NT 4.0.

- Restartable file copy

    When a RAS connection has been lost, this feature will automatically restart file transfer upon reconnection. Restartable file copy addresses the problems of re-establishing connection only to start the file transfer all over again. Restartable file copy remembers the status of your file transmission and continues the transfer from the point where the file transfer was lost.

- Idle disconnect

    After a set time period has passed and if there has been no activity over the remote dial-up link, the Idle disconnect will automatically disconnect the RAS connection. The time allotment can be set by the user or an administrator.

- Auto-dial and Log-on dial

    An association can be now be mapped and maintained between a Dial-Up Network entry and a network address for seamless integration of Dial-Up networking files and applications. This means that if a user opens a file and that file is only accessible over a dial-up connection, Dial-Up Networking will be initiated automatically.

- Client and server API enhancements

    To extend RAS capabilities on NT Server 4.0 and Dial-Up Networking with NT Workstation 4.0 a number of new APIs were developed. Third-party developers can now add value to RAS and Dial-Up Networking because of the APIs making the Remote access and communications platform friendlier.

- Windows 95 look and feel

    Microsoft has given Windows NT Server and Workstation 4.0 the on-screen look and feel of Windows 95. The RAS client component is now referred to as Dial-up Networking for consistency between operating system (Windows 95 and NT) platforms. The interface for Dial-Up Networking and RAS also have the Windows 95 look.

RAS Server Installation

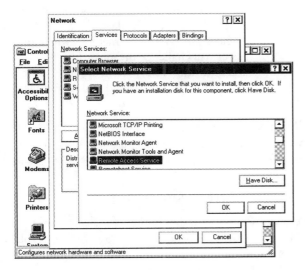

The Control Panel Network utility lets you add support for RAS. Select the **Services** tab and click on **Add**. Select Remote Access Service from the Network Services list and click on **OK**.

The system prompts for the location of the installation source media. This can be either a drive path or a UNC name and path. After verifying that the path is correct, the system will transfer the files necessary for your selected options.

As part of the installation process, the system will search for a modem or other connection device. If not configured, RAS setup will walk you through modem setup and configuration.

You will be prompted to configure access security and to set access levels for remote users for each protocol you are supporting through RAS.

After transferring files, you are returned to the Network Settings dialog. Click on **Close** to complete the installation and configure the selected services.

You are prompted to restart your system. You must restart the system for the changes to take effect.

Modem Setup

When you install RAS server or client, if you do not already have a connection device (a modem, for example) configured on your system, you will be prompted to install one at that time. Since a modem is the most common connection device for RAS, let's step through the configuration procedures as an example.

The first step is to launch the Control Panel Modem utility. If you do not have a modem installed, this will launch the Install New Modem Wizard. You have the option of letting Windows NT attempt to detect your modem or select the modem from a list of those supported by Windows NT. Before letting Windows NT detect the modem, make sure that the modem is turned on and connected, and that there are no applications using the modem.

Modem Detection

Windows NT will check each available COM (serial) port to see if a modem is attached. If one is found, it will query the modem to try to determine the modem type.

The Wizard will display the detected modem. If the one displayed is incorrect, click on **Change** to display a list of supported modems.

Windows NT will install the drivers for the modem. You will next be taken to the modem properties. Once the modem is installed, you can run the Control Panel's Modems utility at any time to configure the modem.

Modem Configuration

The **General** tab on the Modems Properties page displays the installed modem(s) and the selected dialing preference. Click to select the modem, then on **Properties** to modify modem properties.

Properties pages are somewhat modem specific. The examples shown here are typical. The **General** tab lets you set speaker volume and maximum speed.

The **Connection** tab shows default connection properties. Your communications software can override these settings.

RAS Network Configuration

Additional configuration parameters are available when setting up a RAS server. In the example, Dial-out Protocols are greyed and unavailable. These will only be available if you configure the server to support dialing out in addition to receiving calls.

The Server Settings area lets you configure the client protocol connections that will be allowed and Encryption settings. This is also the area when you can enable Multilink.

The encryption settings determine how username and password encryption is supported.

- Any authentication including clear text

  Any client authentication request is accepted. This may be necessary when supporting non-Microsoft clients, but can lead to compromised security. Since usernames and passwords may be passed clear text, they can be intercepted.

- Require encrypted authentication

  Encrypted passwords are required for clients. The client requests the encryption.

- Require Microsoft encrypted authentication

  Only MS-CHAP authentication is accepted. This is the preferred method when supporting Microsoft clients. MS-CHAP is a challenge-and-response method, where the server will challenge the client for authentication information and the client will automatically respond with a username and encrypted password.

If you require Microsoft encryption for authentication, you can also require data encryption for all data transfers.

NetBEUI Client Configuration

You can set configuration options for client protocols. Click on **Configure** next to each supported protocol. Client access is the only option choice available for NetBEUI clients. You can allow clients access to the entire network or the current server only.

TCP/IP Client Configuration

For TCP/IP clients, you can set both the access option and the method for assigning IP addresses. You can assign addresses through DHCP or from a static address pool. You also have the option of letting clients request a predetermined IP address.

Use DHCP to assign remote TCP/IP client addresses
Choose this option if a DHCP server is available and you want the RAS server to assign IP addresses to remote clients.

Use static address pool
>Choose this option when a DHCP server is not available. Specify a valid range of IP addresses in the subnet in which the RAS server resides. The RAS server will assign addresses from this range to remote clients. The administrator can set addresses to be excluded from the range, as well.

Allow remote clients to request a predetermined IP address
>Checking this will allow clients to request a specific IP address from the RAS server.

IPX Client Configuration

In addition to access options, IPX protocol configuration also supports protocol-specific options. You can have RAS allocate network numbers automatically or provide a static range. By default, all IPX clients will be assigned the same network number. Clients may optionally be allowed to request an IPX node number.

As an added note for Windows clients connecting through IPX, you must enable NetBIOS Broadcast Propagation for NWLink to function properly. By default, this will be enabled during RAS server installation.

Remote Access Admin

The Remote Access Admin, which is installed under Administrative Tools (Common), lets you configure Remote Access services.

If run from the RAS server, the local server is displayed by default. Run **Select Domain** or **Server** from the **Server** menu to display additional servers. Only trusted domains will be listed.

Managing Communication Ports

Run **Communication Ports** from the **Server** menu to display the Communications Ports dialog. All communication ports on the current server will be listed. From this dialog, you can complete any of the following:

- Check port status

  Select a port and click on **Port Status** or double-click on a port to open the Port Status dialog. This will display port and connection statistics, error information, and remote station name, IP address, and IPX address.

- Disconnect User

  Choose **Disconnect User** to release the remote user from that port. Highlight the port from which you want to disconnect the remote user and click on **Disconnect User**. A Disconnect User dialog box will appear. Check **Revoke Remote Access Permission** to keep the user from reconnecting, then click on **OK**.

- Send a message to a user

  Choose **Send Message** to send a message to a single user. Highlight the user's port to which you want to send the message, then click on **Send Message**. The Send Message dialog box will appear. Type in the message you want to send and click on **OK**.

- Send a message to all users

  Highlight the server or domain to which you want to send a message and click on **Send to All**. The Send Message dialog box will appear. Enter the message you want to send and click on **OK**.

Service Management

Selections in the **Server** menu let you manage the Remote Access Service. You have command selections to start, stop, pause, and continue RAS. Each of these commands will run specific to the selected server.

Start Remote Access Service

This is used to choose the server on which the Remote Access Service will run. It can be used to restart RAS on a server that has been stopped.

- Choose **Start Remote Access Service** from the **Server** menu.

- The Start Remote Access Service dialog box will appear.

- Enter in the server name that you want started.

- Click on **OK**.

The system will attempt to start the Remote Access Service.

Stop Remote Access Service

This is used to stop the Remote Access Service on a selected server. You should pause the server first and send a message to all connected users to give them a chance to disconnect. Otherwise, you should manually disconnect the users before stopping the service.

- Highlight the server whose Remote Access Service you wish to stop.

- Choose **Stop Remote Access Service** from the **Server** menu.

The system will attempt to stop the remote access service.

Pause Remote Access Service

This is used to pause the Remote Access Service on a selected server. While paused, new incoming calls are blocked but connected users will be able to keep working.

- Highlight the server whose Remote Access Service you wish to pause.

- Choose **Pause Remote Access Service** from the **Server** menu.

The system will attempt to pause the Remote Access Service.

Continue Remote Access Service

This is used to start any paused Remote Access Service on a selected server. After continuing the service, the server will once again accept new connections.

- Highlight the server whose Remote Access Service you wish to resume.

- Choose **Continue Remote Access Service** from the **Server** menu.

The system will attempt to resume the Remote Access Service.

User Access Permissions

Run **Permissions** from the **Users** menu to set user access permissions. Remote access may be granted by user, or for all users by clicking on **Grant All**. Click on **Revoke All** to revoke remote access from all users.

There are three Call Back options supported for users:

- No Call Back

   The user is given access to the server, and if so configured, to the network when validated.

- Set By Caller

  The caller will be prompted for a Call Back number. This will have the server call the user back, avoiding long distance charges at the client end.

- Preset To

  This is the most secure option. The user will be called back at a specified number.

Set the option as appropriate for user support and security requirements.

User Dialin Settings

You can also set dialin information through User Manager for Domains. Display user properties and click on **Dialin**. The same user status will be displayed here and in Remote Access Admin. The same Call Back options are also supported.

Configuring RAS for TCP/IP

Remote RAS Clients are supported by all the TCP/IP networking benefits, including access to the WINS and DNS. Configuring a RAS client to use PPP (Point-to-Point Protocol) or SLIP (Serial Line Internet Protocol) allows dial-up support for Internet and existing TCP/IP internetworks. When a RAS Server is configured for PPP, RAS clients have a server that functions as a router. SLIP client software does not support multiple protocols. It is used to support older software implementations.

Bandwidth is important when designing and installing a RAS server. Even though RAS uses effective compression methods to increase the amount of data that is sent over a communication line, as a rule of thumb allow for protocol and timing overhead. The transfer rates should be estimated using the 10-bit byte. For example, approximately 1 KBps, 60 KB/minute, and 3.5 MB/hour can be supported through a 9600-bps (uncompressed) connection. With data compression you should expect a throughput of about 7 MB per hour. This is an adequate rate for a single client, but it is not as feasible for an intersite line. For this, an ISDN or other higher-speed connection would be more ideal. Basic Rate Interface (BRI) ISDN supports 128 Kbps or 45 MB/hour, assuming no compression. Primary Rate Interface (PRI) ISDN supports transfer rates of 1.544 Mbps in the United States and 2.048 Mbps in most other countries.

Point-to-Point Protocol (PPP)

PPP is a set of industry-standard framing and authentication protocols which are supported by the NT operating system under RAS. Multiple layers of the OSI model configuration parameters are negotiated by PPP. What this means is that NT 3.5 or later (and Windows 95) stations can dial into a remote network through any server that complies with the PPP standards. This compliance allows NT Server to receive calls from other vendors' remote-access software, giving them network accessibility. PPP gives clients the capacity to load any combination of IPX, TCP/IP, and NetBEUI.

Serial Line Internet Protocol (SLIP)

Found in UNIX environments, SLIP is an older communications standard. Unlike PPP, SLIP does not provide encrypted authentication and automatic negotiation of network configuration because it needs the client's intervention. RAS does not provide a SLIP server, but it can be configured as a SLIP client to allow a client to dial into an existing SLIP server.

Point-to-Point Tunneling Protocol (PPTP)

Many companies are looking at the Internet as a means of supporting some, if not all, of their communication needs between corporate locations. One of the major concerns, however, is security. A possible answer is PPTP, a way of creating multiprotocol, Virtual Private Networks (VPNs) across the Internet.

In the past, a corporation would invest in communications lines like ISDN to communicate between corporate sites. With PPTP a remote client can access the corporate network across the Internet securely. You can even configure PPTP filtering on a network adapter so that only PPTP packets are allowed.

PPTP operates across PPP connections. PPTP data is encrypted and encapsulated inside of PPP packets. The PPTP packets can include TCP/IP, IPX, and NetBEUI packets. A session key used for the encryption is negotiated between the RAS server and client when the initial PPP connection is made.

Currently, PPTP is only supported on NT 4.0 RAS servers. It is supported on Windows 95 clients. In addition, there are third-party implementations of PPTP for Windows 3.1 and Macintosh clients. You must install the PPTP protocol on both the server and the client.

PPTP Installation

PPTP is installed through the **Protocols** tab of the Control Panel Network utility. Click on **Add**, click to select Point-to-Point Tunneling Protocol, then click on **OK.** You will be prompted for the path to the NT installation files.

You will be prompted for the number of Virtual Private Networks you want to support. You must configure one VPN for each concurrent PPTP connection. Each of these must also be added to the RAS server as a RAS connection device.

The Remote Access Setup dialog will display automatically. Click on **Add** to add the VPNs.

Once added, you can configure each VPN. Standard configuration parameters are supported, using the same configuration dialogs as when setting up modems or other physical communication devices.

Dial-Up Networking

Run **Start/Programs/Accessories/Dial-Up Networking** to launch Dial-Up Networking and call out through RAS. Dial-up numbers are managed as phonebook entries. Click on **Add** to create a new entry. Click on **More** to:

- Edit settings for the entry and modem.
- Copy settings for the entry and modem.
- Delete an entry.
- Create a desktop shortcut to the entry.
- Open the monitor.
- Call using operator assistance.
- Set user preferences.
- Set Logon preferences.

You can also configure multiple Dialing from: locations. This allows a mobile user to simply select the proper location rather than having to fully reconfigure dial-up networking.

RAS Clients

RAS clients using TCP/IP can be configured to use the default gateway on the remote network while they are connected to a RAS server. This default gateway overrides any local network default gateway while the RAS connection is established. The override is accomplished by manipulating the IP route table. Any local routes, including the default gateway, get their metric (hop count) incremented by one, and a default route with a metric of 1 hop is dynamically added for the duration of the connection. One-hop routes are also added for the IP multicast address (224.0.0.0), for the local WAN interface, and for the network to which the PPP server is attached.

This can present a problem connecting to resources by using the local network default gateway, unless static routes are added at the client. The following are sample route tables for a Windows NT workstation before and after connecting to a remote network using PPP.

Route table before dialing a PPP Internet provider:

Network Address	Netmask	Gateway Address	Interface	Metric
0.0.0.0	0.0.0.0	172.16.112.1	172.16.112.11	1
127.0.0.0	255.0.0.0	127.0.0.1	127.0.0.1	1
172.16.112.0	255.255.255.0	172.16.112.11	172.16.112.11	1
172.16.112.11	255.255.255.255	127.0.0.1	127.0.0.	1
172.16.112.255	255.255.255.255	172.16.112.11	172.16.112.11	1
224.0.0.0	224.0.0.0	172.16.112.11	172.16.112.11	1
255.255.255.255	255.255.255.255	172.16.112.11	172.16.112.11	1

Route table after dialing a PPP Internet provider:

Network Address	Netmask	Gateway Address	Interface	Metric
0.0.0.0	0.0.0.0	172.16.112.1	172.16.112.11	2
0.0.0.0	0.0.0.0	172.16.16.243	172.16.16.243	1
127.0.0.0	255.0.0.0	127.0.0.1	127.0.0.1	1
172.16.112.0	255.255.255.0	172.16.112.11	172.16.112.11	2
172.16.112.11	255.255.255.255	127.0.0.1	127.0.0.1	1
172.16.112.255	255.255.255.255	172.16.112.11	172.16.112.11	1
204.182.66.0	255.255.255.0	172.16.16.243	172.16.16.243	1
172.16.16.243	255.255.255.255	127.0.0.1	127.0.0.1	1
224.0.0.0	224.0.0.0	172.16.16.243	172.16.16.243	1
224.0.0.0	224.0.0.0	172.16.112.11	172.16.112.11	1
255.255.255.255	255.255.255.255	172.16.112.11	172.16.112.11	1

Packet Structure

All conversations between machines take place between their MAC (physical adapter) addresses. Alternate addressing, such as IP addresses, are processed at higher levels in the architectural model.

As data moves down through the model, each layer adds information that helps ensure delivery and data integrity. Upon receipt, each layer is unwrapped and checked, ending eventually with the original data.

The formats involved in this process vary drastically from protocol to protocol, even between protocols within the TCP/IP protocol suite. Each is designed to provide the information required for that protocol to manage its conversations.

About Headers

TCP/IP Packet Structure

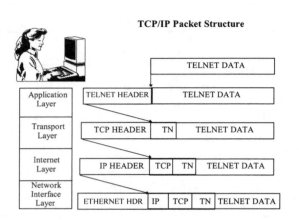

			TELNET DATA		
Application Layer	TELNET HEADER		TELNET DATA		
Transport Layer	TCP HEADER	TN	TELNET DATA		
Internet Layer	IP HEADER	TCP	TN	TELNET DATA	
Network Interface Layer	ETHERNET HDR	IP	TCP	TN	TELNET DATA

The TCP/IP protocol suite is based on four levels; each has its own protocol support components and header formats.

- Network Interface Layer

  The Network Layer adds the source and destination MAC addresses during transmission and checks the addresses during receipt. Only network interface protocol definitions containing an Ethertype field can support TCP/IP.

- Internet Layer

  ARP, IP, and ICMP are supported at the Internet Layer.

- Transport Layer

  The Transport Layer supports TCP and UDP protocols.

- Application Layer

  DHCP and WINS are supported at the Application Layer.

Let's take a look at some examples from each of these.

Network Interface

Ethernet Frame Types

Ethernet II

Preamble /SFD [8]	Dept. Address [6]	Source Address [6]	Ether Type [2]	Data

Ethernet 802.3 /802.2

Preamble /SFD [8]	Dept. Address [6]	Source Address [6]	Length [2]	DSAP [1]	SSAP [1]	Control [1]	Data

Ethernet 802.3 SNAP

TCP/IP is only supported on network interface protocol definitions with a two-octet Ethertype field, including:

- Ethernet_II
- Ethernet_SNAP
- Token-Ring_SNAP

Why? TCP/IP was originally developed on an early version of Ethernet, Ethernet_II. One feature of this protocol was a two-octet Ethertype field, indicating higher-level protocol type, following the source address. A later standard, 802.2, was incompatible because it used one octet DSAP (Destination Service Access Point) and SSAP (Source Service Access Point) to identify protocols. This standard is known as IEEE 802.2 LLC (Logical Link Control).

A new standard was developed to allow continued support of TCP/IP and to enable TCP/IP over Token Ring. This standard, which gave us Ethernet SNAP (Sub Network Addressing Protocol) and Token Ring SNAP, supported TCP/IP by adding a two-octet Ethertype field at the end of the frame.

Ethernet Frames

Before leaving Ethernet frames, let's look at some special notes:

- Addresses

    All supported frame types provide MAC destination and source addresses. Each of these is a six-octet (six-byte) address, normally represented in hexadecimal. Broadcast packets will have a destination of FFFFFFFFFFFF (all ones in binary), indicating that they should be processed by all hosts receiving them.

- Ethertype values

    TCP/IP supports one of two values in the Ethertype field. IP is identified as 0800h and ARP is identified as 0806h.

- Frame type

    Microsoft Windows for Workgroups, Windows NT, and Windows 95 default to using an Ethernet_II frame type. If the network and other network clients use Ethernet_SNAP, it is necessary to reconfigure Windows NT to use the same frame type. Use the Registry Editor to change the following subkey:

    ```
    HKEY_LOCAL_MACHINE\SYSTEM
        \CurrentControlSet
        \Services\Tcpip\Parameters
    ```

Change the keyword value for ArpUseEtherSNAP to 1.

ARP

Address Resolution Protocol is used to determine the MAC address when a remote host's IP address is known. The process used for address resolution was discussed earlier. It includes:

- ARP request sent

    The ARP request contains the destination host's IP address, as well as the sending host's IP and MAC addresses. This information is either broadcast on the local subnets or passed to its eventual destination through routers.

- ARP request received

    Each host receiving the ARP request will compare the packet destination with its own IP address. If they match, the host will generate and transmit an ARP reply. It will also cache the IP address and MAC address of the transmitting station.

- ARP reply sent

    The ARP reply contains the destination host's IP address and MAC (NIC hardware) address. When the original sending host receives this information, it is stored in the ARP cache.

At that point, the stations can communicate.

ARP Header

0	1	2	3
Hardware		Protocol	
Length of HW Address	Protocol Length	Operation	
Source Hardware Address (Bytes 0 - 3)			
Source Hardware Address (Bytes 4 - 5)		Source IP Address (Bytes 0 - 1)	
Source IP Address (Bytes 2 - 3)		Destination Hardware Address (Bytes 0 - 1)	
Destination Hardware Address (Bytes 2 - 5)			
Destination IP Address (Bytes 0 - 3)			

ARP Protocol Header

The requesting system sends an ARP packet with the field for the information it lacks left blank.

Hardware   This field contains the hardware type value, using a value defined in RFC 1340.

Protocol   The protocol field identifies the address structure.

HLEN   The hardware address length identifies the adapter address length in octets.

Protocol Length
    This is the length of the protocol address in octets.

Source hardware address and
Source IP address
    These addresses identify the sending system.

Destination hardware address
    When broadcasting an ARP request, this field is set to all zeros. In the ARP reply, the requested information is inserted in the field.

Destination IP address
    This is used to identify the system from which address resolution is requested.

ARP Request

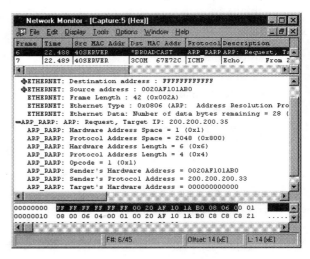

Our example shows an Ethernet packet containing an ARP request. In the upper part of the packet details (the center window) we can see the destination MAC address set to FFFFFFFFFFFF, identifying this as a broadcast.

Most of the ARP header is taken up with addressing information. The destination (target) hardware address is unknown and so has been set to all zeros.

ARP Reply

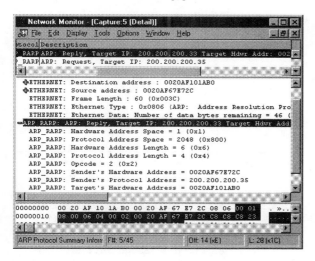

The ARP reply is sent as a datagram. The packet has MAC address values in the Ethernet source and destination address fields. All of the fields in the ARP header are now filled in. The source and target values have been transposed since the message is now going in the other direction, returning to the requesting system.

IP Header

```
 0                   1                   2                   3
 0 1 2 3 4 5 6 7 8 9 0 1 2 3 4 5 6 7 8 9 0 1 2 3 4 5 6 7 8 9 0 1
```

Version	IHL	Type of Service	Total Length	
Identification			Flags	Fragment Offset
Time to Live		Protocol	Header Checksum	
Source Address				
Destination Address				
Options				Padding

Internet Datagram Header

Internet Protocol is the basic TCP/IP transport protocol. It provides the source and destination IP addresses, support for packet fragmentation and reassembly, and the upper-level protocol used for information transfer.

Version
: This identifies the current IP version.

IHL
: The IP header length field reports the IP header field length in 32-bit words. The minimum length is five words (20 octets).

Type of service
: The type of service octet identifies the relative precedence of the datagram, delay, throughput value, and reliability.

Total length
: This reports the length of the complete IP datagram in octets.

Identification
: If it becomes necessary to fragment the datagram to compensate for maximum frame sizes, all fragments will be given the same identification value.

Flags
: The flags field identifies how fragmentation will be handled.

Fragment offset
: This is a fragment count. It identifies where the fragment belongs within the message. This field is used for proper sequencing and to detect lost fragments.

Time to live
> This is the maximum life of the datagram in either hops or seconds. If this value goes to zero, the datagram is destroyed. This is to keep undeliverable datagrams from wandering lost through the internetwork forever.

Protocol
> This identifies the higher-level protocol in use.

Header checksum
> The checksum is used to verify header integrity.

Source address and
Destination address
> These fields contain the source and destination IP addresses.

The rest of the header identifies any options and fills the remaining space with pad characters.

IP Example

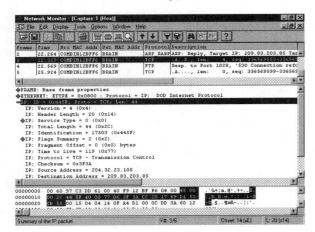

In the example above, you see a sample IP packet. You can clearly see the source and destination IP address in the IP header. The detailed Ethernet header fields, including those containing the MAC addresses, are not shown in the example.

ICMP Header

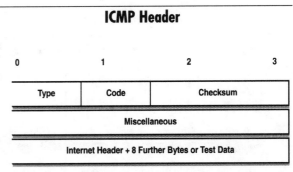

Basic ICMP Message Structure

ICMP is used to report datagram delivery errors.

Type
> This identifies the message as one of thirteen unique message types.

Code
> The code further identifies the message. The code values are message type specific.

Checksum
> The checksum is used to verify header integrity.

Miscellaneous
> The use of this field is defined by the message type.

The remaining message will contain the internet header and additional data. In case of an error in datagram delivery, it will have the first 8 octets of the datagram. It can also include timestamp or address mask information.

ICMP Types

Thirteen unique message types are supported:

0   Echo reply

This is sent in response to an Echo.

3   Destination unreachable

The destination IP address could not be reached. Refer to the code to see why the message couldn't be delivered.

4   Source quench

This is used to reduce traffic when a route becomes congested.

5   Redirect

This is used to advise of a better route.

8   Echo

This is sent to request an echo reply.

11   Time exceeded

The TTL value was reduced to 0 and the datagram destroyed.

12   Parameter problem

A parameter problem was detected in the datagram.

13   Timestamp

This is a timestamp request.

14   Timestamp reply

This is the reply sent to a timestamp request.

15   Information request

This field is obsolete.

16   Information reply

This field is obsolete.

17   Address mask request

This is used to request address mask information.

18   Address mask reply

This is sent as the reply to an address mask request.

ICMP Example

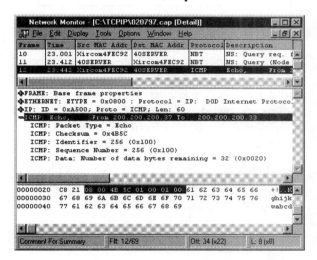

The example above shows an ICMP header. The packet type is identified as ECHO. Notice that the first byte in the highlighted hexadecimal listing is 08. This denotes a packet type of ECHO.

TCP Header

```
 0                   1                   2                   3
 0 1 2 3 4 5 6 7 8 9 0 1 2 3 4 5 6 7 8 9 0 1 2 3 4 5 6 7 8 9 0 1
```

Source Port	Destination Port

Sequence Number

Acknowledgment Number

Data Offset	Reserved	U R G	A C K	P S H	R S T	S Y N	F I N	Window

Checksum	Urgent Pointer

Options	Padding

Data

TCP Header Format

TCP is a sophisticated, connection-oriented protocol. The protocol handles data transfer, reliability, flow control, multiplexing, connections, and security. It supports acknowledged communication and uninterrupted data flow between two hosts. TCP headers are at least 20 octets in length.

Source port   This identifies the source's logical host process.

Destination port
This identifies the destination's logical host process.

Sequence number
This is used to ensure proper sequencing of data octets. A one-up numbering system is used at the source and verified at the destination. The initial values are chosen randomly and synchronized during the initial handshaking process.

Acknowledgment number
Data receipt is verified by this field. The value is set to the next sequence number expected from the other end of the connection.

Data offset   This identifies the length of the header in 32-bit words.

NOTE: *The next six bits are set to zero, followed by the Urgent Pointer field significant, Acknowledgment field significant, Push function, Reset the connection, Synchronize sequence numbers, and No more data from sender flags. These flags are used for connection and data flow control.*

Window   This is used with end-to-end flow control and identifies the number of octets the sender of the segment can receive. End-to-end flow control supports a transfer method called sliding windows which is discussed later in this chapter.

Checksum   The checksum allows data integrity verification.

Urgent pointer
This identifies urgent data within the data segment.

Options   This identifies TCP host required options.

TCP Example

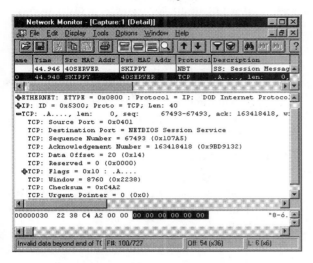

An example TCP header is shown above. You can see the source port, destination port, and window size, as well as other values.

Acknowledgment with Data

A typical TCP conversion between two hosts (identified here as A and B) might go like this:

	Seq. No.	Ack. No.	Flags	Data (Bytes)	Comments
A>B	A	0	SYN	0	Session initialization–A wants B to synchronize.
B>A	B	A+1	ACK SYN	0	Acknowledgment from B–B wants A to synchronize.
A>B	A+1	B+1	ACK	0	Acknowledgment from A–all systems go!
B>A	B+1	A+2	ACK	100	B sends 100-byte packet to A.
A>B	A+2	B+101	ACK	200	A sends 200-byte packet to B and acknowledges the previous packet by increasing the Ack No by 100.
B>A	B+101	A+202	ACK FIN	0	B acknowledges receipt of 200 bytes and wants to end the session.
A>B	A+202	B+102	ACK FIN	0	A acknowledges and wants to end the session also.
B>A	B+102	A+203	ACK	0	B acknowledges–session over.

The sequence numbers keep track of octets within a message. The number transmitted is the number assigned to the first data octet. The acknowledgment number is the next expected sequence number, verifying that the correct number of octets were received. That is why the sequence number for B jumps from B+1 to B+101 when a 100-byte (octet) data packet is sent.

No data is transmitted during session initiation or termination. The initiating handshake is used to synchronize sequence numbers and acknowledge numbers. The closing handshake ensures that each host has acknowledged that the other wants to end the session.

Sliding Windows

TCP uses the sliding windows concept to support transmission of multiple packets before receiving acknowledgment. On a reliable network, this can mean improved throughput on data transmissions. The first step is to set transmission parameters. During the initial handshake:

- The segment size is agreed upon, based on the maximum packet size of intermediate routers.

- Each system will send its receive buffer size.

- Each system will set its transmit buffer (send window) to the other's receive buffer size.

During data transfer, the sending system can send as many segments as will fit in the send window without waiting for acknowledgment. As each packet is sent, a retransmit timer is started. If acknowledgment is not received for that packet before the time expires, the packet is retransmitted.

The receiving system will send acknowledgment when:

- Two or more sequenced segments are received.
- The window has filled to 50%.
- When 50% of the window is freed by passing data to the client application.

When acknowledgment is received for specific packets, those packets are removed from the send window (buffer). The window is then slid along the queue to include the next segments waiting to be transmitted. At that point, the only packets in the window are those waiting for acknowledgment or waiting for transmission. Those waiting for transmission are sent immediately, continuing until the entire data block has been transmitted.

Exception Handling

Sliding windows have the ability to adjust for changing conditions and recover from transmission errors.

- Window size

    The receiving system has dynamic control over the window size. It can send a different window size during its acknowledgment and the sending station will automatically adjust. If the receiving station becomes congested, it will set the window value to zero to suspend transmission. Transmission will restart when a non-zero window value is received by the sending station.

- Lost segments

    If segments are received out of order (three, four, and six, but not five) the receiving station starts a Delayed-ACK timer. If this timer expires before the packet is received, only packets received in order are acknowledged (three and four, but not six). When the retransmit time expires on the sending station, the missing packet will be retransmitted.

- Retransmit timer

    The retransmit timer dynamically adjusts itself based on the packet Smooth Round Trip Time (SRTT). This value cannot be adjusted manually.

NOTE: The Delayed-ACK timer value should also be less than the retransmit timer value.

Ports and Sockets

The IP header takes care of getting data to the right destination host. TCP makes sure that the packet gets to the correct application on the receiving host by using its port address. Well-known application protocols have a Well Known Port address. Examples include:

Port	Application
20	FTP
23	Telnet
25	SNMP
53	DNS
69	TFTP
79	FINGER

In the previous example, packets would be addressed to port 20, the FTP daemon.

UDP

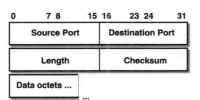

User Datagram Header Format

As you can see by the protocol header, UDP is less sophisticated than TCP. It is used for connectionless transmissions, transmissions where acknowledgment is not required.

Source port   This identifies the source port for the transmission. If not used, this field is filled with zeros.

Destination port
This is the destination port, identifying the destination application.

Length   This is the length of the UDP datagram.

Checksum   The checksum is used to validate data integrity. This is optional under UDP. If not used, the checksum is filled with zeros.

The IP header routes the packet to the correct destination, and the UDP header to the correct process.

UDP Example

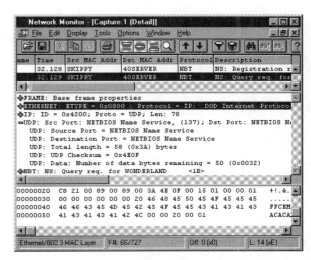

The example above shows a UDP packet. In this case, the optional checksum is being used. You can tell this because its value is not set to zero.

Windows Sockets

Before leaving the discussion of transport layer protocols, some mention should be made of Windows Sockets. Windows Sockets is a standard application interface defining communications between Windows and the underlying protocol stack. As long as the application and the protocol stack both comply with the Windows Sockets standard, they should be able to communicate.

Before the introduction of this standard, there was a significant chance that applications and protocol stacks coming from different vendors would not work together. In 1992, work began on defining a standard for communication between a Microsoft Windows application and the underlying protocol stack using a universal service addressing scheme. This address was based on the protocol ID, host address, and port/socket ID.

There are two types of sockets available:

Stream   This is used for reliable, two-way sequenced flow. It is typically used with TCP.

Datagram   Less reliable, this supports unsequenced two-way flow. It is typically used with UDP.

Microsoft Windows NT supports Windows sockets for 16-bit and 32-bit applications.

DHCP

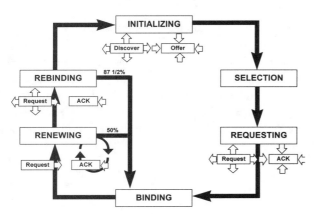

DHCP operates at the application level. The sequence of events relating to DHCP were discussed earlier. Let's review them now, this time going into a little more detail. The states associated with DHCP are:

- Initialization

    This is when the client first broadcasts its request and DHCP servers respond with address offers.

- Selection

    The client reviews and accepts an offer packet while in this state.

- Request

    This is when the client sends a request, attempting to lease the address it has selected from those offered.

- Bound

    After the client receives its address lease and related configuration information, it enters the bound state and will not communicate with the DHCP server until T1 time.

When T1 time, approximately 50% of the lease period, is reached, the client station will attempt to renew its address. If unable, it will enter the Rebinding state at the T2 time, 87.5% of the lease period. If still unable to renew its lease, it will attempt to bid for a new address at the end of its lease period.

Initialization

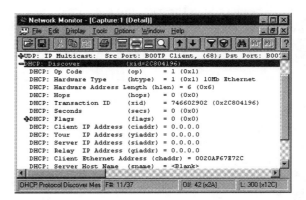

The client's first packet is a Discover packet. It shows the client's current address as 0.0.0.0, indicating that the client has not received an IP address.

Other key fields in the Discover packet include:

Transaction ID

> This number is used to identify DHCP packets belonging to this session. All packets in this session will use the same transaction ID, up until the client enters the bound stage.

Giaddr

> The Relay IP Address is used by the DHCP server to determine the appropriate scope. If an RFC 1542 BOOTP-enabled router receives the packet and the giaddr (Relay IP Address) is blank, the router will place its own address in that field. If a DHCP server receives the packet and the giaddr is blank, the local subnet is assumed.

Requested Address

> If the client had a previous address, it will request the same address again. If available within the appropriate scope, that is the address the DHCP server will send in its offer. If the station did not have a previous IP address, this field is set to zero.

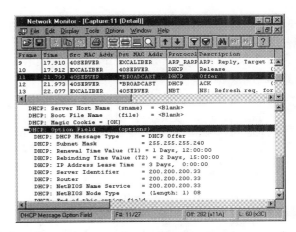

The offer packet contains an IP address, subnet mask, and lease details. There are three time periods with which you need to be familiar:

- T1

  > The renewal time is equal to approximately 50% of the lease period. This identifies when the client will begin its attempts to renew its license.

- T2

  > The T2 period occurs if the address has not been renewed by the time 87.5% of the lease period time has elapsed. Most attempts at resolving addresses don't get to this period. During the T2 time, the host will broadcast to all DHCP servers in attempt to find one that can renew its address.

- Lease period

  > This is the period for which the station will have its assigned address. If not renewed, the address can be reassigned.

Most clients will renew their IP addresses before the T2 time.

Selection

The DHCP client will select from one of the offers it has received. If it did not have an IP address before, it will usually take the first address offered. If no appropriate offers are received:

- The client will send four additional Discover packets at 2, 4, 8, and 16 seconds.

- The client will wait 5 minutes and then try again.

- The client will continue this process until it receives a valid offer.

Once the client has selected an offer, it moves into the request phase.

Request

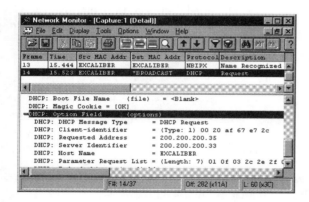

The client will broadcast its Request. This accepts the selected offer and, since it is a broadcast, informs any other DHCP servers that it has accepted an offer.

The Request will contain the DHCP server's IP address and the requested IP address. At this point, the client can also request other parameters. The example includes:

01	Subnet mask
03	Router
0f	Domain name
2C	NBNS\WINS server
2E	NetBIOS node type
2F	NetBIOS Scope ID

The DHCP server will pass any available parameters configured as global or scope options.

Bound State

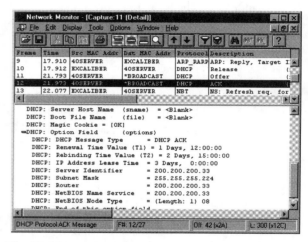

The DHCP server responds to the Request with an ACK, once again as a broadcast. This response is sent as a broadcast to let any other DHCP servers on the network know that their offers have been declined. After the ACK is sent, the DHCP server treats the IP address as assigned. The ACK will include:

- IP address and subnet mask

- DHCP server IP address

- Lease, T1, and T2 times

- Requested parameters, if available

When it receives the ACK, the client has an IP address for at least the duration of the lease.

Renewal/Rebinding

At T1 time, the client will attempt to renew the address. The client will send a Request, this time as a datagram, and wait for an Ack in response. The Ack will have the lease renewal information as well as any changes to requested parameters.

If an Ack is not received, the client will continue trying until the T2 time is reached. It then switches from sending a datagram to broadcasting its request. It will wait for an Ack from any server, which is unlikely, since that would mean that at least two servers had overlapping scopes. Usually a client will only receive an address due to T2 broadcasts if the machine from which it received the original address has failed and a new machine is handling its scope.

If unable to renew before the end of the lease, the client will begin the bid process, starting with a Discover broadcast, as soon as the lease expires.

Additional Messages

DHCP supports three additional messages. These are:

- DECLINE

    The DHCP client will send a Decline if it finds an invalid parameter in an ACK. This releases the IP address at the server. The client will have to start over from initialization.

- NAK

    The DHCP server sends a NAK to indicate invalid information received in a packet. Once again, the client must start over at initialization.

- RELEASE

    If a client no longer needs an IP address, it can issue a Release. This allows the DHCP server to reassign the address. You can force a release by running the following at the command prompt:

    ```
    ipconfig /release
    ```

WINS

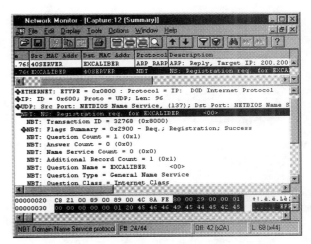

WINS also operates at the application level. The service automatically registers client host names as they come online.

As the client initializes, it sends a Name Registration Request to the WINS server. NetBIOS names are somewhat encrypted, using an encryption compliant with RFC 1001. This helps to ensure compatibility with other forms of NetBIOS Name Server.

If there are no problems, the WINS server will respond with a positive Name Registration Response, similar to the one in our example. This includes a Time to Live (TTL) value, the period for refreshing the registered name.

The client is responsible for refreshing the name entry. It will make its first attempt at 1/8 the TTL period, then continue at every 1/8 until able to refresh.

Query Requests

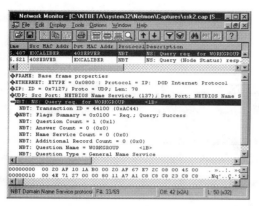

When a host needs to resolve a NetBIOS name, it sends a query request. An example is shown above.

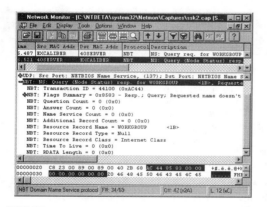

The WINS server name query response returns the requested name.

Stepping Through

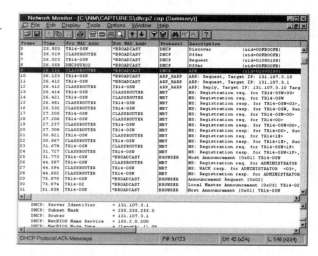

As TCP/IP initializes at a client, it broadcasts its DHCP Request. In this example, there are two DHCP servers, both with appropriate addresses, issuing offers. After negotiation of the IP address there are three ARP packets. One of these is the client host requesting its own address. This is done to verify that the address is unique. The other two are used to locate the WINS server.

After locating the WINS server, frames 13 through 24 show registration and response of the client's NetBIOS names. In frame 25, the system is announcing itself to the local Browser. Frames 26 through 28 show that a user, Administrator, is logged on. The final frames are the client requesting the name of its Master Browser.

Basic Troubleshooting

In the real world, it isn't *if* problems occur, but *when*. A large industry has grown up around providing support tools for networking and, more specifically, for TCP/IP networks. Even if you don't have access to specialized tools, a number of basic tools are built into Microsoft TCP/IP.

When problems occur:

- Collect all possible information.
- Try to determine the root cause of the problem.
- Change only one variable at a time and test.
- Document the problem and its solution.

A key point to remember is: *Fix the business problem first.* Get the most critical system going first. Do whatever is necessary to keep everyone working, then correct the underlying problems.

Event Viewer

The Event Viewer, part of the Administrative Tools (Common) program group, is one of the first places to look when problems occur. The system will write an entry into the System log when an error occurs.

When dealing with a network problem, you will often see a series of errors. If a lower-level service fails to start, any services that bind to that service will not start.

You should usually look at the oldest entry in the series to see what started the failure. Double-click on any entry to view details about the error.

Event Details

Viewing details about the entry will give you additional information about the error. This is often a good place to start in troubleshooting.

Types of Errors

Let's look at some error types you may encounter and the tools available to help you correct them.

- Installation

    For our purpose, these are errors that keep the installation from running or the protocol from initializing the first time.

- Configuration

    These are any errors relating directly to configuration settings and not covered in another error.

- Routing

    Errors in contacting hosts on remote subnets fall into this category.

- Name resolution

    This refers to any type of host name error.

- NetBIOS name resolution

    This includes anything relating to Microsoft network NetBIOS applications, including browsing, resource management, and name resolution.

- Other

    Errors not fitting into any of the other categories have been listed here.

Windows NT provides tools to assist in troubleshooting each of these error types.

A Note on PING

The PING utility was discussed earlier in the course as a way to test for the existence of a specified IP address. It is also a powerful diagnostic tool. It provides an easy way to step through a problem to see where a failure might be occurring:

- Ping yourself or your loopback address.

    This is to verify that you have a working TCP/IP stack. It also lets you know if your IP address is what you think it is.

- Ping someone local

    Once you can see yourself, try to contact another host in the same subnet. This verifies your subnet mask.

- Ping the default gateway

    If the router responds, then you have the correct gateway address and the router appears to be working.

- Ping each hop to the remote host

    If you are having trouble communicating with a remote host, this is a quick way to check each of the intermediate routers.

- Ping the remote host

    This tells you that you can directly communicate with the remote host. If you are still having other problems communicating with the host, they aren't related to the IP address, subnet mask, or intermediate router addresses.

- Ping the host name

    If you can ping the host by its IP address, but not by its host name, you most likely have a problem with your host name resolution method. If you are using HOSTS, make sure the domain is listed and that you have the appropriate aliases. If you are using DNS, make sure the DNS server is running, that you can connect to it, and that the entry for the host you are trying to reach is correct.

- Ping the NetBIOS name

    If you can ping the host by its IP address, but not by its NetBIOS name, you most likely have a problem with your NetBIOS name resolution method. If you are using LMHOSTS, check to make sure the entry for the host is correct. If you are using WINS, make sure the correct WINS server has been identified for your machine and for the host you are trying to reach. Make sure the WINS server is running.

Because of its simplicity, it is easy to overlook PING as a troubleshooting tool.

Installation

Installation errors include errors that keep TCP/IP and related services from being installed or keep them from initializing after installation. Common causes include:

- Network adapter

    Network adapter failures are likely due to incorrect driver settings or a bad adapter.

- Network hardware

    Bad cable, bad connectors, or loose physical connections can keep an adapter from initializing. This is usually reported in the System log as an adapter failure.

- Installation media

    If the source media is bad, the software can't install properly. Also make sure that you are using the correct version of the installation media.

- Wrong selections

    Sometimes, you just choose to install the wrong thing. Use the Network utility to remove any incorrect software and install the services you need.

Use the Event Viewer to view the System Log contents to look for hardware or software initialization failures. You must fix any hardware errors first. You can then reinstall any or all TCP/IP components through the Control Panel Network utility.

Configuration

The most common causes of configuration errors are that you either didn't have the right information, or you had the right information but typed it in wrong. Either way, this can result in problems on the network including:

- Duplicate addresses

    If the other host is active on the network, you should find out about this immediately. The duplicate address should be detected at initialization. NT will disable the TCP/IP stack and generate an error message.

- Inability to communicate

    Incorrect values in the IP address or subnet mask can keep you from communicating with other hosts.

- Cannot find network devices

    A common cause of not finding devices, such as WINS servers or the default gateway, is that address information has been entered incorrectly.

One way to reduce the possibility of configuration-related errors is to use DHCP. As long as the client hosts can communicate with the DHCP server and the server is configured properly, problems should be kept to a minimum.

About Duplicate Addresses

Duplicate addresses are usually one of the easiest problems to locate. Let's look at an example.

Assume that two stations, named STA1 and STA2, have the same address. STA1 is already up and running on the network. STA2 comes online. An error message will be generated on both systems stating that there is an address conflict. On each system, the message will list the other system's MAC address.

The TCP/IP stack will not initialize on STA2. The station will be unable to communicate via TCP/IP. STA1 will continue to operate normally after the error dialog is cleared.

Correcting Configurations

You have already seen two utilities that can be helpful in diagnosing and correcting configuration errors. They are:

IPCONFIG Run **ipconfig /all** to list all important IP configuration parameters for the host. A good start at verifying the correctness of the address and subnet mask is to compare them to those assigned to other systems on the subnet.

If you have a DHCP client with an address of 0.0.0.0, it has been unable to get an address from the DHCP server. Correct any problem with the server or intermediate path (if any), then run **ipconfig /renew** to bid for an address.

ARP   Run **arp -a** to view the ARP cache. If an attempt to contact a local host has generated an entry for the default gateway, your IP address or subnet mask are incorrect.

If the ARP cache includes any invalid entries, they may be deleted by running:

```
ARP -d IP_address
```

Routing

Routing errors can come from a number of sources, including:

* Network hardware

    Bad or marginal hardware, bad cabling, loose connections, and so forth can cause a break in your communication path.

* Invalid subnet mask or default gateway

    Contact will fail if either value is incorrect at the local or remote host end.

* Routing tables

    Incorrect router information in intermediate routers will keep packets from reaching the proper destination. Take special care when entering routing information for static routers.

* Correcting routes

    Remember that TRACERT can be used to trace the route between source and destination, listing all intermediate routers. This can help in trying to build better routes manually.

* Transient conditions

    Only OSPF routers can automatically compensate for transient conditions, such as a line temporarily down or short-term congestion.

Remember that PING can be used to test communication paths. Ping each router along the path to the remote host to locate at which point the failure is occurring.

NETSTAT

The **netstat** command was discussed earlier in the course as a tool for viewing the contents of the routing table. After you have a list of intermediate routers, you can use the **netstat** command to view the contents of the table. Let's quickly review selected options. You should remember:

netstat -a   All connections and listening ports

netstat -e   Ethernet statistics (may combine with **-s**)

netstat -n   IP addresses and port numbers reported numerically with no name lookup attempted

netstat -p   Statistics for TCP or UDP (TCP, UDP, or IP if the **-s** option is also included)

netstat -s   Per protocol statistics, defaulting to TCP, UDP, and IP (**-e** or **-p** may also be specified)

You will need to run **netstat** for each intermediate router on which a problem is suspected. You may want to use REXEC or a similar utility to facilitate this.

Name Resolution

Host name resolution means either a problem with the HOSTS file or access to a DNS server. Key points to remember when working with a HOSTS file include:

- Only one entry per IP address

    If multiple host names are supported at the same IP address, enter all names on the same line as aliases.

- Case-sensitive

    The HOSTS file uses case-sensitive entries. Enter both uppercase and lowercase entries as aliases.

- File accuracy

    As always, if you've edited the file recently, the problem may be that the wrong information was supplied or that it was entered incorrectly. Check the file entries and verify that they are correct.

If DNS fails, it could be that the DNS server has failed or that you are unable to establish contact with the server.

NetBIOS Name Resolution

The potential problems with NetBIOS names depend on the method you are using for name resolution:

- Broadcast

    Hosts will only be able to see and access hosts configured on the same subnet.

- LMHOSTS

    Make sure that LMHOSTS contains tables that are complete and accurate, and that do not contain duplicate entries. Use #DOM entries to support trust relationships and validation outside the subnet.

- WINS

    Registration and many resolution problems are often signs that you cannot consistently communicate with the host. Missing entries can be a sign of communication failure between replication partners, or that replication needs to occur more often. Any devices other than Windows for Workgroups, Windows NT, or Windows 95 require static mappings and a WINS proxy agent.

NBTSTAT was discussed earlier in the course as a tool for diagnosing NetBIOS name resolution problems. Command options provide the NetBIOS name cache (-c), local NetBIOS names (-n), and name resolution statistics (-r). You can list both workstation and server sessions, listing remote hosts by IP address (-S) or attempting to find and display their host names (-s). The command can also purge the NetBIOS names cache and reload the LMHOSTS file (-R).

Miscellaneous Tips

When you consider the number of systems, operating systems, applications, support devices, and transmission media involved in even a medium-sized network, the number of variables is staggering. A number of tools are available to help you tame the problem:

- Performance Monitor

    Performance Monitor provides an easy way to gather basic performance statistics.

- Protocol Analyzer

    A protocol analyzer lets you take your investigation down to looking into individual packets. Choose carefully, since the products are specific not only to protocol, but often to manufacturer implementation.

- TELNET

    Often overlooked, the direct connection provided with TELNET is a flexible and powerful, though sometimes cumbersome, tool.

- SNMP

    Simple Network Management Protocol is a comprehensive diagnostic and management tool.

SNMP Overview

SNMP is one of the most comprehensive tools available for TCP/IP network management. It operates through conversations between SNMP agents and management systems. Through these conversations, the SNMP management systems can collect statistics from and modify configuration parameters on agents.

Agents are any component running the SNMP Agent service and capable of being managed remotely. Agents include:

- Minicomputers and mainframes
- Workstations
- Servers
- Bridges, routers, and gateways
- Terminal servers
- Wiring hubs

Management stations are typically more powerful workstations. Common implementations are Windows NT or UNIX stations running a product such as HP OpenView, IBM Systemview/6000, or Cabletron Spectrum. They provide a graphic representation of the network, letting you move through network hierarchy to the individual device level.

SNMP Conversations

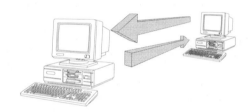

There are three basic commands used in SNMP conversations:

- GET

    The **get** command is used by the management station to retrieve a specific parameter value from an SNMP agent. If a combination of parameters are grouped together on an agent, **get-next** retrieves the next item in a group. For example, a management system's graphic representation of a hub includes the state of all status lights. This information is gathered through **get** and **get-next**.

- SET

    The management system uses a **set** to change a selected parameter on an SNMP agent. For example, a **set** would be used by the management system to disable a failing port on a hub.

- TRAP

    SNMP agents send TRAP packets to the management system in response to extraordinary events, such as a line failure on a hub. When the hub status light goes red on the management system's representation, it is in response to a TRAP.

Get and **set** are generated by an SNMP management station. Agents are able to respond to **set** and **get** and to generate a TRAP.

MIBs

The term Management Information Bases (MIB) refers to objects available for management via SNMP, containing unique identifiers for every manageable object in a network device. MIBs are required for every object used as a statistics source or managed by a management system. MIBs can be defined as read-only, only responding to **get** commands, or read-write, able to respond to both **get** and **set** commands.

Windows NT comes with four MIBs:

- Internet MIB II

    Defined by RFC 1213, this MIB is present on all management systems. It defines 171 fault and configuration management objects. SNMP requests for objects in this MIB are serviced by the TCP/IP DLL.

- LAN Manager MIB II

    About 70 objects are defined by this MIB, the majority being read-only. The management system must be running the Windows NT version of this MIB, which is different from the OS/2 version, before they can be used. Requests are serviced by the appropriate DLLs.

    Objects in this MIB are divided into four groups: Common, Server, Domain, and Workstation. They are used to return network service and domain-specific information.

- DHCP MIB

    Approximately fourteen objects are defined in this MIB. They are used to monitor the DHCP server and its configured scopes.

- WINS MIB

    Over 70 objects are defined in the WINS MIB. They are used for WINS server monitoring and configuration.

Third-party manufacturers may define other MIBs and associated DLLs for management and control of other objects under Windows NT.

MIB Hierarchy

Reference to MIB objects is based on a hierarchical system. Ownership of a name space is granted to a manufacturer. Through this, the manufacturer can develop its own MIBs defining unique IDs for objects that will not conflict with those developed by other manufacturers.

Each MIB object is defined by an address using a sequence of numbers separated by periods. At the root are three values, CCITT (0), ISO (1), and JOINT-ISO-CCITT (3). At the next level, the significant path to use is ORG (3), followed by DOD (6), and then Internet (1).

All objects on a TCP/IP network are prefixed with the number 1.3.6.1 (ISO.ORG.DOD.Internet). Two paths you may encounter below this are MGMT (2), and Private (4). Name spaces are allocated for organizations under Private.Enterprise (1.3.6.1.4.1). Microsoft has been allocated numbers 77 for LAN Manager and 311 for Microsoft.

For example, a GET command for a list of Scopes defined for a DHCP server would address the unique object:

```
1.3.6.1.4.1.311.1.3.2.1
```

    - or -

```
iso.org.dod.internet.private.
    enterprise.microsoft.software.
    Dhcp.DhcpScope.scopetable
```

SNMP

Simple Network Management Protocol is a powerful diagnostic and management tool. When installing SNMP on a Windows NT station, you need to gather your configuration information before installation. This includes:

- Community

    A community is a group of hosts to which your station belongs. You can specify to have your system send traps to one or more communities.

- Trap destination

    These are either names or IP addresses to which the SNMP service will send traps with the community name.

SNMP installs an SNMP service agent and API, an API for a third-party SNMP manager, and a selection of Performance Monitor performance counters.

SNMP Installation

SNMP is installed through the Control Panel Network utility.

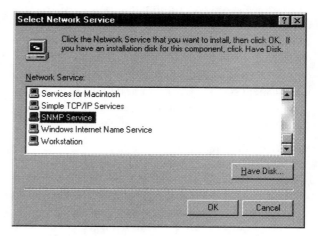

To install the SNMP Service:

1. Launch Control Panel Network utility.

2. Select the **Services** tab and click on **Add**.

3. Select SNMP Service and click on **OK**.

4. Identify the path to the installation files and click on **Continue**. You are next prompted for configuration information.

SNMP Security

If there is any potential drawback to SNMP, it is security. It would be possible for a person to generate a SET command to force a system to change configuration settings. All it would take is the agent's IP address and a knowledge of MIBs.

The main requirements to do this would be determination and patience. SNMP packets are sent clear text. Anyone with a network monitor would be able to capture and view the packets.

SNMP does have some very basic security, based around the community concept. Much like NetBIOS packets and their scope IDs, each SNMP packet contains a community ID. If a packet does not contain the correct community ID, it is rejected. However, most networks are set up to use the default community ID, public.

There are more secure versions of SNMP available, but not in common use. As one way of avoiding potential security problems, most Windows NT MIB objects are read-only. Management systems can view, but not change, configuration parameters.

SNMP Configuration

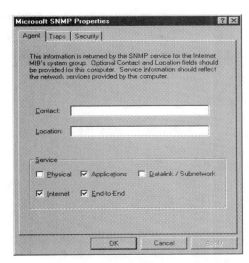

Earlier in the course, you saw how to install SNMP agent services on Windows NT. Now that you have seen how SNMP works, let's take a closer look at some of the configuration parameters available on the Microsoft SNMP Properties sheet.

Agent

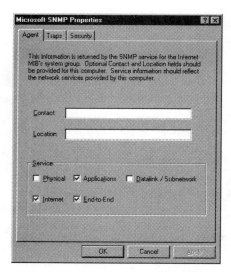

The Contact and Location fields are optional. The contact person for this host's TCP/IP configuration should be listed in the Contact field. The Location field is used for identifying the host's physical location. The selections under the Service field identify the capabilities of your system. These are:

Physical   This identifies that your computer manages a physical TCP/IP device, such as a repeater.

Applications
             If your system includes any TCP/IP applications, such as electronic mail, this selection should be checked. It should be checked on all NT systems.

Datalink/Subnetwork
             This identifies that your computer manages a TCP/IP subnetwork or Data Link devices, such as a bridge.

Internet   Only check this box if your system acts as an IP gateway (router).

End-to-End This should be checked on any system acting as an IP host.

End-to-End and **Applications** are default selections. **Internet** will be a default selection if your system is configured to act as a router.

Traps

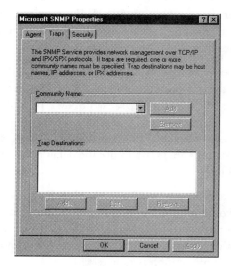

The **Traps** tab of the SNMP Properties sheet includes options for:

Community Name
             This is the community ID to send with trap packets. Multiple community names may be specified. Community names are case-sensitive.

Trap Destinations
             This is the IP address of the management system to receive Traps for the specified community. Destination addresses are set separately for each community, and a community may have multiple destinations.

Click on the **Security** tab to set security features relating to communities.

Security

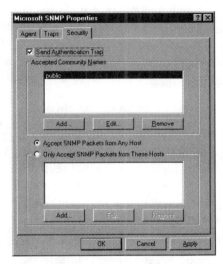

Click on the **Security** tab to configure SNMP Security.

Send Authentication Trap
> If enabled, SET or GET requests that do not contain an authorized community name or come from an authorized IP address, generate a trap indicating a failed authentication.

Accepted Community Names
> This list identifies communities from which the host will accept requests. The default entry is public, to which typically all hosts belong.

Accept SNMP Packets from Any Host
> If enabled, SNMP packets will not be rejected due to source host ID.

Only Accept SNMP Packets from These Hosts
> This selection is used to specify a list of hosts from which SNMP packets are accepted.

Performance Factors

When looking at network performance and potential bottlenecks you have to look beyond your local LAN or subnet. You need to consider the network as a whole, especially in large WAN configurations. Tuning considerations include:

- Network performance
- Network capacity
- Network reliability
- Microsoft TCP/IP Optimization

Careful consideration and tuning of these factors will help you maximize use of your available bandwidth, allowing you to stream information. This refers to the ability to transmit data continuously without having to wait for acknowledgments or retransmissions.

Some of the performance parameters in this chapter require you to edit the registry using Registry Editor. You should always exercise extreme caution when directly editing registry contents.

Network Performance

There may be little you can do about overall performance. Large wide area networks often include a combination of link types and line speeds. Local connections typically have high-speed links: 10 Mbps for Ethernet, 16 Mbps for Token Ring, or 100 Mbps for FDDI. Wide area links are significantly slower, typically in the 64-Kbps range. Low-speed links, such as X.25 and standard modem links, provide the poorest performance.

Any time traffic has to travel across one of the lower speed links, performance suffers. Performance can sometimes be improved through careful routing. Of course, if there is only one route to a destination, there is nothing you can do to adjust the route taken.

Optimizing Routes

You can sometimes improve overall performance by routing your heaviest traffic requirements across your fastest links.

- Static routers

  You set the routes on static routers through router table entries. When supporting large amounts of traffic, use the speed of the intermediate routes rather than the number of hops as a guideline. Keep in mind that static routers cannot compensate should the route become congested.

- Dynamic routers (RIP)

  If a router uses RIP, all routes are determined by lowest hop count. Some routes can be adjusted by giving them a higher apparent cost. You also have the restriction that routes will not dynamically readjust if a route becomes congested.

- Dynamic routers (OSPF)

  The best performance is offered by OSPF routers. Routes are calculated based on real performance and are dynamically adjusted if a route becomes congested.

In all situations, but especially when working with manual routes, regular performance tests and careful documentation are critical.

Network Capacity

The speed at which data is transmitted across a network link directly affects the amount of data the link can carry. Overload the capacity of the link and packets must be buffered, may end up out of sequence, and can end up lost completely. This leads to retransmissions, which in turn increases the level of traffic. Careful network design can help minimize this problem:

- Physical subnets

  Divide the network into physical subnets linked by routers. Design the subnets so that most of the resources the workstations need are available locally. Most traffic is across the local, high-speed link and traffic routed out of the subnet is kept to a minimum.

- Balance loads

  As described earlier in this chapter, use routers to help balance the load across subnet links. Whenever possible, keep the majority of the traffic on higher speed links.

- Application planning

  The location of applications and data files is significant. If possible, install applications on the local hard disk. Data files can be kept on network servers.

This is a situation where it is much easier to plan around the problem than to try to correct the problem after the network is in place.

Bridges vs. Routers

Routers should be given preference over bridges when designing and configuring WANs. Bridges, by design, can escalate a transient reliability problem into a serious network failure.

Frequently, a host will use broadcast transmissions if there is an unexplained loss of contact with another host. Typically, these broadcasts are not propagated by routers.

Remote bridges, on the other hand, pass on all broadcasts. Every host receiving the broadcast must process it, if only to reject it. As broadcasts go above a certain level, the performance loss due to broadcasts can lead to further broadcasts. This can lead to a broadcast storm, a complete breakdown of network communications.

Network Reliability

Network reliability problems can result in lost packets and retransmissions, generating artificially high traffic levels. The problem can come from marginal transmission media (cable), bad WAN links, and so forth. It can be further aggravated by failing hardware or environmental factors. Packet fragmentation and congestion also affect reliability.

One of the first steps is to make sure that the network hardware is all working properly. Replace or repair marginal hardware. Replace marginal transmission media whenever possible. Make sure that all cabling is installed within accepted specifications.

On WANs, line problems and router congestion can be announced to the sending host by ICMP, if supported by your routers. On receiving the error reports, the host will either try a different route, slow down the rate of transmission, or return the error to the application.

NT System Parameters

Windows NT 4.0 is primarily a self-tuning system. However, on occasion a situation may arise when the default system parameters must be adjusted in order to optimize network performance.

System parameters that may affect network performance include:

- TCPWindowSize [REG_DWORD]

    This registry parameter sets the size, in bytes, of the receive window. The size of the receive window regulates how many bytes a sender can transmit without receiving an ACK from the receiver. The default for Ethernet is 8760. Increasing the size of the receive window should improve performance on high bandwidth networks that experience many delays. This parameter must be created to alter the default value.

    This parameter should be added to:

    ```
    HKEY_LOCAL_MACHINE\System
        \CurrentControlSet\Services
        \TCPIP\Parameters
    ```

- ArpCacheLife [REG_DWORD]

    Windows NT 4.0 automatically adjusts the size of the ARP cache. However, the ArpCacheLife parameter was added to allow control over cache aging. This parameter sets the age of the ARP cache, defaulting to two minutes on unused entries and ten minutes on used entries. This parameter must be created to alter the default value.

    This parameter should be added to:

    ```
    HKEY_LOCAL_MACHINE\System
        \CurrentControlSet\Services
        \TCPIP\Parameters
    ```

- MaxPreLoad [REG_DWORD]

    This sets the size of the LMHOSTS cache, defaulting to 100 entries. It may be necessary to increase this for hosts on large networks where WINS is not implemented to cut down on the use of NetBIOS name resolution broadcasts. This parameter must be created to alter the default value.

    This parameter should be added to:

    ```
    HKEY_LOCAL_MACHINE\System
        \CurrentControlSet\Services
        \NetBT\Parameters
    ```

The Windows NT Resource kit documents these, and other, network parameters.

NT Services

Before leaving the subject of network performance, let's consider the effect of the services provided by Windows NT on the network.

- NT Domains

    The way in which NT domains are configured, including the physical location of network servers, can have an impact on network performance.

- DHCP

    The placement and number of DHCP servers is an important part of network planning.

- WINS

    Not only must WINS server planning include general performance factors, reliability factors must also be considered.

These are all issues that have been touched upon in earlier chapters. A review is worthwhile, however, as a reminder of how these factors can affect Microsoft clients, as well as the network as a whole.

NT Domains

When designing the setup for an NT domain, you have to consider some of the major traffic sources involved. These include:

- Logon validation
- File services
- Print services
- File replication

Most of the traffic generated will be between the domain controllers and domain workstations. It is normally suggested that you keep the domain controllers, any additional servers, and domain workstations on the same physical subnet.

If primary and backup domain controllers are placed across multiple subnets, you must either use WINS or modify the LMHOSTS file on domain controllers to ensure proper communications.

When splitting a domain across slower wide area links, it is suggested that a backup domain controller be placed in each location. This allows local logon validation and a local source for shared resources.

DHCP

As discussed earlier, network size will have an effect on DHCP planning and implementation. Configuration factors are somewhat determined by network size.

Small Network

For our purpose, a small network is one with no subnets or routers. Planning requirements include:

- DHCP hardware and storage requirements
- Dynamic clients
- Static clients
- DHCP options

A small network is normally best served by a single DHCP server.

Large Network

A large network is one that includes subnets and has routing requirements. During planning, consider:

- Router/DHCP compatibility
- Physical subnets
- Physical placement of DHCP servers
- DHCP option types

There is no limit placed on the number of clients a single DHCP server can support. Disk capacity, traffic levels, and CPU load will act as limiting factors in real-world applications.

WINS

The planning criteria mentioned earlier in this chapter for DHCP servers also applies to WINS servers. In fact, it is common to have a machine act as both a DHCP and a WINS server.

Typically, a WINS server can handle 1,500 registrations and 760 queries per minute. Use these values to help determine the number of servers you will need. When setting up multiple servers, there are two common models:

- Central server

    One server is designated as the central server. All other servers act as both push and pull partners with this server, but not with each other.

- Endless chain

    Each server acts as both a push and pull partner with nearby servers. The servers at each end of the chain act as push and pull partners with each other.

Adjust replication to meet user requirements and available communication bandwidth. Typically, replication is set to occur every fifteen to thirty minutes. When transmitting over slow links, you may want to cut this down to as low as twice a day.

Performance Monitor

When you install SNMP support, you also add TCP/IP-related counters to the Performance Monitor. These counters can be used like any other in Performance Monitor, are supported by all views, and can be used for defining alerts.

Performance Monitor lets you add other systems to your view. This lets you monitor performance counters from multiple systems at your station.

TCP/IP Counters

As with other counters, those supported by TCP/IP are grouped by object. Selecting an object, such as FTP Server, displays a list of counters which can be added to your Performance Monitor view. Click on the **Explain** button to receive a short description of each of the counters at the bottom of the dialog.

The dialog for all views is similar, letting you select the object, counter, and instance, when appropriate. When selecting counters for the Alert view, you will also set the threshold value and the program to run, if any, when an alert occurs.

TCP/IP Objects

The following object types are added to Performance Monitor when you install SNMP:

ICMP   The ICMP counters provide information about ICMP message rates, error counts, and selected status information.

IP
The IP counters track rate information for IP datagrams and related error conditions.

Network Interface
Network interface counters track information about bytes and packets transferred. It will also provide an estimated current bandwidth value.

TCP
The TCP counters provide connection and segment count information.

UDP
The UDP counters track information relating to UDP datagram transfers and related errors.

Network Monitor

Network Monitor provides administrators with the means to detect and troubleshoot problems with the network. Administrators can capture and display packets (or frames) directly from the network.

Network Monitor captures packets by copying them from the network stream to memory. To facilitate this process, your network interface card must support promiscuous mode. In most network environments, with the exception of Token Ring and subnets, computers "hear" all of the traffic on the network, but they only pass on to the operating system packets that are specifically addressed to them. Promiscuous mode simply means that the network adapter will pass along all network traffic to the operating system. You can check the documentation that came with your network adapter card to see if it supports promiscuous mode.

NOTE: *Windows NT Server Network Monitor will only capture packets that are sent by or designated for the local computer. If you want to capture packets sent between other computers on the network, you must use the version of Network Monitor that ships with Microsoft Systems Management Server (SMS).*

Network Monitor is installed through the Control Panel Network utility. Click on the **Services** tab, then click on **Add**. Select Network Monitor Tools and Agent and click on **OK**. Provide the path to the installation files and click on **Continue**. Exit the Network utility and restart your computer if prompted to do so.

Capturing Data

Network Monitor provides a great deal of control over the type of data that is captured. You can take a sampling of all of the network traffic sent to or from the local computer or design a capture filter that will capture specific information.

Network Monitor Capture Window

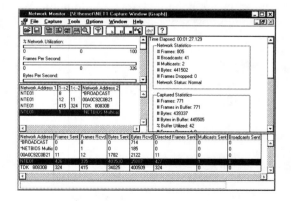

When a capture is performed, information about the frames is displayed in the Network Monitor Capture window. The following is an overview of the different sections of the capture window:

- Graph pane

    The graph pane is the upper-left section of the window. It provides a graphical representation of the percentage of network utilization, number of frames per second, and number of bytes per second.

- Session Statistics pane

    The session statistics pane is the left-center section of the window. It provides information about the individual sessions that are taking place on the network.

- Station Statistics pane

    The station statistics pane is located at the bottom of the window. This section provides information about sessions involving the computer that is running Network Monitor.

- Total Statistics pane

    The total statistics pane is located on the right side of the window. It displays a summary of the network activity.

Follow these steps to capture network data:

- Run **Start/Programs/Administrative Tools/ Network Monitor.**

- When the Capture window appears, run **Start** from the **Capture** menu.

- To end the data capture, display the **Capture** menu and click on **Stop**.

Data capture can be paused by running **Pause** from the **Capture** menu.

You can also define a capture filter. A capture filter allows you to capture only specific network information. You can use a capture filter to specify the types of protocols or data patterns to capture, or through the use of an address database you can monitor the network traffic between the local computer and a particular computer address.

Creating a Capture Filter

To design a capture filter, run **Filter** from the **Capture** menu and provide the appropriate information. Click on **OK** to continue past the warning dialog. The Capture Filter dialog box contains three elements:

- SAP/ETYPE

- Address Pairs

- Pattern Matches

Any or all of these can be used in defining a capture filter.

SAP/ETYPE

This line is used to specify which protocols to capture. To capture frames in a certain protocol, you must enable the protocol. To exclude a certain protocol, you must disable it.

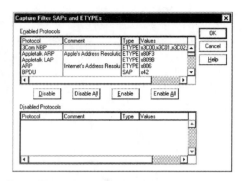

To enable or disable a protocol:

- Select the SAP/ETYPE line and click on **Line.**

- When the Capture Filter SAPs and ETYPEs dialog box appears, select the protocol you wish to enable/disable and click on the **Enable** or **Disable** button.

- Click on **OK** to return to the Capture Filter dialog box.

Address Pairs

This line is used to specify particular computer addresses for data capture. Four address pairs can be monitored simultaneously.

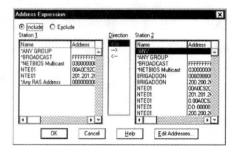

To define address pairs:

- Select the Address Pairs line and click on **Address** under Add to display the Address Expression dialog box.

- Select the first computer of the pair from the Station 1 box.

- Select the second computer of the pair from the Station 2 box.

- Determine the direction of traffic that will be monitored by selecting the appropriate arrow symbol in the Direction box.

- Click on **OK** to return to the Capture Filter dialog box.

Pattern Matches

This line is used to limit the capture to include only the frames that contain specific ACSII or hexadecimal data patterns.

To specify a pattern:

- Select the Pattern Matches line and click on **Pattern** under Add to display the Pattern Match dialog box.

- In the Offset box, enter the beginning byte number.

- Indicate whether Network Monitor should begin the search at the beginning of the frame or where the topology header ends by selecting either the **From Start of Frame** or the **From End of Topology Header** option button.

- Choose the format by selecting either the **Hex** or **ASCII** option button.

- Enter the pattern you want to match in the Pattern box.

- Click on **OK** to return to the Capture Filter dialog box.

When you have finished designing the Capture Filter, click on **OK**. If you want to save the filter for future use, click on **Save**. To open an existing filter file, click on **Load**.

Viewing Captured Data

Now that you know the various steps involved in capturing data, let's discuss how to view the data that was captured. When performing a data capture, there are two ways to stop the capture and view the data:

1. Stop the capture and view the data immediately by choosing **Stop**, then **View** from the **Capture** menu.

2. Stop the capture and save the data to a file for later viewing. To do so, choose **Stop** from the **Capture** menu and **Save As** from the **File** menu. To view the data, choose **Open** from the **File** menu and enter the filename.

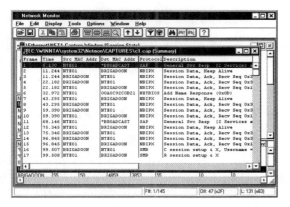

Either method of viewing the data will open the Network Monitor Frame Viewer window. The Frame Viewer window defaults to the Summary pane. To view more specific information about a frame:

- Remove the check mark from the **Zoom** option on the **Window** menu.

- Enlarge the window by clicking on the maximize button in the upper-right corner of the Frame Viewer window.

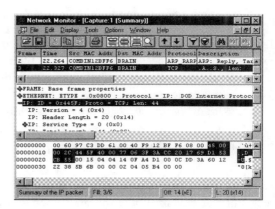

The Frame Viewer window should now be divided into three separate panes:

Summary Pane
: This is the top section of the window. It contains a list of the frames, and related information, in the order in which the frames were captured.

Detail Pane
: This is the middle section of the window. It contains the contents of the packet and the protocols that were used.

Hex Pane
: This is the bottom section of the window. It displays the captured data in hexadecimal and ASCII form.

To view a particular frame, select the frame in the Summary pane and the corresponding information will be displayed in the Detail and Hex panes.

Display Filters

A display filter is used to eliminate extraneous data and allow you to focus on specific types of data. It filters data that has already been captured, and displays frames based on source or destination address, the types of protocols used, or specific protocol properties. Only frames that meet the criteria of the display filter will be displayed in the Frame Viewer window.

To design a display filter, open the Frame Viewer window and run **Filter** from the **Display** menu. The Display Filter dialog box should appear. It contains two main elements:

- Protocol
- ANY <--> ANY

Protocol

This line is used to specify the protocols or protocol properties that will be viewed. Only these protocols will pass through the filter.

To specify the protocols to display:

- Open the Display Filter dialog box.

- Select the Protocol line and click on **Expression** under the Add section to display the Expression dialog box.

- Click on the **Protocol** tab to access the Protocol dialog box.

- To add (or enable) a protocol, select the desired protocol from the Disabled Protocols section and click on **Enable**.

NOTE: *By default, all supported protocols are enabled.*

- To remove (or disable) a protocol, select the protocol from the Enabled Protocols section and click on **Disable**.

- Click on **OK** to return to the Display Filter dialog box.

The chosen protocol should now be listed on the Protocol line.

To specify which protocol properties to display:

- Open the Display Filter dialog box.

- Select the Protocol line and click on **Expression** under the Add section to display the Expression dialog box.

- Click on the **Properties** tab to access the Properties dialog box.

- To display the properties for a protocol, double-click on the protocol name.

NOTE: *To hide the properties displayed for a protocol, double-click on the protocol name again.*

- Select a property.

- Choose a relation symbol in the Relation box.

- Specify whether the value is hexadecimal or decimal by selecting either the **Hex** or **Decimal** radio button.

- Enter a byte value (hex or decimal) in the Value box.

- Click on **OK** to return to the Display Filter dialog box.

When you have finished defining the display filter, click on **OK**.

ANY<--> ANY

This line is used to specify a particular computer address. With this feature you can view the frames that were transmitted to/from a particular computer.

To specify which computer addresses to display:

- Open the Display Filter dialog box.

- Select the ANY<-->ANY line and click on **Expression** under Add.

- Click on the **Address** tab (if not already selected) to access the Address dialog box.

- Choose a computer name from each of the Station boxes.

- Specify the direction of network traffic by choosing the appropriate arrow in the Direction box.

- Click on **OK** to return to the Display Filter dialog box.

When you have finished designing the display filter, click on **OK**.

The data that meets the display filter criteria should now be displayed in the Frame Viewer window.

Module 2—Exam #70-087
Implementing and Supporting Microsoft Internet Information Server 4.0

This study guide is designed to help you prepare for Exam #70-087, Implementing and Supporting Microsoft Internet Information Server 4.0. The following criteria were obtained from Microsoft's Web site as of June 1998:

- Choose a security strategy for various situations. Security considerations include:

  Controlling anonymous access

  Controlling access to known users and groups

  Controlling access by host or network

  Configuring SSL to provide encryption and authentication schemes

  Identifying the appropriate balance between security requirements and performance requirements

- Choose an implementation strategy for an Internet site or an intranet site for stand-alone servers, single-domain environments, and multiple-domain environments. Tasks include:

  Resolving host header name issues by using a HOSTS file or DNS, or both

  Choosing the appropriate operating system on which to install IIS

- Choose the appropriate technology to resolve specified problems. Technology options include:

  WWW service

  FTP service

  Microsoft Transaction Server

  Microsoft SMTP Service

  Microsoft NNTP Service

  Microsoft Index Server

  Microsoft Certificate Server

- Install IIS. Tasks include:

  Configuring a Microsoft Windows NT Server 4.0 computer for the installation of IIS

  Identifying differences to a Windows NT Server 4.0 computer made by the installation of IIS

- Configure IIS to support the FTP service. Tasks include:

  Setting bandwidth and user connections

  Setting user logon requirements and authentication requirements

  Modifying port settings

  Setting directory listing style

  Configuring virtual directories and servers

- Configure IIS to support the WWW service. Tasks include:

    Setting bandwidth and user connections

    Setting user logon requirements and authentication requirements

    Modifying port settings

    Setting default pages

    Setting HTTP 1.1 host header names to host multiple Web sites

    Enabling HTTP Keep-Alives

- Configure and save consoles by using Microsoft Management Console.

- Choose the appropriate administration method.

- Install and configure Certificate Server.

- Install and configure Microsoft SMTP Service.

- Install and configure Microsoft NNTP Service.

- Customize the installation of Microsoft Site Server Express Content Analyzer.

- Customize the installation of Microsoft Site Server Express Usage Import and Report Writer.

- Create and share directories with appropriate permissions. Tasks include:

    Setting directory-level permissions

    Setting file-level permissions

- Create and share local and remote virtual directories with appropriate permissions. Tasks include:

    Creating a virtual directory and assigning an alias

    Setting directory-level permissions

    Setting file-level permissions

- Create and share virtual servers with appropriate permissions. Tasks include:

    Assigning IP addresses

- Write scripts to manage the FTP service or the WWW service.

- Manage a Web site by using Content Analyzer. Tasks include:

    Creating, customizing, and navigating WebMaps

    Examining a Web site by using the various reports provided by Content Analyzer

    Tracking links by using a WebMap

- Configure Microsoft SMTP Service to host message traffic.

- Configure Microsoft NNTP Service to host a newsgroup.

- Configure Certificate Server to issue certificates.

- Configure Index Server to index a Web site.

- Manage MIME types.

- Manage the FTP service.

- Manage the WWW service.

- Configure IIS to connect to a database. Tasks include:

    Configuring ODBC

- Configure IIS to integrate with Index Server. Tasks include:

    Specifying query parameters by creating the .idq file

    Specifying how the query results are formatted and displayed to the user by creating the .htx file

- Configure IIS to support server-side scripting.

- Configure IIS to run ISAPI applications.

- Maintain a log for fine-tuning and auditing purposes. Tasks include:

  Importing log files into a Usage Import and Report Writer database

  Configuring the logging features of the WWW service

  Configuring the logging features of the FTP service

  Configuring Usage Import and Report Writer to analyze logs created by the WWW service or the FTP service

  Automating the use of Usage Import and Report Writer

- Monitor performance of various functions by using Performance Monitor. Functions include HTTP and FTP sessions.

- Analyze performance. Performance issues include:

  Identifying bottlenecks

  Identifying network-related performance issues

  Identifying disk-related performance issues

  Identifying CPU-related performance issues

- Optimize performance of IIS.
- Optimize performance of Index Server.
- Optimize performance of Microsoft SMTP Service.
- Optimize performance of Microsoft NNTP Service.
- Interpret performance data.
- Optimize a Web site by using Content Analyzer.
- Resolve IIS configuration problems.
- Resolve security problems.
- Resolve resource access problems.

- Resolve Index Server query problems.
- Resolve setup issues when installing IIS on a Windows NT Server 4.0 computer.
- Use a WebMap to find and repair broken links.
- Resolve WWW service problems.
- Resolve FTP service problems.

Essential Terms

The following are brief definitions of Internet terms. Most of these are described in greater detail in the following paragraphs and chapters.

Dial-up Client

A computer with a temporary Internet connection that cannot act as a server and has a temporary IP address.

Domain Name

The textual name identifier for a specific Internet host, i.e., www.microsoft.com.

Domain Name Server

An Internet host dedicated to the function of translating fully qualified domain names into IP addresses.

File Transfer Protocol (FTP)

The protocol used to transfer files between TCP/IP hosts.

Home Page

The default HTML document returned by an HTTP server when a URL containing no specific document is requested.

Host

A node on a TCP/IP network. This term can be used to refer to a client, a server, or a computer that acts as both a client and a server. It can also be used to refer to other network devices that have at least one IP address, such as routers.

HyperText Transfer Protocol (HTTP)

A client/server interprocess communication protocol used by "Web sites" (server) and "Web browsers" (client).

HyperText Markup Language (HTML)

The language used to construct documents for distribution by HTTP servers.

Internet

The global interconnection of networks based on the TCP/IP protocol suite.

Internet Protocol (IP)

An Internet (Network) layer protocol used to perform route discovery, packet routing, fragmentation, and re-assembly of packets on TCP/IP internetworks.

Intranet

A privately owned network based on the TCP/IP protocol suite.

Java

A cross-platform programming language developed by Sun Microsystems used to create applications that can run in a Web browser or as stand-alone programs.

Java Virtual Machine (JVM)

Software that allows a computer to execute applications written in the Java programming language.

Multipurpose Internet Mail Extensions (MIME)

Extensions to standard electronic mail protocols that support rich content such as animation, audio, and video.

Request for Comments (RFC)

A document describing each existing/proposed Internet protocol. The Internet Engineering Task Force (IETF) establishes subcommittees to evaluate Internet protocols. RFC documents are circulated throughout the Internet community to elicit user feedback. Each RFC document is assigned a unique number.

Search Engine

A Web site dedicated to responding to requests for specific information, searching massive locally stored indexes of HTML documents. Popular search engines include Yahoo!, Excite, AltaVista, and InfoSeek, among others.

Simple Mail Transfer Protocol (SMTP)

The protocol used to exchange electronic mail messages between TCP/IP e-mail servers.

Spider

A program that searches the Internet for Web servers, retrieves HTML documents found on each server, indexes the documents, and stores the indices in a database used by search engines.

Transport Control Protocol (TCP)

A connection-oriented transport layer packet transport protocol that utilizes virtual circuits, packet sequencing, and acknowledgment to provide reliable packet delivery on TCP/IP networks.

Uniform Resource Locator (URL)

A location and document specifier that uniquely identifies a resource on a server. URLs contain the domain name of the Internet host serving the resource, the path to the resource, and the resource name. URLs are defined in RFC 1738.

User Datagram Protocol (UDP)

A connectionless transport layer packet transport protocol designed to provide high-performance, low-overhead packet delivery.

Web Browser

An application that requests documents from an HTTP server and formats HTML documents for display on user workstations. The most popular Web browsers are Netscape Navigator and Microsoft Internet Explorer.

Web Page

An HTML document on an HTTP server.

Web Site

A collection of HTML documents located on an HTTP server. Pages typically contain HyperText links that allow users to easily navigate through available pages.

World Wide Web

A collection of rich content documents maintained by millions of HTTP servers located throughout the world.

Connecting to the Internet

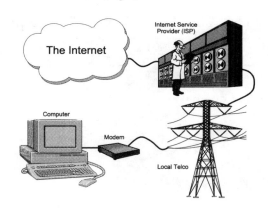

What do you need if you want to connect to the Internet? The answer depends on what you want to accomplish. While the vast majority of Internet users participate as clients who view available information, the number of servers on the Internet has exploded in recent years. Basic system requirements for Internet connectivity include:

- Computer
- Modem, Integrated Services Digital Network (ISDN), Asymmetric Digital Subscriber Line (ADSL), or cable adapter
- TCP/IP-capable operating system, such as UNIX, Windows 95, Windows NT, or Macintosh operating system
- TCP/IP Communications Protocol
- Archie, FTP, Gopher, SMTP mail, Telnet, or an HTML browser application
- Internet Service Provider (ISP)

This chapter provides an introduction to these tools and technologies, with more detailed information later in the course. Our emphasis in this course is server implementation, but any server discussion requires that you understand available clients as well.

What is the WWW?

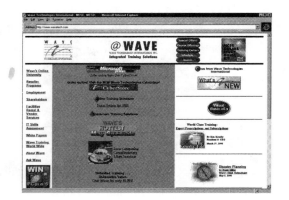

The Internet is the largest computer network in the world. It links computers of every model and operating system together to facilitate the sharing of information.

Every Web site (such as http://www.wavetech.com) on the Internet is assigned a unique address similar to the way that all of the buildings located on a particular street have an address. Computers that connect to the Internet use Internet Protocol (IP) addresses, which are understood by the TCP/IP protocol suite.

Each IP host is also assigned a Domain Name System (DNS) name. This is the name referred to by users who wish to access a particular host. Web servers typically have names in the following format:

```
www.domain_name
```

To access a particular Web server, users launch a Web browser application and specify the Uniform Resource Locator (URL) with which they wish to connect. URLs that refer to Web servers always begin with "http://". This is the URL designator for a HyperText Transfer Language (HTTP, a.k.a. "Web") server. The remainder of the URL refers to the host (typically "www") and domain information, such as "wavetech.com."

The client browser running on a user's computer generates HTTP requests for documents based on user selections.

Prior to the introduction of the HyperText Transfer Protocol and the World Wide Web (WWW), some universities and other agencies tried to organize information in a format that allowed you to find , view, and access information in a non-graphical format with protocols like Archie, Veronica, and Gopher. With the development of the WWW, HTML, HTTP, search engines, and graphical Web browsers, the Internet has become increasingly user-friendly. This has led to the explosive growth of Internet traffic in recent years.

The WWW provides access to text, pictures, sounds, and multimedia content from anywhere in the world. By using hypermedia and hypertext, users are able to retrieve information by a simple mouse click. Currently, there are over 34 million users accessing the Internet. Clearly, the WWW is the fuel feeding the incredible growth of the Internet.

Web Clients

The browser is the client component required to view documents stored on an HTTP Web server. When designing a Web site, your content should be formatted to support both of the popular browsers (Netscape Navigator and Microsoft Internet Explorer). Documents must provide consistent functionality across both application platforms.

Both Internet Explorer 4 and Netscape Navigator 4 provide support for Java applets and JavaScript. This allows you to create dynamic, moving Web pages. Java is becoming the language of choice for program development (like C++) and also for applet development. The primary reason for this is that, provided it does not depend on operating system Application Programming Interfaces (APIs), a Java program or applet can run on any platform that has a Java Virtual Machine. In other words, it is a platform-independent program requiring only a Java-enabled browser. JavaScript is the embedding of simple Java statements in your HTML code.

Microsoft Internet Explorer

In addition to support for the Java language, Internet Explorer 4 supports programs, or components, written to the ActiveX specification. This allows ActiveX components to be automatically downloaded to the browser and executed on a client. ActiveX components can be written in any Windows programming language, one of the most popular being Visual Basic 5.0, or its predecessor, Visual Basic–Control Creation Edition.

VBScript is similar to JavaScript in that it is the embedding of simple VB statements in your HTML code. Internet Explorer 4 supports VBScript.

Adding Support for Rich Content

One final way to enhance the client is called *Netscape Plugins*. These are programs that add functionality to the browser. They are downloaded from a server and installed on the client computer. Subsequently, Web browsers can use these programs to access documents containing an infinite variety of content types. Examples of popular plugins are Macromedia's Shockwave and Apple Computer's QuickTime.

Web Servers

A basic Internet server provides Web documents over HTTP and files over FTP. In addition, certain programs can run on the Web server to enhance the information sent to the browser. These are:

- Common Gateway Interface (CGI)
- Internet Server Application Programming Interface (ISAPI)
- Active Server Pages (ASP)

The primary difference between CGI and ISAPI is that with CGI programs, a new copy of the program is loaded into memory on the server every time a client browser requests the page containing the program. With an ISAPI program, one copy is loaded into memory and shared by all applications.

While CGI and ISAPI are usually written in either Perl or C (for CGI) or C++ (for ISAPI), an Active Server Page is a script that is interpreted by a dynamic link library that is loaded in the Internet Information Server's memory. This means that an Active Server Page can be written in any Active scripting language, including VBScript and JavaScript. An Active Server Page can also run ActiveX components, making it a very powerful tool for server-side Web solutions. Active Server Pages will be covered in more detail later in the course.

ASP, CGI, and ISAPI programs can provide many types of services to client browsers including:

- Database lookups
- Capturing information and updating a database
- Page hit counters
- Online shopping and order processing

What Happens When you Click on a HyperLink?

The following is a description of the events behind the operation of a typical HTTP server and client:

1. The client browser translates the URL embedded in the user-specified URL into a fully qualified domain name and path to the document.

2. The browser requests name resolution for the domain name and path from a DNS Server. The DNS server returns an IP address, which is the IP address of the server containing the requested document.

3. A TCP/IP connection is established to the server's IP address.

4. The browser uses HTTP to request the document from the server.

5. The server transmits the HTML document at the path indicated in the URL to the browser.

6. The TCP/IP connection to the Web server is broken. Each page request makes a unique, temporary TCP/IP connection.

7. The HTML document is formatted by the browser and presented to the user. Because HTML pages may contain many embedded objects such as graphics and frames, the request-response process is repeated until all objects have been retrieved.

   NOTE: *You can watch this process occur by watching the bottom left corner of your browser window. Connections are made and broken as the various elements of a document are retrieved.*

Microsoft Internet Information Server (IIS)

Microsoft provides support for Web applications through the Microsoft Internet Information Server. IIS transmits documents in HyperText Markup Language (HTML) pages using the HyperText Transfer Protocol (HTTP). It listens for requests from users and responds by providing the information that satisfies the request. With it you can provide a wide variety of services, including:

- Publish information about your business on the Internet.

- Publish a catalog and take orders.

- Create interactive programs that provide real time information to people visiting your site.

- Provide access to your databases for your employees and/or customers.

You can also use IIS in an intranet to provide internal access to company information, methods and procedures, and forms for your employees.

With IIS 3.0, Microsoft introduced server-side scripting. Many functions that formerly had to be done with a compiled application could now be done with text files that were interpreted by the Web server. Documentation and program example files are included with IIS 3.0 and IIS 4.0.

IIS 4.0 provides support for the Distributed Component Object Model (DCOM), JavaScript, Java applets, VBScript, and ActiveX programs that run on the server. (As opposed to being downloaded to the browser and running on the client.)

The latest version of IIS, version 4, offers so much flexibility in providing dynamic information, that previous versions should be used only until version 4 is installed.

Using Internet Information Server

Internet Information Server allows you to create powerful Web solutions, provided you understand the technologies available to you. For example, you could:

- Create client/server applications using the Microsoft Internet Server Application Programming Interface (ISAPI).

- Create and run Common Gateway Interface (CGI) applications.

- Create HTML scripts that interface with Microsoft SQL Server.

- Develop server-side scripts (ASP) to add dynamic information to your Web pages.

- Enhance your HTML pages with ActiveX, Java, VBScript, and JavaScript, on the server as well as the browser.

NOTE: *Some of these terms and technologies may be unfamiliar to you. Don't let that concern you. At least initially, you only need a general understanding of many of these.*

Microsoft Windows NT Server 4.0

The Microsoft Internet Information Server 4.0 runs on the Microsoft Windows NT Server 4.0 or higher operating system. Windows NT provides fast performance, good security, and the ability to integrate IIS with Microsoft's SQL Server.

IIS 4.0 requires that you first install Service Pack 3 and Internet Explorer 4.0. IIS 4.0 is available with the Windows NT 4.0 Option Pack, which can be downloaded from the Microsoft Web site at www.microsoft.com/windows/downloads/contents/products/nt4optpk/ or installed from the Microsoft TechNet or MSDN Universal CD-ROMs. These components are also included in Microsoft BackOffice Suite 4.0.

Microsoft Windows NT 4.0 Internet Client Tools

Windows NT 4.0 includes a complete set of Internet client application tools including:

- Internet Explorer

    This is a full-featured Web browser.

- Internet Mail/Exchange

    This is an e-mail utility that can be configured to send and receive e-mail over the Internet via the SMTP and POP protocols.

- FTP

    This is a standard File Transfer Protocol client utility.

- Telnet

    This is a utility that provides a command-line interface to connect to a remote host and access character-based applications as if connected via a local, serial terminal.

- Finger

    This is a utility used to look up information about users on a remote system.

- Ping

    This is a utility that is used to test connectivity to other systems. Ping is actually an acronym for Packet Internet Groper.

- Nslookup

    This is a utility used to resolve host names to Internet Protocol addresses.

- Rsh

    This is a utility that is used to access a remote shell program, allowing you to execute commands on remote UNIX hosts that support running the rsh service.

- Tftp

  The Trivial FTP utility allows you to upload and download files between two computers on a network.

- Tracert

  This is a utility that allows you to trace the route and track the number of router "hops" between your computer and any TCP/IP host computer.

Finding an ISP

The first step is to create a list of ISPs that serve your area.

There are three ways to find ISPs:

1. Whenever you attend an Internet conference or training, ask people who they're using.

2. Use the search engines on the Internet. Search for "ISP," "Internet Service Provider," and your city name.

3. Read your local newspaper. ISPs tend to advertise in the sports, business, and entertainment sections. You might have to search the paper for a week or two, but ISPs do advertise.

There are national ISPs, but usually they contract with a local ISP for their presence. Skip the nationals unless it is a big phone company and is a true provider instead of a middleman.

Connectivity Options

You should become familiar with connectivity terminology: The first thing that you want to be able to assess is your bit transfer rate requirements. You will need to weigh the cost of high transfer rates against the benefits. Next you'll want to look at options for sending and receiving those bits: ISDN, Frame Relay, and ATM.

The industry standard bit transfer rates for various transmission media are as follows:

T-Class Carriers

T-carriers are a type of high-speed leased telephone lines used for voice and data transmission. There are four service levels:

T1	1.544 Mbps	1 Channel
T2	6.312 Mbps	4 Channels
T3	44.736 Mbps	28 Channels
T4	274.176 Mbps	168 Channels

FT1

This is a subdivision of T1, which is less expensive and is based on 64 Kbps channels. This service is the most commonly used where you need an inexpensive, continuously open channel. This is called Fractional T1.

ISDN

This is a switched digital service that is usually sold on a time and distance rate schedule just like phone calls. Most ISDN is provided by phone companies that have converted some of their analog lines to integrated voice and digital. ISDN lines are available with bandwidth increments of 56/64 Kbps, 1.544 Mbps, and 2.048 Mbps.

The most common service options are Basic Rate and Primary Rate. Basic Rate divides its available bandwidth into three data channels: Two B channels and one D channel. The B channels transmit data at 64 Kbps each and the D channel transmits signaling and link management data at 16 Kbps. Since the third channel is used for signaling overhead instead of actual data transmission, the available bandwidth is 128 Kbps. In the United States, Primary Rate ISDN is 23 B channels at 64 Kbps and a D channel that operates at 64 Kbps. This yields a total of 1.544 Mbps T1 bandwidth. In Europe, Primary Rate ISDN includes 30 B channels and one D channel. This yields an available bandwidth of 2.048 Mbps.

> NOTE: *If your ISDN rate is a measured rate and ISDN is used continuously, it is generally more expensive than dedicated leased lines FT1 (Fractional T1) and T1.*

Frame Relay

This is a packet-switching network service that provides high-speed data transmission rates. Frame relay uses permanent virtual circuits (PVCs) to establish stable end-to-end circuits.

ATM (Asynchronous Transfer Mode)

This is a packet-switching network service that can transmit data in excess of 600 Mbps. Its high-speed advantage is due to the fact that it transmits uniform data packets that are subdivided into data frames. Each frame is enclosed within an addressable 53-byte cell and routed by hardware switching.

ATM is the backbone of major telecommunications companies. It is becoming more and more popular in private industry because prices are falling and hardware is more easily accessible.

> NOTE: *The above information is important to understand, but the bandwidths listed are those you will get under the best possible conditions. What you need from your ISP once you have chosen your data transfer rate and method of transfer is a guaranteed CIR (Certified Information Rate). A CIR guarantees that no matter how much traffic the lines support you are guaranteed that your data will always have a specific bandwidth.*

Connection Concerns

Your biggest long-term cost will be what you pay your ISP each month for the connection and what you pay the phone company for the line. The type of phone line you choose is dependent on geography and politics. Some phone companies price services like ISDN cheaply; others charge much more. Your ISP should already have an intimate knowledge of the local phone company's structure and pricing policies and should guide you.

If your company is new to the Internet, you may be able to get by with a 56-Kbps connection to your ISP. You might choose a frame relay connection or an ISDN connection. A 56-Kbps connection will be the least expensive and will give you the opportunity to learn more about IIS and your ISP. Your ISP and your customers will alert you when more bandwidth is required.

Another area of concern is your ISP's connection to the Internet and how many people are using it. If your ISP only has a 56-Kbps line and is the ISP for a few companies, your throughput may not be very good. Access their Web site and check out the response.

How far is your ISP from the Internet backbone? The Internet backbone is the 12 (or so) Network Access Points (NAPs) in the United States that are connected to each other at 45 Mbps. Everyone else connects to these NAPs. For example, the best situation would be a provider who connects to one of these 12 backbone connections, such as StarNet (Washington University in St. Louis, Missouri). How many hops does your ISP have to go through to get to the backbone?

The three major long-distance companies all have their own version of the Internet backbone. Selecting one of these as your ISP can yield improved performance.

You will need to make sure your new ISP provides any add-on services, like mail, news, or DNS.

Terminal Adapter vs. Router

While talking with ISPs, they may mention using either a terminal adapter or a router for your connection. Each device connects to your network interface card and the telephone line. A router is more expensive but allows all of the computers on your network to connect directly to your ISP's router, then out to the Internet. A terminal adapter would connect one of your computers to one of your ISP's servers, then out to the Internet. With a terminal adapter, if the particular ISP server to which you are connected was to go down, your connection would also be down.

With ISDN, some routers can *spoof* the line. This means they actually connect to your ISP as needed while your server thinks the line is up all of the time. If your phone company is charging you for connection time, this can save money.

If you believe that your Web site has the potential to be very popular, consider buying a multiple ISDN connection router. Then as you grow, you can just add another ISDN line instead of having to purchase another router.

Domain Name System Server

The Domain Name System is described later in this course. Microsoft included a DNS server as part of the TCP/IP support shipping with Windows NT Server 4.0. In brief, a DNS server is a database of Internet domain names and their associated IP addresses.

You would normally run your own DNS to resolve any inquiries for your domain name, and any other names similar to it. For example, you can surf to www.wavetech.com, or you can surf to dhill.wavetech.com. If you surf to the latter, the DNS system will eventually contact the Wave DNS server to find out where dhill.wavetech.com is located.

Your ISP should provide your secondary DNS address which will point to your ISP's DNS server.

Changing ISPs

If you become dissatisfied with your ISP, you can go through the process of finding another provider. It is important to register your own domain name. Smaller organizations are sometimes tempted to rely on an ISP's domain name as the path to their Web site. This leaves you locked into one vendor, or forces you to reroute anyone looking for your site.

In the long term, it is much easier if you have your own registered domain name. Once you find a new ISP, you can fill out an electronic form and submit it to have your domain name registered to the new ISP's network address. To do this, you must contact the InterNIC in Herndon, Virginia or submit your request electronically via the InterNIC Web site at http://www.internic.net.

Windows NT Server Installation

The first step in preparing to install a Microsoft Internet Information Server is knowing how to install and configure Windows NT Server. You will also need to install Service Pack 3 and Internet Explorer 4.01.

Before installing Windows NT Server you need to determine if you will need a 10- to 20-MB FAT partition for DOS-based device drivers and utilities. With older motherboards that could not perform automatic detection or assign interrupts (IRQs) and I/O addresses to devices, it was necessary to create a FAT partition that could be used to run MS-DOS configuration and diagnostic utilities. These devices might include network adapters, modems, sound cards, CD-ROM drives, and SCSI controllers. With advances in motherboard and BIOS technology there is little or no need for a FAT boot partition.

Installing NT for an Internet Information Server

Windows NT currently ships with three setup diskettes, a Windows NT CD-ROM, and a Service Pack 3 CD-ROM. You can use the three setup diskettes to begin an NT installation. If you have a newer motherboard in which the BIOS supports a bootable IDE CD-ROM, you can install directly from the CD. If the latter is true you can configure the BIOS to boot to the CD-ROM drive first. The process for installing Windows NT Server by booting from the CD-ROM is the same, but faster than if you boot from diskette.

To install Internet Information Server 4.0 correctly, you must follow the appropriate installation order. That order is:

- Install Windows NT Server 4.0.
- Configure TCP/IP.
- Install Service Pack 3 (or a more recent version).
- Install Internet Explorer 4.01.

- Install Windows NT 4.0 Option Pack.

Directory Structures and Sharing

An in-depth discussion of security issues will be provided later in the course. Click on the **Start** button and select **Settings/Control Panel/Server/Shares**.

The Shared Resources list allows you to view the shared file systems on your Windows NT Server computer. The drives and directories whose names end with a $ are called administrative shares. There will always be some shares of this type present.

The significance of administrative shares is that they do not appear in browse lists. These are used by the system and network for their own purposes. This does not mean, however, that they are completely unavailable. In fact, you can set up your own *hidden* shares by creating them as administrative shares. For users to access these shares, they will have to know and manually enter the share name.

Initially, you will want to prevent all remote logins, except anonymous (more on this later), so these administrative shares do not pose a security risk at this point.

User Management

Next, you should view information about the users and groups that have been defined on your server. Click on the **Start** button and select **Programs/Administrative Tools/User Manager for Domains**.

When User Manager for Domains launches, double-click on the Administrator user to display the User Properties page.

This is where you can change the password for the Administrator user. It is strongly recommended that you change your administrator password to something very difficult to guess.

For added security, you can change the Administrator account to a different name through User Manager for Domains.

In addition, review all user names on the system and make sure you don't have other administrators. The easiest way to do this is to view the member list of the Administrators (on a stand-alone server) or Domain Admins (on a domain controller) group.

TCP/IP Installation and Configuration

You should have installed the TCP/IP protocol when you installed the Windows NT Server 4.0 operating system. If not, you can add TCP/IP support at any time, as long as you have access to the Windows NT Server installation files.

TCP/IP is the protocol you use when connecting your Windows NT Server computer to the Internet. Setup is straightforward once you have the necessary information from your Internet Service Provider (ISP).

TCP/IP installation and configuration tasks are performed using the Network utility.

You may also be using additional protocols such as NetBEUI or IPX to provide or gain access to resources on a LAN. It is recommended that you disable these other protocols before connecting your server to the Internet. Once you feel comfortable with the Windows NT Server security system, you can enable additional protocols as required.

Network Utility

To install or configure TCP/IP, click on the **Start** button and select **Settings/Control Panel/Network**. Or right-click on Network Neighborhood, then select **Properties**.

You can view the Computer Name and Workgroup values that were assigned during the server installation process. To edit these values, click on **Change** and enter the new information.

Network Adapters

Click on the **Adapters** tab. You should notice one or more entries in the Network Adapters field. If it is blank, you will need to click on **Add** and install the appropriate drivers. The drivers are located on the Windows NT Server 4.0 CD-ROM.

If you are using an unsupported network interface card you will need access to the Windows NT Server 4.0 driver diskette supplied by the card's manufacturer.

Communications Protocols

Click on the **Protocols** tab. Scroll through the list to locate the TCP/IP Protocol entry. If it is not listed, click on **Add** and install the appropriate files. The files are located on the Windows NT Server 4.0 CD-ROM.

Depending on your server's configuration there may be additional communications protocols listed. The only protocol required to use Internet Information Server is TCP/IP.

TCP/IP Properties

To check your TCP/IP configuration, select TCP/IP Protocol, then click on **Properties**.

The listed Adapter should be the network interface card that you will be using to connect to your ISP. Do not enable **Automatic DHCP Configuration**. Your ISP should have provided you with values for the IP Address, Subnet Mask, and Default Gateway fields.

> *NOTE: Do not connect your server to the Internet until these values are properly configured!*

Domain Name System Configuration

The Domain Name System is a client/server protocol that translates TCP/IP host names into numeric IP addresses. DNS maintains a set of tables that map host names to IP addresses. If a certain DNS server does not find a host name in its tables, it passes the DNS query to another DNS server for resolution.

A DNS server can be installed on your Windows NT Server 4.0 computer, on one of your ISP's servers, or elsewhere on the Internet. A typical configuration maintains a local DNS for your LAN, in addition to a DNS provided by your ISP, for resolving Internet host names.

To view Domain Name System information, click on the **DNS** tab.

Your ISP should have provided you with the addresses of one or more DNS servers. You will need to enter the information in the DNS Service Search Order list. Also enter a host and domain name. If you have registered a domain name with InterNIC, enter it here.

Click on **OK** when done. Return to the Network Settings window, then click on **OK**. If any parameters were modified you will be prompted to restart the server.

Name Resolution and WINS

A critical issue in networking is the resolution of host names, especially in a Microsoft networking environment. Microsoft's implementation of TCP/IP supports the following:

- HOSTS file

  This method uses a text file to associate a host name with an IP address. This method does not support NetBIOS-based applications.

- DNS

  The Domain Name System supports fully qualified host names including an IP domain, subdomain, and host name.

- NetBIOS broadcasts

  This method resolves NetBIOS names and IP addresses through broadcasts. However, broadcasts are not propagated past the local subnetwork, severely limiting the usefulness of this method.

- LMHOSTS file

  Similar to the HOSTS file method, this method specifically supports NetBIOS names. Name resolution is maintained via a text file located on the local machine or accessed through network shares.

- WINS

  This is an automated NetBIOS name resolution method. WINS clients automatically register themselves with the WINS server, which can then be queried for name resolution. NetBIOS names can also be manually entered into the database.

Each of these methods will have its place in a mixed network environment.

Additonal Utilities

Microsoft includes three tools with Windows NT Server 4.0 that are vital for testing your TCP/IP installation and Internet connectivity. These are:

- PING.EXE

  The Packet Internet Groper utility is used to test TCP/IP connectivity by transmitting ICMP packets to a TCP/IP host. The host should then echo the packets back to the originating IP address.

- IPCONFIG.EXE

  The Internet Protocol Configuration utility is used to view TCP/IP configuration information from a command prompt.

- TRACERT.EXE

  This utility is used to check the availability of routes to a given destination network. It also provides timing information that can be used to identify bottlenecks in an internetwork or on the Internet.

Each of these utilities is located in the \WINNT\SYSTEM32 subdirectory.

Windows NT 4.0 Service Pack 3

The Windows NT 4.0 Service Pack 3 is required by Internet Information Server 4.0. This is a self-installing Service Pack that *must* be reapplied anytime changes are made to operating system services or hardware configuration.

Service Pack 3 contains the following components:

- Updated Dynamic Link Libraries (.DLL)
- Windows NT Kernel Updates
- Windows NT Driver Updates
- Windows NT Service Updates

Because several parts of Internet Information Server must run as a service, if IIS 2.0 is already installed, Service Pack 3 will automatically update the service to IIS 3.0. Service Pack 3 is available on Microsoft's Web site or on the Windows NT 4.0 Option Pack CD-ROM.

The Microsoft Internet Explorer (IE)

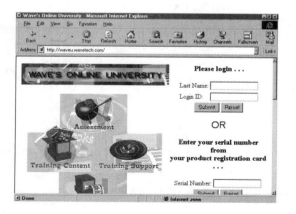

Included on the Windows NT Server 4.0 CD-ROM is an earlier version of the Microsoft Internet Explorer Web browser. This is a tool for navigating and accessing information on the Web. Web surfers can use any Web browser for accessing your site and this is a major consideration when designing your Web pages. Internet Explorer is also available for the Macintosh.

Microsoft Internet Explorer 4.0 and higher supports HTML 1 through HTML 4.0. Netscape Navigator currently supports HTML 1 through HTML 3.2. Each browser may display pages slightly differently. Both also have special enhancements that enable *cooler* looking pages and better functionality, but are proprietary to that particular browser.

If you use HTML commands that are browser specific, you may restrict many potential customers from gaining access to you. Later in the course, publishing information is discussed in more detail.

The latest version of IE can be downloaded from the Microsoft Web site (http://www.microsoft.com/ie). According to Microsoft, IE Service Packs will be made available for download from the same site.

Internet Explorer 4.01 is also available on the Windows NT 4.0 Option Pack CD-ROM. It is necessary to install Internet Explorer 4.01 before installing Internet Information Server.

Windows NT 4.0 Option Pack and IIS 4.0 System Requirements

Most Internet Information Servers will probably be up and running 24 hours a day, 7 days a week. It is important to select a high-quality hardware platform. The following is a list of the minimum hardware and software requirements for running IIS 4.0. You may also have additional requirements depending on the applications you are running or services you want to support.

Minimum IIS 4.0 Requirements

The following is a list of minimum and recommended requirements for an Internet Information Server:

- CPU: Pentium 66 (minimum), Pentium 90+ (recommended)

- Hard Disk: 200 MB of disk space (minimum), SCSI Controller with 2+ GB hard drive (recommended)

- Memory: 32 MB RAM (minimum), 64+ MB (recommended)

- CD-ROM drive

- VGA, Super VGA, or video graphics adapter compatible with Windows NT Server 4.0

- Microsoft mouse or other pointing device

- Windows NT Server 4.0

- Windows NT Service Pack 3

- Internet Explorer 4.01 (or greater)

- Windows NT 4 Option Pack

- Network Interface Card

- An Internet connection and an Internet Protocol (IP) address from your Internet Service Provider (ISP), unless you're setting up an intranet

- Router or terminal adapter for connecting to your ISP

- A registered Internet Domain Name

IIS Directory Structure

By default, the Windows NT 4.0 Option Pack/IIS 4.0 installation process creates the following directory structure on the drive where Windows NT was installed:

> \InetPub\wwwroot
>
> \InetPub\ftproot
>
> \InetPub\scripts
>
> \InetPub\Mailroot
>
> \InetPub\nntpfile
>
> \InetPub\Catalog.wci
>
> \InetPub\iissamples
>
> \InetPub\Mail
>
> \InetPub\News

NOTE: *You are provided with the option of installing to a different drive but most installations use the default IIS parent directory of \InetPub.*

Making Sure It's Running

To verify that your installation was successful, launch Internet Explorer and type the following URL:

```
http://localhost
```

If your Web service is running, the default document on the local machine will be displayed.

You can also tell if the Web service is running by opening the Services utility in Control Panel.

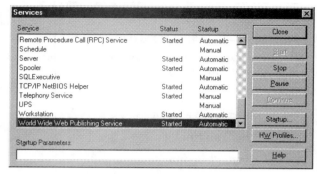

Benefits of the MMC

In Windows NT 4.0, every management tool you use has a different interface. This requires you to think about how to use the tool's interface. By consolidating all management functions into a uniform interface, you can more easily concentrate on the job that needs to be done instead of worrying about which menu or button you need to select to get you where you want to go.

The Microsoft Management Console solves that problem. The MMC is a shell that provides the user interface to management tools called *snap-ins*. Windows NT 4 Option Pack installs the snap-ins that are used to manage the services you select to install. For example, the Internet Service Manager snap-in allows you to administer the Internet Information Server. The Microsoft Transaction Server snap-in allows you to administer the Microsoft Transaction Server.

MMC Feature Tour

To launch the Microsoft Management Console utility, run **Start/Programs/Windows NT 4.0 Option Pack/Microsoft Internet Server/Internet Service Manager**.

The MMC has an Explorer-like interface with a hierarchical TreeView control on the left-hand side and a ListView control on the right-hand side. The left-hand side is known as the *scope* pane. The right-hand side is the *contents* pane. As with Explorer, the information in the contents pane can be displayed in either Large Icon, Small Icon, List, or Detail views.

The snap-ins that have been added to the console are listed under the Console Root folder in the scope pane. They can be expanded to reveal the objects they contain. To change which snap-ins are displayed, run **Add/Remove Snap-In** from the **Console** menu.

You can add either a stand-alone snap-in, such as the Microsoft Index Server snap-in, or an extension, like the SMTP extension for Internet Information Server. If you choose to add a stand-alone snap-in, you will be prompted to select whether the snap-in will be used to manage a local service or a service on another computer.

Once you click on **Finish**, the snap-in will be added to the scope pane of the current console.

Saving Consoles

When MMC is first loaded, the default console is displayed. However, you can customize consoles for yourself and for other administrators and users. Benefits of doing this include:

- Using your customized console on various machines.

- Limiting which snap-ins a particular user can load.

To save a console you have created, run **Save As** from the **Console** menu. Give the console a name. The file will be saved with the .msc extension. It can then be copied to a disk or to the network and shared with the appropriate permissions. One example of this would be if you have developers who need to manage the Microsoft Transaction Server and you want to restrict them from accessing other servers. In this case, you could create a console with only the Microsoft Transaction Server snap-in and save it to a shared directory. Then give the Developers group read-only access to that directory.

Getting Help

The **Help** menu of the Microsoft Management Console allows you to access help files for the console itself, as well as for the currently selected snap-in.

If you are connected to the Internet, you can also select **Microsoft on the Web** to directly access URLs that provide you with access to a gallery of snap-ins, product news, frequently asked questions, and the ability to send feedback on the product. You can also access Microsoft's Home Page.

Management Tasks

Examples of common management tasks you might need to perform through the Internet Service Manger include:

- Controlling anonymous login
- Configuring authentication methods
- Configuring directory restrictions
- IP Filtering

NOTE: *When using NT Explorer to alter directory permissions, User Manager to add or change user names and groups, or the Internet Service Manager to configure IIS 4.0, it may be necessary to stop and restart the WWW and FTP services for changes to take effect.*

Objects and Icons

Before you can use the Internet Service Manager to administer your Web server, you need to understand some of the objects that are created beneath the Internet Information Server. These are:

- Computer

    This object's icon resembles a computer. It is used to set properties that apply to all of the sites running on a particular computer. Some of these properties can be overridden by properties set on child objects.

- Sites

    Beneath the Computer object are all of the sites running on that server. One of the powerful features of Internet Information Server 4.0 is that you can run multiple sites on the same computer and manage them easily through the MMC. When Internet Information Server is installed, the following sites are created automatically:

    Default FTP Site

    Default Web Site

    Administration Web Site

    If you installed extension services, such as SMTP, a site for that service will appear as well. In addition, you can add multiple sites to your server. You will see how that is done later.

- Applications

    Applications can be added to each Web site. In Web usage, an application defines the directories in which a file being executed runs. All files within an application can share context information and variables. For example, you may have an order entry application that includes several forms. By including those forms in an application, each form can have access to variables set on the other forms. An application is defined by its starting point. Directories added beneath that starting point belong to the application. However, if an application starting point is added inside of one of those directories, a new application tree is started.

- Virtual Directories

    A virtual directory is a directory that can be located on the local computer running Internet Information Server or on a different machine. They will be discussed in detail later in the course.

- Directory

    A directory is a path on the local computer or one that can be accessed by a URL.

Inheritance

Each object has a set of properties associated with it. By default, all child objects inherit properties from the parent object. For example, when Internet Information Server is first installed, the Connection Timeout value for the FTP connections on the Computer object is set to 900. Therefore, all FTP sites beneath the server have a Connection Timeout set to 900 as well. You can change this default value on the Computer object. If you do, it will affect any FTP site objects that have not had their Connection Timeout value set explicitly.

However, if you set a property on a child object explicitly, that value will override any value set on an object above it in the hierarchy. In the previous example, suppose you were supporting an FTP site for users that you knew would be dialing over poor lines with slow modems. You could increase the timeout value for that site only to 1500. Even if the Computer object's Connection Timeout value was later changed to 300, the site with the explicitly set value would remain unchanged.

It is important to note that for properties that contain lists of values, such as users who have permission to an object, the lists are replaced, not merged.

Server Properties

You can display the Computer object's properties by right-clicking on the Computer object and running **Properties** or by selecting the Computer object and clicking on the **Properties** button. To set default properties for either WWW sites or FTP sites, select the appropriate service from the drop-down list and click on **Edit**. The appropriate property pages will be displayed.

You can also set bandwidth throttling properties and mime types globally from this property page. Keep in mind that these are global to all sites running on the server except those for which properties have been explicitly set.

Web Site

The Web Site property page allows you to define the Web site name, specify the IP address of the Web server, control the number of connections, enable/disable logging, and configure the TCP Port number used for the Web site and any SSL you may have selected.

The IP address can be selected from those configured in the Network utility. A special value of All Unassigned is the default. This means that the site will respond to any IP address that is configured in the Network utility, but that is not being used by another WWW site on the server. This is useful for computers with multiple network adapter cards.

The Port is another important field. The default port for the WWW service is port 80. If you change the port number for a particular Web site, users will have to append the port number to the URL in order to reach the site.

Operators

This page allows you to specify the users who possess rights to control certain aspects of the Web site. By default, the Administrators group is given this right.

Operators cannot do everything. They are not allowed to:

- Modify a Web site's host header, IP Address, or port.
- Make changes to the IUSR_*ComputerName* account.
- Change bandwidth throttling settings.
- Create virtual directories.
- Relocate virtual directories.

In order to be assigned as an operator, a user account must be created in either User Manager (for a stand-alone system) or User Manager for Domains (for a domain member).

Performance

This property page allows you to configure the performance of the Service based on the expected number of users per day. If you are a corporation that has an Internet link you can configure the bandwidth that you are willing to allow for the Web server so that e-mail and other network traffic is not adversely affected by Web traffic. Performance properties will be discussed in more detail later in the course.

ISAPI Filters

An ISAPI filter is a dynamic link library that executes in response to a particular event. ISAPI filters can be specified on a Server level or on a Site level. When they are specified at both levels, the lists are merged. When you configure an ISAPI filter, you must specify the path to the DLL, the event with which the filter is associated, and the filter's priority. If an event is associated with multiple filters, the filter with the highest priority executes first. If two filters have the same priority, the filter that was loaded first is the one executed first.

A filter loads into memory when the server or site that uses it starts. They are loaded in the order in which they appear in the list. To promote or demote a filter, use the arrow buttons to the left of the list.

Home Directory

This property page allows you configure the home directory for your Web site. The default directory for IIS 4.0 is *systemdrive:*\Inetpub\wwwroot. This directory could exist as a share on a separate Windows NT Server computer by enabling redirection. You can also control user rights and permissions to the contents of this directory along with application settings.

The Home Directory property sheet is used to configure the default directory for your home page and other Web content. When a user enters the URL for your Web site such as http://www.wavetech.com, a default document is returned to them. If the URL specifies a subdirectory on your server without specifying a particular document, a default document from that subdirectory is returned to them, if available.

Documents

This property page allows you to define the default HTML document name for your Web site. When users connect to your Web site, if they haven't asked for a specific document, your server will send them the default document from your \Inetpub\Wwwroot directory.

Two sample HTML pages are created in \InetPub\wwwroot directory during the NT 4.0 Option Pack installation process. They are:

- default.htm
- default.asp

If more than one document is specified, IIS 4.0 goes down the list until it locates one of them. If you don't specify a default document and the Directory Browsing property on the Web site property page is checked, the user will receive a directory listing when a document is not specified. If Directory Browsing is disabled, the user will receive an error.

In the UNIX world, the default document name is index.html. In the world of IIS 4.0, the default document name is generally default.htm. You can change this name to anything you desire (usually index.html).

You can also specify a file containing a footer on this property page. This is useful in a situation where you want to have an identical footer on every Web page that is displayed. For example, you might use a footer to display a copyright notice on all content.

Directory Security

This allows you to configure the type of security that is established on the Web site. You can also choose to make global directory security changes to other IIS 4.0 Services. You can configure anonymous logon, Windows NT logon with directory security, IP restrictions, or combinations of all three. Security will be discussed in detail later in the course. However, let's take a brief look at it now.

Anonymous Access

The anonymous user account is the account that the WWW Service uses when accessing content on your server. The default anonymous user account IUSR_*Computername* is appropriate for most situations. During creation, this user is added to the member lists of the local Guests group and the Domain Users global group. Later in this chapter, you will see how to verify that the Windows NT permissions for this account are properly configured.

When a user clicks on a URL that points to your server, the IUSR_*Computername* account is used by IIS 4.0 to determine access to directories and files containing Web content. Access is controlled by the Windows NT and IIS 4.0 permissions granted to this account. If you wish to limit site access to certain users, you can require users to supply a valid account name and password. If you enable this option, all users that connect to your Web server will require NT user accounts and passwords.

Authentication Methods

Authentication is used to restrict directory access to certain users. Overall user access is determined by the combination of IIS security, Windows NT directory permissions, and user rights.

For example, if you wish to enable access to your Web site for Internet users you would configure the directory permissions to the wwwroot directory for the IUSR_*Computername* account to Read. If you then wanted to prevent anonymous users from accessing certain subdirectories below wwwroot, you would not grant any NTFS permissions to the IUSR_*Computername* account for those subdirectories. If you have a user that requires access to a restricted subdirectory, you will need to create a Windows NT user account, assign a password, and grant the user Read permission in the subdirectory.

IIS 4.0 provides two user-level authentication options:

Basic Authentication

Basic Authentication can be used by all browsers. This authentication method transmits usernames and passwords through a network as simple unencrypted ASCII text. This might be considered a security problem since anyone with a network analyzer could capture packets containing usernames and passwords. However, if you do not select this option, you will disallow access to secured directories for users with a browser other than Internet Explorer. When you enable this option, you are warned that this is a possible security issue. Ignore the warning and enable Basic Authentication.

Windows NT Challenge/Response

This authentication method is for users who use the Internet Explorer browser. This method encrypts usernames and passwords during transmission and is considered secure.

HTTP Headers

Allows you to configure custom HTTP headers, Multipurpose Internet Mail Extensions (MIME types), content expiration, and content ratings. These will be discussed later in the course.

Custom Errors

This property page allows you to create custom error messages for your Web site.

FTP Service Properties

You configure the FTP Service through a collection of five properties pages. These are:

- Ftp Site
- Security accounts
- Messages
- Home Directory
- Directory Security

FTP Site

In the **FTP Site** properties page you can:

- Enter a description of the FTP Site and the IP address of the FTP server.
- Configure the TCP/IP Port on which the service is listening. This defaults to Port 21.
- Limit the maximum number of concurrent connections the site should allow.
- Enable or disable logging.
- Display a list of users who are currently connected to the site.

Security Accounts

In the **Security Accounts** properties page you can:

- Allow anonymous connections using the Internet guest account IUSR_*Computername.*

- Enable or disable automatic password synchronization and allow only anonymous logons.

- Assign FTP site operators.

By enabling the **Allow Anonymous Connections** option you allow browsers and FTP clients to connect to your server without an explicit user account name and password. You must use NTFS permissions in conjunction with FTP server directory permissions to control access to the FTP server.

If you enable the **Allow only anonymous connections** option you prevent anyone from logging on to your server with a valid username and password. For example, with this option disabled, a user might successfully guess your Administrator password and would have access to directories with the same permissions as the Administrator user.

Messages

In the **Messages** properties page you can configure three types of messages to be displayed by your FTP server:

- A Welcome message that is displayed when a client connects to the FTP server.

- An Exit message that is displayed when a client disconnects from the FTP server.

- A Maximum Connections message that is displayed when the site has reached the maximum number of user connections allowed.

Home Directory

In the **Home Directory** properties page you can:

- Specify where FTP content is stored, either locally or on another server.

  If the FTP content is stored on another server it is accessed through a share.

- Configure the default parent directory for the FTP Service.

  This is the path to the directory that will store the files. It is recommended that it be on an NTFS partition.

- Configure the access permissions for the FTP root directory.

  The initial default configuration for this directory is read-only with logging enabled. There may be a time when you want to designate a subdirectory to allow clients to upload files. Then you would select both read and write for that subdirectory only.

  If the directory is on an NTFS partition and the permissions set here do not match the NTFS permissions granted to the user, the most restrictive settings will be applied. For example, if the IUSR_*ComputerName* account is granted read-only permission to the directory and the FTP Site is set up with write permission, an anonymous user will only be granted read permission to this site.

- Directory-style listing

  Select from either UNIX or MS-DOS directory-style listings. The default is MS-DOS.

When a user connects to your FTP server with a valid Windows NT user account and password, the FTP service will look for a subdirectory under \InetPub\ftproot or a virtual directory that matches the user's name. If one exists, the FTP service will set that directory as the default for this user.

Directory Security

The **Directory Security** properties page allows you to configure IP Filtering.

When most people connect to the Microsoft FTP site, they do so anonymously. The username is "anonymous" and the password is usually their e-mail address. By allowing anonymous connections, Microsoft can distribute updates and new software without having to maintain millions of user accounts. Many companies allow read permission to some directories for the anonymous user and limit writing to one directory called incoming.

The anonymous user account (IUSR_*Computername)* is created during the Windows NT 4.0 Option Pack installation process and is the default user account used by the FTP Service. The Internet standard username used by clients is "anonymous" and IIS 4.0 recognizes this.

Connecting Without a Firewall

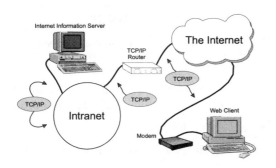

There are many options available for connecting your Web server to the Internet. In the example shown above, the Web server is connected to the corporate intranet. The intranet is connected to the Internet via a TCP/IP router. This configuration allows access to the server by both internal users and Internet users. Although flexible and easy to implement, this configuration may be difficult to secure from outside intruders.

Connecting With a Firewall

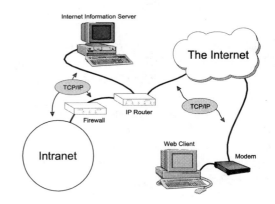

In the above example, the corporate intranet connects first to a firewall and then to a port on a TCP/IP router. The Web server connects to a different router port and is located on a separate subnet. This configuration also allows access to the Web server by internal corporate users as well as external Internet users. The primary difference between this configuration and the previous example is the introduction of a firewall to secure the corporate intranet.

A firewall is capable of providing a much more sophisticated level of security than is available in most routers or the Windows NT Server 4.0 operating system. IP Filtering is the primary method available to IIS 4.0 administrators for keeping out unwanted intruders. Most firewalls combine IP Filtering, circuit-level proxy, and application-level proxy functions to virtually eliminate network security breaches.

A circuit-level proxy operates at the OSI Session layer by substituting the firewall's IP address in place of the client computer's. All packets leaving the firewall appear to the Internet as coming from a single IP address.

An application-level proxy operates at the OSI Application and Presentation layers and is generally considered to offer the highest level of security.

Access Overview

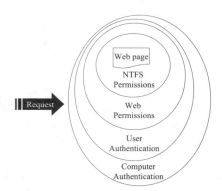

Depending on your needs, you can enable up to four layers of security to protect a document on a Web server. If all four layers are implemented, an access request must be approved at each of them. If any of the security criteria are not met, the request for access will be denied. The four criteria you can use to configure access are:

- Computer authentication

    You can select to grant or deny access based on the identity of the computer making the request.

- User authentication

    You can select to grant or deny access to the Web site based on whether the user can correctly enter the user name and password of a known Windows NT domain user. Another way to provide user authentication is through verifying that the user holds a valid certificate that grants him or her access. Certificates will be discussed later in the chapter.

- Web permissions

    You can specify that a Web site, directory, virtual directory, or file has a particular set of permissions, regardless of who is trying to access it.

- NTFS permissions

    You can take advantage of Windows NT's security model by assigning NTFS permissions to resources. This provides you with the ability to control access based on a user's identity.

Let's look at each of these, beginning with NTFS permissions.

NTFS Permissions

NTFS permissions consist of two components:

- Directory Access Permissions

    Directory Access permissions determine a user's rights to a directory or subdirectory.

- File Access Permissions

    File Access permissions determine a user's rights to a particular file.

Directory Access Permissions

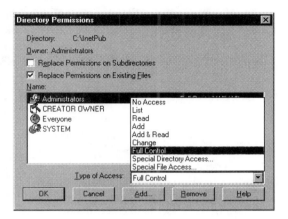

Windows NTFS security includes several pre-configured directory permissions sets. These make it easy to assign directory rights without needing to select individual permissions.

You can set the following directory permissions:

- No Access (None) (None)

    Prevents access to the directory. If a user or group to which a user belongs is assigned No Access, the user will not be able to access the directory, regardless of the permissions specified by other group memberships.

- List (RX) (Not Specified)

    Allows viewing file names, subdirectory names, and changing to the directory's subdirectories. Does not provide access to files.

- Read (RX) (RX)

    Allows viewing file names, subdirectory names, and changing to the directory's subdirectories. Allows viewing of file contents and program execution.

- Add (WX) (Not Specified)

    Allows adding files and subdirectories to the directory. Does not provide access to files.

- Add & Read (RWX) (RX)

    Allows viewing file names, subdirectory names, and changing to the directory's subdirectories. Allows adding files and subdirectories to the directory. Allows viewing of file contents and program execution.

- Change (RWXD) (RWXD)

    Allows viewing file names, subdirectory names, and changing to the directory's subdirectories. Allows adding files and subdirectories to the directory. Allows viewing and changing of file contents and program execution. Allows deletion of the directory and its files.

- Full Control (All) (All)

    Allows viewing file names, subdirectory names, and changing to the directory's subdirectories. Allows adding files and subdirectories to the directory. Allows viewing and changing of file contents and program execution. Allows deletion of the directory and its files. Allows deletion of the directory and its files. Allows changing ownership and taking ownership of the directory and its files.

NOTE: *When you set a directory permission, a set of abbreviations for individual permissions is displayed next to it. For example, when you set Add & Read permissions on a file, you see (RWX) (RX), signifying Read, Write, and Execute permissions.*

Special Directory Access

You can also configure Special Directory Access permissions, which allow you to select from a list of permissions rather than use one of the pre-configured Type of Access sets.   Special Directory Access permissions are:

- Full Control (All)

    Includes Read, Write, Execute, Delete, Change Permissions, and Take Ownership permissions.

- Read (R)

    Allows viewing of file names and subdirectories.

- Write (W)

    Allows adding files and subdirectories to the directory. Does not provide access to files.

- Execute (X)

    Allows changing to subdirectories in the directory.

- Delete (D)

    Allows deletion of the directory.

- Change Permissions (P)

    Allows changing the directory permissions.

- Take Ownership (O)

    Allows taking ownership of the directory.

File Access Permissions

Windows NTFS security also includes several pre-configured file permissions sets. These simplify the assignment of file rights. You can set the following file permissions:

- No Access (None)

    Prevents access to the directory.

- Read (RX)

    Allows viewing of file contents and execution.

- Change (RWXD)

    Allows viewing of file contents and execution. Allows writing to the file and file deletion.

- Full Control (All)

    Allows viewing of file contents and execution. Allows writing to the file and file deletion. Allows changing ownership and taking ownership of the file.

- Special Access

    Allows user-selectable permissions.

Special File Access

You can also configure Special File Access permissions, which allow you to select from a list of permissions rather than use one of the pre-configured Type of Access sets. Special Directory Access permissions are:

- Full Control (All)

    Includes Read, Write, Execute, Delete, Change Permissions, and Take Ownership permissions.

- Read (R)

    Allows viewing of the file's contents.

- Write (W)

    Allows changing the file's contents.

- Execute (X)

    If the file is a program, allows execution of the file.

- Delete (D)

    Allows deletion of the file.

- Change Permissions (P)

    Allows changing the file's permissions.

- Take Ownership (O)

    Allows taking ownership of the file.

Default Directory Access Permissions

The above graphic shows the default permissions that the Windows NT 4.0 Server operating system assigns to an NTFS directory upon creation. These permissions are inappropriate for a Web server. From a security standpoint, Web server access is treated as local access. Anyone who visits your Web site could add, change, and delete files. Obviously, you are going to want to change these permissions.

User Authentication

You have already been introduced to the anonymous user and to two of the options available for user authentication. However, let's take a closer look at some key points.

IUSR_Computername

By default, the Internet Guest account is named IUSR_*Computername*, where *Computername* is the machine name of your Internet Information Server. When you install Internet Information Server, this account is created automatically. You can modify the account in User Manager for Domains, but if you change the username or password, you will have to change it in Internet Information Server as well. Select the server or site for which you want to change the guest user. Display **Properties**. Click on Directory Security. Click on the **Edit** button for Anonymous Access.

Browse to select the new account. Notice that you can synchronize the passwords so that if the anonymous user's password is changed in User Manager for Domains, the change will automatically be changed in Internet Information Server.

Basic Authentication

If you need to support browsers other than Internet Explorer, you will only be able to validate users with Basic Authentication. This method involves sending a username and password as clear text and is not as secure as using Windows NT Challenge/Response. However, this security hole can be eliminated by requiring that password information be sent over Secure Sockets Layer (SSL). SSL will be discussed later in the chapter.

Windows NT Challenge/Response

When a user is validated through Windows NT Challenge/Response, the username and password are not actually sent across the wire. Instead, the browser and the server communicate using a cryptographic technique. This is more secure than Basic Authentication, but requires that users have Internet Explorer 2.0 or higher. If a browser supports both Windows NT Challenge/Response and Basic Authentication, Windows NT Challenge/Response is used as the preferred authentication method.

Client Certificates

You can associate a client certificate with a particular Windows NT user account. Public key encryption and certificates are discussed in detail later.

When is Authentication Used?

Users are prompted for logon when the site they request does not allow anonymous access. This is configured through the Web Site property page. Users will also be prompted for logon if they attempt to access a resource for which NTFS permissions have been configured, but the anonymous user has not been granted the necessary permission.

Internet User Configuration

Windows NT user management is performed using the User Manager for Domains utility. To launch this utility, run **Start/Programs/Administrative Tools/User Manager for Domains**.

Now check the properties of the anonymous user account, IUSR_*Computername*.

Double-click on the IUSR_*Computername* user account.

Click on the **Groups** button.

Verify that the anonymous username is a member of only the Guests group. If the Web server has an account in a Windows NT Domain, the Domain Users group will also be listed.

> NOTE: *Even though not explicitly listed, membership in the group Everyone is assumed for all users.*

When you are setting file and directory access permissions, you can set them for Everyone, Guests, or just for the anonymous username. From a security standpoint, it would typically be considered best to avoid assigning any permissions to Guests.

Next, we'll check the User Rights policy for the anonymous user account. The User Rights policy determines the rights granted to groups and user accounts. A right authorizes a user to perform certain actions on the system. A user who logs on to an account to which the appropriate rights have been granted can carry out the corresponding actions. When a user does not have appropriate rights, attempts to carry out those actions are blocked by the system. User rights apply to the system as a whole and are different than permissions, which apply to specific objects.

Select **User Rights** from the **Policies** menu.

Set the Right option to Log on locally. Verify that the IUSR_*Computername* user account is listed. This is the only special rights assignment that should be given to the anonymous user. If you continue to view the different policy rights you will notice that the IUSR_*Computername* user account is listed only under Log on locally.

The rights granted to a group are also provided to the members of that group. In most situations, the easiest way to provide rights to a user is to add that user's account to a group that already possesses the needed rights.

> NOTE: *If an appropriate group does not exist, create one. It is more efficient to manage the server on a group basis than managing individual user rights.*

If you choose to create a new group, assign the group the following rights:

- Log on locally
- Access this computer from a network

User Account Passwords

Even though the Web server is primarily accessed via the anonymous user account, it is important to review all of your Windows NT domain and server security policies when setting up for Internet access. Make it as difficult as possible for someone to guess another user name and password on your server.

It is common knowledge that the default superuser account on a Windows NT Server computer is Administrator. It is critical that this account is always password protected. You could also rename this account for additional protection.

The password for the Administrator, as well as all other users on your server, needs to be difficult to guess. If this is a new Windows NT Server computer that is used only for Internet connectivity, you should have only a handful of user accounts to review.

You can configure the Account Policy for your server with the User Manager for Domains utility. Select **Account** from the **Policy** menu.

The above figure shows recommended settings for username and password policies. Though a detailed discussion of policy issues is beyond the scope of this course, some areas of concern should be mentioned:

- Always force periodic password changes.
- Minimum password ages should be used.
- Force a minimum length long enough to help make passwords difficult to guess.
- Keep a password history to limit reuse of passwords.
- Use account lockout to detect attempts to break into your system.

While these will not make your system impenetrable, they will help. Remember that part of your protection plan is teaching users to create good passwords.

Miscellaneous Security Issues

Limit the members of the Administrators group–the fewer the better. Also limit membership of other default groups to only those users needing special rights or access permissions.

By default, when an NTFS directory is created, the group Everyone has full control of all files in it. Change or remove the permissions for the group Everyone by using **Properties/Security/Permissions**.

Enable auditing if you suspect that a user is attempting to hack into your system. You can enable auditing by using **Properties/Security/Auditing**. You should audit any NTFS directories where you are concerned about user access. You can have auditing track successful attempts, failed attempts, or both.

Web Permissions

Permissions that are not sensitive to user identification can be granted on the Home Directory property page. Most of these settings will be discussed later in the course. For now, let's look at those that specifically apply to whether a user is granted access.

Access Permissions

You can specify whether the contents of a directory are available for Read (download) access or Write (upload) access. Most HTML documents should only be available for Read access. FTP sites and directories can also be assigned Read and/or Write access.

Application Permissions

You can configure whether or not the applications or server-side scripts that exist in the directory can be run. Available settings are:

- None

  This prevents files located in the directory from being executed. This does not prevent HTML from being downloaded and executed by the browser. This is the default value.

- Script

  This allows scripts, such as CGI scripts, Internet Data Connector (IDC), and ASP scripts, to be executed by the server.

- Execute

  This allows both applications, dynamic link libraries, and scripts to be executed in this directory. This setting should never be combined with the Write permission because it would effectively allow a hacker to upload an application and execute it on your Web server.

These settings are only available for Web sites and directories. They do not apply to FTP sites.

Directory Permission Guidelines for IIS 4.0

The following guidelines will help you determine which permissions to assign for various Web server content directories. The following options are configured using the Web site's Home Directory properties page.

- HTML Content

  These are directories containing HTML content.

  Set the Access Permissions value to **Read** and the Applications Settings Permissions to **None**.

- Executable Programs

  These are programs that users can run.

  Set the Access Permissions value to **Read** and the Applications Settings Permissions to **Execute**.

- Scripts

  These are CGI or other types of scripts that users can run.

  Set the Access Permissions value to **Read** and the Applications Settings Permissions to **Script**.

- Database Files

  These are SQL or other types of database files.

  Set the Access Permissions value to **Read** and **Write** and the Applications Settings Permissions to **None**.

IP Filtering

You may have a situation that warrants either granting or restricting access based on the IP address or domain name of the machine sending the request. You can choose to either grant access to all computers except those explicitly listed or deny access to all computers except those explicitly granted. This option is available on the Directory Security property page.

To add an entry to the list, click on the **Add** button.

You can choose to add:

- A single computer

  Specify the IP address of the computer you wish to add. If you don't know the IP address, you can click on **DNS Lookup** to specify it by host name.

- A group of computers

  You will need to specify the Network ID and the subnet mask of the group of computers you wish to add. This option is useful if you are building a Web site that should be accessed only by members of a particular department and that department is in its own subnet.

- A domain name

  You can specify that computers with a particular domain name be granted or denied access. However, this will adversely affect performance, since the DNS server will have to be consulted for a reverse lookup with each access request.

The Secure Sockets Layer (SSL) Protocol

The Secure Sockets Layer (SSL) protocol is a low-level authentication and encryption method used to secure transactions in higher-level protocols such as HTTP and FTP. It is supported by IIS 4.0 and both Netscape Communicator/Navigator and the Microsoft Internet Explorer browsers.

To properly configure and manage the IIS 4.0 Secure Sockets Layer (SSL) implementation you must understand the following concepts:

- Securing transmissions
- Keys
- Generating a key pair
- Certificates

SSL is an available option for supporting encrypted communications across the Internet.

Securing Transmissions with Secure Sockets Layer

The SSL protocol uses an initial client/server handshake process to decide on the type of security to be used during a conversation. Once the security level has been determined, all subsequent communications between the server and client are encrypted.

SSL includes provisions for server authentication (verifying the server's identity to the client), encryption of data in transit, and optional client authentication (verifying the client's identity to the server).

By employing SSL-enabled servers and clients, it is possible to send encrypted messages across the Internet without fear of interception. In order to implement SSL you must first apply for and obtain a verification certificate from a certificate authority (CA), such as Verisign (www.verisign.com) or Cardservice (www.cardservice.com). You can also use Microsoft Certificate Server to act as your own certificate authority. This will be discussed later.

SSL should be enabled only for virtual directories containing highly sensitive information, as SSL encrypted transmissions are slower due to the overhead of the encryption/decryption process.

The latest version of SSL, version 3, offers improved performance over earlier versions due to a streamlining of the client/server handshaking process. SSL3 is compatible with SSL version 2.

Clients requesting documents stored in SSL-enabled directories must use the https:// URL format instead of the standard http:// format.

Digital Envelopes

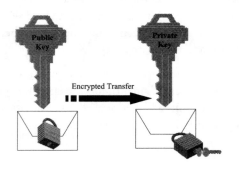

SSL works by utilizing the concept of digital envelopes. In order for a digital envelope to work, a key pair is required. One of the keys is a public key and is used to lock the envelope before it is sent. The other key is a private key and is used to unlock the envelope after it is received. This guarantees that the only one who can open the envelope is the recipient who has the private key. Let's look at a practical example.

Suppose you have a Web page that accepts credit card information from clients. In order to secure that transaction, you send the client the public key of your key pair. The client then uses that key to lock the envelope containing his credit card information. No one except the owner of the private key (you) can unlock that envelope. When you receive the envelope from the client, you use your private key to unlock it.

Implementing SSL

The tasks required to implement SSL are:

- Generate a key pair and a request file.
- Request a certificate from a certificate authority (CA).
- Install the certificate on your server.
- Enable the SSL security on a folder.

Generate a Key Pair and Request File

The first step in implementing SSL is to generate a key pair and request file. The key pair is created with the Key Manager. When generating the key pair, you provide the following information:

- Key name
- Password
- Encryption key length
- Organization
- Organizational unit

- Common name
- Country
- State
- City
- Administrator name, e-mail address, and phone number

You can elect to save this information in a file, which you must then send to the selected CA or allow the Key Manager utility to automatically send the request to an online CA. The CA will then send you a certificate to be installed on your server.

To generate a key pair and request file, run **Start/Programs/Windows NT 4.0 Option Pack/Microsoft Internet Server/Internet Service Manager**.

Right-click on Default Web Site and select **Properties**. Click on the **Directory Security** tab. Click on the **Key Manager** button.

Single-click on WWW. From the **Key** menu, select **Create New Key**.

Select a request file option and click on **Next**.

The Key Name field is used to assign a name to the new key. You might have multiple keys if you are hosting Web sites for other companies. The password is used to encrypt the key. If you downloaded the International version of IIS 4.0 from the Microsoft Web site, your only choice will be a key that is 512 bits. The key pair in the U.S. version can be up to 1,024 bits long. Enter the appropriate values, then click on **Next**.

Enter your company name in the Organization field. Enter your department or division in the Organizational Unit field. Enter the DNS name for your Web server, such as www.wavetech.com, in the Common Name field. Click on **Next**.

Enter the two-letter ISO country code in the Country field. Enter your state or province and city information in the appropriate fields. Click on **Next**.

Enter your site administrator's name, e-mail address, and phone number. Click on **Next**.

After all information has been entered, click on **Finish**. Depending on the request file option you selected, a request file will be created locally or one will be automatically sent to the CA you specified.

Key Request Tips

- Never use commas in any of the fields. Commas signal the end of a field and will cause an improper certificate request to be created.
- VeriSign will not accept any punctuation or abbreviations. For Example:

   You must spell out "Street" instead of "St."

   You must spell out "Incorporated" instead of "Inc."

   You must spell out "Saint Louis" instead of "St. Louis," and so on.

Acquiring a Certificate

When you contact either VeriSign or Cardservice, you will need to enter information about your organization and your server. The current cost for a server ID certificate from Verisign is $349.00 (U.S.) for the first server and $249.00 for each additional server.

You can also apply for a certificate by filling out the appropriate online forms at Verisign or another CA.

The online application process at Verisign presents you with a seven-step process.

You will need to provide the CA with all of the information discussed in this section.

Installing a Certificate

Once your application has been processed by the CA, the certificate digital ID file will be e-mailed to you. After you receive your certificate file, you must run the Key Manager utility and select the key to which you will be adding the certificate.

To install the certificate, run **Start/Programs/Windows NT 4.0 Option Pack/Microsoft Internet Server/ Internet Service Manager**.

Right-click on Default Web Site and select **Properties**. Click on the **Directory Security** tab.

Click on the **Edit** button next to Secure Communications.

> *NOTE:* *After you have created a key using Key Manager, this dialog box changes and the Key Manager button is replaced by the Edit button.*

The default encryption strength is 40 bits. If you require 128-bit encryption, click on the **Encryption** button, select the **Require 128-bit encryption** option, then click on **OK**. At the time of this writing, 128-bit encryption was only available in the United States and Canada.

The Client Certificate Authentication option allows you to configure your Web server to accept, require, or reject client certificates as a method of establishing a connection to Web content directories that are SSL enabled.

If you select the **Enable Client Certificate Mapping** option, certificate-bearing clients who connect using a valid Windows NT user account name and password will be automatically mapped to that account and its corresponding access restrictions.

Click on the **Key Manager** button.

Click on the key you wish to authorize, then select **Install Key Certificate** from the **Key** drop-down menu.

Browse to locate the certificate file. When you select the file, you will be prompted to enter the same password that you specified when you created the key pair. Enter the IP address for your server or use the Any Unassigned option to apply the certificate to all of the unassigned IP addresses on your server. Click on **OK**.

> *NOTE:* *If you use a proprietary e-mail system, the text file containing your digital ID could be corrupted when received. If you try to install your key and you get a message about an invalid password, the digital ID might have been corrupted by the mail system, or in transit. To resolve this problem, contact Verisign Technical Support and request that they send the digital ID to a standard SMTP/ POP3 mail server.*

The double red line that was displayed through your key should now be gone indicating that the key has been certified.

Select **Commit Changes Now** from the **Computers** menu, then click on **OK**. Restart your server to continue.

Enabling SSL

After completing the process of obtaining a certificate and installing it on the server, enable SSL on a per directory basis.

To enable SSL, launch the Internet Service Manager utility and open the properties for your Web site. Right-click on any of the folders in your Web server's directory structure and select **Properties**. Click on the **Directory Security** tab, then click on the **Edit** button next to Secure Communications.

Select the **Require Secure Channel when accessing this resource** option. Finally, select the desired Client Certificate Authentication option and select **Enable Client Certificate Mapping**, if required.

> *NOTE: From this point on, all client references to documents in this directory must specify a URL format of "https://" instead of "http://."*

Back Up Your Key File

You will want to back up your key file and keep it in a safe place. Key Manager allows you to export your key from the registry into a file.

Select the key you wish to back up and click on the **Key** menu. Select **Export Key**, then **Backup File**. Specify a destination and click on **OK**.

Suggestions for Using Certificate Server

If your goal is to use SSL to enable you to accept credit cards from users over the Internet, running your own certificate server is probably not your best option. In order for a certificate to be accepted, the client needs to trust the authority. Internet Explorer is already configured to trust several well-known certificate authorities.

However, if you need to use SSL to provide a secure channel to your corporate intranet or if you have a well-known set of customers for whom you'd like to provide a secure site, you might want to consider creating your own certificates by using Certificate Server.

While the architecture of Certificate Server is beyond the scope of this course, it is important to point out that the policies for granting certificates are entirely at your discretion. You can write applications that interface with Certificate Server to perform any sort of business logic you require to validate a user. They can even be written so that they store the certificate request so that you can perform manual validation.

Installing Certificate Server

Before you install Certificate Server, you will need to create a shared directory in which you will store the configuration information.

Certificate Server is part of Windows NT 4.0 Option Pack. To install it, insert the Option Pack CD-ROM in your CD-ROM drive. It automatically displays Internet Explorer. Click on **Install**. Click on **Install Windows NT 4.0 Option Pack**. Select to open the file from its current location and click on **OK**. When the Option Pack welcome screen displays, click on **Next**. Click on **Add/Remove**.

Select Certificate Server and click on **Next**.

Here you can select the location in which to store the CA configuration information, the certificate database, and the log. The CA configuration information includes the CA certificate that users can download and install in their browsers. This information must be stored in a shared directory on the machine where Certificate Server is installed.

If you select **Show Advanced Configuration** and click on **Next**, you will be prompted to select the following options:

- Cryptographic Service Provider

  This allows you to select alternate CSPs. By default, the CSP installed will be Microsoft Base Cryptographic Provider.

- Hashing algorithm

  Hashing is a numeric computation that is used to encrypt the data. Different CSPs will support different hashing algorithms. You can even develop your own CSP to provide a custom hashing algorithm.

> *NOTE: The current release of Certificate Server only supports Microsoft Base Cryptographic Provider and the MD5 hashing algorithm*

- Use existing keys

  This option is useful if you are upgrading an existing Certificate Server. If Certificate Server can find a matching certificate in the store, it will use that to generate the keys.

- Make this Certificate Server the default

  Select this option if you want this Certificate Server to be the default server when a certificate is requested.

- Choose Certificate Hierarchy

  In future releases, you will be able to select whether you are generating a root certificate authority or a non-root certificate authority. This option is not supported in this release.

If you did not choose to go through the advanced options or after you have finished setting them, you will be prompted to enter identification information. This information will be contained in the certificate authority certificate users will download and install in their browsers.

After you have entered the appropriate information, click on **Next**. Your computer will be configured for Certificate Server and the necessary files will be downloaded. After it finishes copying files, click on **Finish** to complete the installation. The Certificate Server will be loaded as a service. It will be configured to start automatically as soon as the computer starts.

You will need to restart your computer or manually start the Certificate Authority service before you can issue certificates.

Customizing Certificate Server

By default, Certificate Server uses the policy file Certpdef.dll. However, you can configure it to use a custom policy. To do so:

- Obtain or build a policy DLL.

  Certificate server exposes some COM interfaces that programmers can use to build policy modules in C++, Visual Basic, or Java. These interfaces are beyond the scope of this course.

- Unregister the current policy file.

  Like any COM server, the policy file is unregistered through the command:

  ```
  regsvr32 /u certpdef.dll
  ```

- Register the new policy file.

  Copy the custom policy module to the *systemroot*\System32 subdirectory and run the **regsvr32** command. For example, to register the policy named corpplcy.dll, you would type the following:

  ```
  regsvr32 corpplcy.dll
  ```

The same basic procedure can be used to customize the way in which the certificate is delivered to the recipient. The module that controls this is known as the *exit module*. The default exit module is certexit.dll. Exit modules are optional.

Processing a Certificate Request

Once you have a certificate request, like the one generated by using Key Manager, you can easily process it. To do so, run **Start/Programs/Windows NT 4.0 Option Pack/Microsoft Certificate Server/Process Certificate Request File**. You will be prompted to locate the .req or .txt file containing the request. After you locate it, you will be prompted for a file name and directory containing the certificate. A valid certificate will be generated, containing the appropriate public key. You can now distribute it for installation or use the Key Manager to install it, as described earlier.

Certificate Server Tools

Certificate Server is managed through a Web page named *certsrv*. To open it, launch Internet Explorer and type the following URL:

```
http://localhost/certsrv
```

This page provides hyperlinks to the following tools:

- Certificate Administration Log Utility

    This utility allows you to view information about the certificates that have been processed and their status. You can view either a list of certificates or view certificates one at a time.

- Certificate Administration Queue Utility

    This utility allows you to get information on the status of issued and pending certificate requests.

- Certificate Enrollment Tools

    This utility allows you to install CA certificates, process certificate requests, and request a client authentication certificate.

- Certificate Server Documentation

    This hyperlink will display help on using Certificate Server.

Configuring a Browser to Recognize a CA

Before a browser will accept a certificate issued by a particular Certificate Authority, that browser must obtain a valid CA Certificate. When Certificate Server was installed, that certificate was created in the shared configuration directory. One of the files created is an HTML document named cacerts.htm. By navigating to that document, users can install the CA Certificate for your server simply by clicking on the hyperlink. Select to open the file. You will be prompted to select whether or not to enable authentication and for which types of services. You will need to close and restart your browser for changes to take effect.

The HTTP Protocol

HTTP Conversation

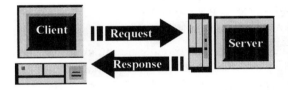

A Web server and Web client communicate by using the HTTP protocol. The client (browser) initiates the communication by sending a Request. The server parses the request and sends a Response. Traditionally, the connection between them would be terminated as soon as the response was sent.

However, since more and more requests result in a number of Response packages, later versions of HTTP made it possible (and in HTTP 1.1, recommended) to keep the connection open until some action indicates that the conversation is over. One of the important features of the HTTP 1.1 specification is that it made persistent connections the default. This is known as HTTP Keep-Alives. In Internet Information Server 4.0, this is turned on by default. It is recommended that you keep it in almost all situations. However, if your scenario warrants turning it off, you can do so on the Performance property page of the appropriate Web objects. However, keep in mind that establishing and closing connections is costly, not only for the client and server machines, but for the network itself.

HTTP Headers

Every HTTP Request or Response has both a header and a body. They can be sent together or the header can be sent independently.

The Request header contains important information the server needs to locate the requested resource and fulfill the response. For example, it contains the Uniform Resource Identifier (URI) for the resource being requested. It can also contain information about preferred languages, conditions on which the content should be downloaded, and information that identifies the type of browser sending the request. The type of browser is passed in the field called the User Agent. One of the most important Request header fields introduced with HTTP 1.1 is the Host field. You'll see more how that is used later in the chapter.

The Response header contains information the client needs to determine whether to accept the response and to properly display the content. For example, it might include information about when the content on a particular Web page expires or which application should be used to display it. Response headers can be set on the HTTP Headers property page of any Web site or directory object.

A number of important fields are defined by the HTTP 1.1 specification. It is available on the Internet at http://www.w3.org/Protocols/rfc2068/rfc2068. Although it is possible to configure additional fields, keep in mind that both the client and the server will need to understand their significance.

Content Expiration

When a browser receives a Response from a server, it normally caches the information so that the next time the page is accessed, the browser simply displays the cached page instead of sending another request. However, depending on how dynamic the information on your Web page is, you may want the cached information to expire after a particular period of time. For example, if you have a special offer that is going to last until July 4th, 1998, you will want the cached page to expire on July 5th, 1998 at 12:01 a.m. If, however, your Web site is updated hourly to show the latest company news bulletin, you will want the cached page to expire after 1 hour.

When a user requests a URL, the browser checks to see if that URL is in the cache. If it is, the browser will check to see if the content has expired. If it has, the browser will request an update from the server. If it has not, the cached content will simply be displayed.

Content Ratings

Depending on the type of data you display on your site, you might want to provide content ratings. If a user is using a browser that supports content ratings, appropriately identifying your content can allow users to filter it out.

You can rate your site based on the level of violence, sex, nudity, or language it uses. This voluntary rating system was developed by the Recreational Software Advisory Council as a way to help parents screen the content their children can access on the Internet. More information is available at www.rsac.org.

MIME Types

A Multipurpose Internet Mail Extension (MIME) type associates a file extension with a particular data type to help the browser know how it should be handled. For example, a file with the extension .jpg is associated with the image/jpeg MIME type by default. You can add new types, remove types, or edit existing types.

A list of MIME types is configured at the computer level. If you add a MIME type to a dependent object, the addition *replaces* the list defined at the computer level. Remember, with the exception of ISAPI filters, properties that are actually lists are replaced, not merged.

Custom Errors

When a Request cannot be fulfilled or if there is additional information, the server will send back a Response containing an error. The error will have an error number that browsers can use to determine the course of action they should take and a user-readable message to let the user know why the request was denied. However, the standard user-readable messages are not very user-friendly or explanatory. Therefore, you can use the Custom Errors property page to reference files or URLs to be used in place of the standard error messages.

To change a message reference, select the error number and click on **Edit Properties**.

Notice that the default text and the error code are listed on the dialog. You can choose whether to use the default text or to reference a file by path or a URL. The URL must point to a resource on the local server.

Microsoft has supplied user-friendly error messages for many errors. These are installed at *systemroot*\help\common\.

However, you still may find it beneficial to provide your own messages for some errors. For example, if your site is geared toward children, you may want to have an error message with simpler language. Another situation where you might want a custom message would be to provide error messages in the same language as the text on the site.

Uses for Virtual Directories

When a client connects to your Web site, IIS 4.0 uses HTTP to send your home page (usually default.asp, default.htm, or index.html) to a browser application. This file is stored in the wwwroot directory. Directories that hold content for the Web server are called *publishing directories*. However, suppose you want to store content in a directory that is not beneath the wwwroot directory. For example, you may want to store content on a second hard drive or even on different servers on your network. These directories are known as *virtual directories*.

Some reasons to use virtual directories are:

- Load Distribution

    When browsers send requests to your IIS 4.0, the server has to retrieve data from its hard drive (or cache RAM). If the requested data must be read from disk, it is then temporarily cached in server memory. This process consumes server memory resources and imposes CPU and bus overhead. Increasing numbers of client requests leads to greater server utilization. By distributing the processing load across multiple servers you can manage the utilization of any given server.

- Content Distribution

    Content distribution is as important as load distribution. For example, if you were a distributor of auto parts you might configure a server that contains an inventory and vendor database. Another server might store information about employees and payroll. A third server could act as a query server, allowing intranet users to access realtime inventory and human resources data.

- Enhanced Security

    You can enhance your system's security by storing content and data on physically separate servers. Users never directly access virtual directories.

Virtual Directory Scenario

Let's examine a scenario that describes virtual directories:

A user points his Web browser to http://www.autoparts.com. Because no specific directory or document name was supplied by the client, IIS 4.0 responds by sending the contents of the default home page, which is located in the C:\InetPub\wwwroot directory.

The auto parts distribution company that owns the Web site maintains inventory information on a separate server named Auto1. The path to the directory containing the inventory information on Auto1 is C:\Parts\Chevrolet. It is shared to the network as ChevyParts. The IIS 4.0 administrator creates a virtual directory below wwwroot on the *AutoWeb* server that references the \\Auto1\ChevyParts share. The administrator also supplies an alias of *Chevy* for the virtual directory.

When Web clients select a hypertext link that points to documents stored on Auto1, the user is unaware that the documents are located on a different Web server. The URL to documents on Auto1 would be entered in the following format:

```
http://www.autoparts.com/Chevy
     /document_name
```

where *document_name* is the name of an HTML document stored in the C:\Parts\Chevrolet subdirectory on Auto1. If no document name is provided, the document specified as a default document will be used.

Universal Naming Convention

To successfully create and manage virtual directories you need to be familiar with the syntax specified by the Universal Naming Convention (UNC) system. The format for a UNC is:

    \\servername\sharename

The *servername* refers to the NetBIOS name of the server containing the desired resource and *sharename* refers to the shared resource used.

For example, the UNC name for the ChevyParts share on the Auto1 server would be:

    \\Auto1\ChevyParts\

Creating Virtual Directories

Let's see how to create a virtual directory on IIS 4.0. First, create a directory named Parts1. Set the appropriate NTFS permissions for the folder. If it is on a computer other than the one running Internet Information Server, share the directory to the network. Make sure the Sharing permissions are the same as the NTFS Security permissions. If they are different, the most restrictive access permissions will be used.

In Internet Service Manager, right-click on the Web site that should contain the virtual directory and select **New/Virtual Directory.**

Enter an alias name for the virtual directory, then click on **Next.**

If the physical directory is on the local machine, enter a path. If it is on a different machine, enter the UNC name. Click on **Next.**

You can also click on **Browse** to locate the directory. Select the desired directory, then click on **OK.** Click on **Next.**

After selecting the physical directory, click on **Next** to continue.

Select the access permissions you wish to assign to the new virtual directory. The default permissions are **Allow Read Access** and **Allow Script Access.** This is appropriate for server-side applications, but the Script access should be cleared for virtual directories that contain HTML files. Clear **Allow Script Access** and click on **Finish.**

The virtual directory is now created and can be viewed with the Internet Service Manager utility.

If you had selected either Script or Execute permissions, the virtual directory would have been configured as an application starting point. Applications will be discussed later in the course.

Right-click on the virtual directory and select **Properties** to view the Virtual Directory properties sheet.

Enable Directory Browsing

Virtual directories will not appear in your directory structure unless you enable the **Directory browsing allowed** option. This option is located on the Home Directory properties sheet.

Redirection

Often when you reorganize your Web site, you find that you have many links that need to be fixed. One way that you can provide your users with the continuing use of your Web site while you find those links is to use browser redirects. The Virtual Directory, Home Directory, and Directory property pages allow you to configure the virtual directory, site, server, or directory to redirect access attempts to a different URL.

Multiple Network Adapters

This method requires that you install a separate network interface card (NIC) for every IP address/Web server that you are hosting.

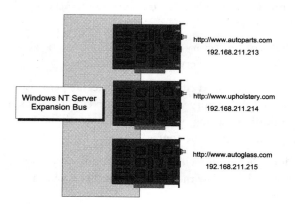

This method requires a separate hub port connection for each individual NIC. You also need a free expansion slot for each board.

The decision to install multiple network interface cards depends on several factors including:

- Available bandwidth on your Internet connection
- Router speed
- Overall network traffic
- Disk channel usage.

Multihoming

Another method of implementing virtual servers is called *multihoming*. This method requires you to bind multiple IP addresses to a single network interface card. Each assigned IP address/domain name is associated with a virtual server possessing a specific home directory on the server. For example:

- 192.168.211.213 = http://www.autoparts.com = c:\autoparts
- 192.168.211.214 = http://www.upholstery.com = c:\upholstery
- 192.168.211.215 = http://www.autoglass.com = c:\autoglass

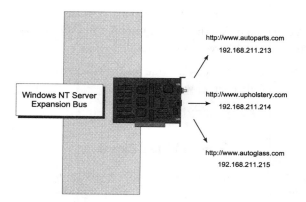

This method requires only one hub port connection and a single expansion slot in the host computer. However, because all network traffic funnels through a single NIC, the NIC is a likely source of data transmission bottlenecks.

Specifying a Host Header

One of the most powerful new features of HTTP 1.1 is the ability to run multiple Web sites off a single IP address. This is done through the use of a new field in the HTTP Request header, the Host field. To configure a virtual server using Host Headers:

Right-click on the Computer object. Run **New/Web Site**.

Enter a description for your site.

Select an IP Address (or keep it at Any Unassigned).

Configure the path for the site's home directory and select whether the site can be accessed anonymously.

Configure access permissions. Once again, Read and Script access are the defaults. However, if you are going to be using strictly HTML, you can clear the Script access. Click on **Finish**. At this point, the new site will be created, but it will not be started.

Right-click on the new Site icon and run **Properties**.

Click on **Advanced**.

Now you can edit the identity for the site. Select the item in the Multiple identities for this Web site list. Click on **Edit**.

Enter a fully qualified domain name as the Host Header Name and click on **OK**. Close all of the dialogs and property pages. Click on the **Start** button to start the site.

> NOTE: *You cannot use host headers to provide multiple sites that use SSL. This is because the host name is associated with the SSL certificate.*

A Note on Name Resolution

As with any Web site, you will need to implement the appropriate host name resolution to enable users to access your Web site. If you are using HOSTS for name resolution, provide an alias to each additional Web site on the line with the IP address. If you are using DNS, you will need to create an additional A record for each host name your Web site supports.

Specifying a Unique Port

You can also create multiple Web sites by specifying unique ports for each site, instead of using the default port of 80. While this works from a technical point of view, it is not as friendly for users because the port must be specified as part of the URL.

However, using ports to identify unique sites is one way to support multiple SSL sites on the same IP address.

Active Server Pages Benefits

Active Server Pages were introduced earlier in the course. However, it is important to revisit their benefits before talking about their specifics. An Active Server Page is compiled by Internet Information Server. Regardless of the scripting language or components used in its code, its output to the client (browser) is vanilla HTML. For this reason, using Active Server Pages will provide you with the following benefits:

- Browser compatibility

  Provided your output is only standard HTML, your Web page can be viewed with any Web browser. In fact, Internet Information Server 4.0 provides a Browser Capability object that can be used from an ASP to tailor your output to take advantage of specific browser features, such as ActiveX, Java, or Dynamic HTML.

- Less network traffic

  If a component manipulates data that is located on the Internet server or on a server connected to the same LAN, it is likely that you will gain performance by running the component on the server side, instead of transferring large amounts of data across slow links.

- Better performance

  Active Server Pages provide better performance than other server-side technologies, such as CGI. Active Server Pages are multithreaded and run inside the Internet Information Server process. This conserves memory and processor time, particularly when multiple users are accessing a Web page.

- Easier maintainability

    The Active Server Page itself is automatically recompiled by Internet Information Server the first time it is accessed after a change. Like an HTML file, it does not need to be explicitly compiled. This makes modifications to business logic easy.

- Logic cannot be viewed

    The only code the browser knows about is that which is downloaded as HTML. Therefore, viewing the source code through the browser will only display the HTML that is transmitted. Any logic in your scripts or components is private.

Intrinsic Active Server Pages Objects

Active Server Pages have several intrinsic objects. These objects will be overviewed, but not discussed in detail. The intrinsic objects are:

- Request

    The Request object allows you to find out information, such as arguments passed in the URL, information from cookies and forms, and any HTTP headers. You will see how to use the Request object to retrieve URL arguments later in the chapter.

- Response

    The Response object can be used to display text or to open a different URL.

- Server

    The Server object is used to access features of the Internet Information Server. As you will see a little later, the Server object is required to create an instance of a server-side component.

- Application

    This object is used to store information that is common to all users accessing the Web. A common use of the Application object is to lock and unlock resources so that they are not modified at the same time by two different users.

- Session

    The Session object is used to maintain state when moving between Web pages. For example, you may have a series of forms that gather various types of information from the user. This information can be stored in the Session object and retrieved by any of the pages until the session is closed.

Creating an Active Server Page

An Active Server Page is like an HTML document, except that it uses some special tags and is saved with an .asp extension. An Active Server Page should contain a header that looks like this:

```
<%@ LANGUAGE="VBSCRIPT" %>
<HTML>
<HEAD>
<META NAME="GENERATOR"
    Content="Microsoft Visual InterDev
    1.0">
<META HTTP-EQUIV="Content-Type"
    content="text/html;
    charset=iso-8859-1">
```

```
<TITLE>Document Title</TITLE>

</HEAD>

<BODY>

<!-- Insert HTML here -->

</BODY>

</HTML>
```

Notice that the language is noted as VBScript. You could also use JavaScript or any other Active scripting language hosted by Internet Information Server.

Scripting an Active Server Page

ASP Component Access

Active Server Pages (ASP) use *properties* and *methods* to access components. Properties control the state of an object. Methods are *functions* that operate on the object.

The example VBScript procedure uses an object that retrieves the date of the user's last order from a database.

```
<%
Dim OrderDate
Set objOrder = Server.CreateObject
   ("OrderWiz.Retriever")
objOrder.LastName = "Reese"
objOrder.FillLastOrderInfo
OrderDate = objOrder.LastOrderDate
Response.Write = "You placed your
   last order on " & OrderDate
%>
```

The <% and %> symbols indicate that the script should be run by the server rather than by the client. The Server object is an intrinsic object. Its **CreateObject** method is called to create an instance of the object of class OrderWiz.Retriever. This is an object class that must be registered properly in the registry of the machine running Internet Information Server. Once the instance of the object is created, its **LastName** property is set. Next the script calls the **FillLastOrderInfo** method, which locates the last order made by someone with the last name of Reese. Next the script retrieves the value of the **LastOrderDate** property. The **Write** method of the intrinsic Response object outputs the text as plain HTML.

This script has been simplified for the purposes of this course. In actuality, you would need more information to reliably locate the last order of the person using your Web site.

However, using ActiveX components on the server deserves a littler closer look.

Creating Object Instances

When you're using ActiveX components from an Active Server Page, you need to specifically ask the server to create an instance of the object for you. The Server object has a **CreateObject** method for this purpose. It has the syntax:

```
Set Variable =
   Server.CreateObject(Libname.Class)
```

The server locates the object's programmatic identifier in the registry and launches the server either in-process (for DLLs) or out-of-process (for EXEs). It is best to use a multithreaded in-process component with Active Server Pages.

Once the instance of the object is created, use the variable containing its reference to access properties and methods.

The first time the server loads the object, it keeps it in memory so that overhead is not incurred every time a user connects to the Web server. While this provides a performance boost, it does mean that the object cannot be replaced unless you specifically unload it. One way to do this is to stop the WWW Publishing Service.

Now let's look at how your Active Server Page can be passed information through its URL.

URL Arguments

It is likely that you may have an Active Server Page that is called via a hyperlink from another Active Server Page or an HTML page. If this is the case, you may want to pass information to the Active Server Page so that it can process the information and return a result to the user. Fortunately, the Active Server Page Request object makes this fairly easy.

An Active Server Page URL can include arguments that are passed as follows:

```
server/directory/
    file.asp?arg1=value&arg2=value
```

The question mark specifies that an argument list follows. Arguments are separated with the ampersand (&). For example, you may want to pass the item number selected to an inventory ASP. The URL you use for the hyperlink would look something like this:

```
www.mystore.com/inventory/
    check.asp?Item=820A
```

Inside the Active Server Page, you would use the **QueryString** method of the Request object to retrieve the value of the argument. Your code would look like this:

```
<%Item=Request.QueryString("Item")%>
```

Once you have retrieved the values, you can use the variable just as you would any other.

Virtual Directory Permissions

The application starting point for an ASP application is a virtual directory that has been configured as an application. In addition to assigning user- and group-specific NTFS permissions to all directories, files, and component files the ASP will need to access, you also need to assign appropriate Web permissions. To determine the appropriate permissions, think about the types of files that are in the virtual directory.

- Only .asp files

    You can get by with either Read or Script permissions.

- Multiple file types, including .asp files (for example, .htm and .asp files)

    You will need to specify both Read and Script permissions.

- Executables or dynamic link libraries (ActiveX component files)

    You will need to specify both Read and Execute permissions.

ODBC

Open Database Connectivity (ODBC) provides an interface that applications can use to talk to various data sources. The ODBC Driver Manager is responsible for finding the appropriate driver to access a database. The examples given in this book reference a SQL data source. However, any source with an ODBC driver could be used, including Oracle, Sybase, or Microsoft Access databases. Let's look at how ODBC datasources can be configured.

ODBC Administrator

The ODBC Data Source Administrator is launched by double-clicking on the ODBC icon in the Control Panel. It allows you to configure data sources on a per-user or per-system basis. To configure a data source, click on **Add**. You will be prompted to choose the driver for your data source. If you choose the SQL Server driver, the ODBC SQL Server Setup dialog will be displayed.

ODBC SQL Server Setup

The ODBC SQL Server Setup dialog box allows users to configure a SQL Server data source. The fields should be filled in as follows:

Data Source Name
> This is the name by which you will refer to the data source when opening the database.

Description
> This is a textual description of the database.

Server
> This is the machine name of the server running Microsoft SQL Server. If SQL Server is running on the local machine, specify "local."

Network Address
> This is the address of the SQL Server. If you are configuring a Microsoft SQL Server data source, you can usually use the default setting.

Network Library
> This is the name of the NetLibrary that the SQL Server driver will use to communicate with the network. If you specify default, it will use the Net-Library that is set up as the default driver in the SQL Server Client Configuration Utility (usually Named Pipes). Using the Named Pipes NetLibrary is sufficient in most cases. Named Pipes runs over TCP/IP, as well as several other protocols and it allows integrated security and trusted connections. However, if your Internet Information Server is on one side of a firewall or proxy server and the SQL Server is on another, you will have to use TCP/IP Sockets as your NetLibrary. The default port for the TCP/IP Sockets library is 1433. If you decide to change it, make sure it is changed consistently on your SQL Server, the firewall, and the Internet Information Server.

Database Name
> This is the name of your SQL Server database. This is optional. If it is not specified, you will need to include it in your call to **OpenDatabase**. Otherwise, master will be opened.

Language Name
> The language for which SQL Server was configured.

Generate Stored Procedure for Prepared Statement
> This option specifies that SQL Server should compile a statement when it is prepared and store it as a stored procedure.

Translation

A translator is usually used to translate data between character sets or to provide encryption or decryption. Click on **Select** to choose a translator if applicable.

Convert OEM to ANSI characters

Select this option if your client application uses a different code page than that used by the SQL Server that manages the data source.

Data Source Registry Entries

If you configure a user-specific data source, information about it will be stored in the Registry under the HKEY_CURRENT_USER\Software\ODBC\ODBC.INI subkey. Data Source Names are listed under ODBC Data Sources. Each Data Source Name also has its own subkey under which the various attributes needed to connect to the data source are listed. The example above shows the entries created when a data source named Personal Warehouse was created.

If you configure a system-specific data source, information about it will be stored under HKEY_LOCAL_MACHINE\Software\ODBC\ODBC.INI.

Internet Data Connector

The Internet Data Connector (IDC) is used to retrieve information from a database, format it using a template, and send the resulting HTML to the browser. It requires an ODBC data source name (DSN).

To use the Internet Data Connector, you need to create two files for your query.

IDC file

This file contains the information necessary to query the database. The syntax of the file will look something like this:

```
Datasource: web sql

Username: sa

Template: sample.htx

SQLStatement:

+SELECT au_lname, ytd_sales from
   pubs.dbo.titleview where
   ytd_sales>5000
```

Notice that the IDC file contains the following four types of information:

- Datasource

  The Datasource is the DSN that has been configured in the ODBC Administrator. Internet Information Server will pass this information to the ODBC Driver Manager. The ODBC Driver Manager will find the DSN in the registry, launch the appropriate driver, and submit the query.

- Username

  This is the name that should be used to log on to the database management system. The username "sa" is the default SQL Administrative name.

- Template

  This is the name of the HTML document that will receive the results of the query.

- SQLStatement

    This is the statement that describes the information that should be returned. This statement is passed on to the database management system, which parses the statement and returns the appropriate results. A detailed discussion of SQL syntax is beyond the scope of this course.

An IDC file is an ASCII file saved with the .idc extension.

Template File

The template file is an HTML document that is saved with the .htx extension. Inside the file, the HTML references the IDC query. The HTML syntax uses special scripting tags <% %>, as well as some keywords to interpret and display the result set. The details of interpreting an IDC result set are beyond the scope of this course.

ADO works in conjunction with an OLE DB provider to give a client application access to any type of data, whether it is relational or not. As long as an OLE DB provider exists for a particular data source, ADO can access it. As you can see, this does not mean that ODBC will go away. The ODBC Manager has an OLE DB provider. Its OLE DB provider implements the interfaces that ADO expects an OLE DB provider to implement and passes the request for a connection or query on to the ODBC Manager. From there it works exactly as it always has.

The real difference is that ADO and OLE DB do not require data sources to include an ODBC driver. For non-relational data sources, this greatly reduces the number of layers through which a request must pass.

Currently, the only OLE DB provider available for ADO is the ODBC provider.

ADO and OLE DB

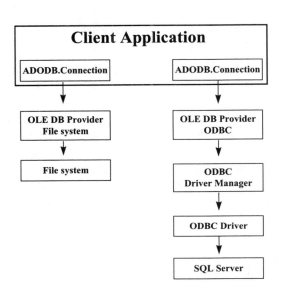

ADO Object Model

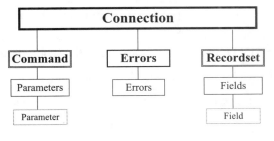

ADO OBJECT MODEL

The ADO object model is composed of ActiveX objects that can be used in any controller, including Internet Information Server, through the use of Active Server Pages. The ADO object model contains seven objects:

Connection This object is used to create a connection with a Database server.

Command	This object is used to issue queries or execute stored procedures. With non-relational data sources, you may not need to use it.
Recordset	This object stores the result of a query or the data source returned by a provider. This is the object with which you will most frequently interface.
Parameter	The Parameter object provides parameter information and data for the Command object.
Field	A Field object allows access to each data column in the current Recordset record.
Property	The Property object provides information about the characteristics of the Connection, Command, Recordset, and Field objects.
Error	The Error object allows retrieval of provider error information when an error occurs.

The ADO object model also contains four collections:

Fields	A collection of Field objects.
Properties	A collection of Property objects.
Parameters	A collection of Parameter objects.
Errors	A collection of Error objects.

The Connection, Command, and Recordset objects are the central objects in the ADO object model.

Remote Data Service

Internet Information Server 4.0 provides support for Remote Data Service (RDS) 1.5. RDS allows for disconnected result sets on the client. This is useful for situations where the user needs to navigate through and manipulate a set of data. Like ADO, RDS uses OLE DB providers to interface with the data source. This version of RDS also uses the same object model as ADO, making it easy for programmers to adapt server-side code to work with a client-cached result set and vice versa. A detailed discussion of the RDS architecture is beyond the scope of this course.

What is a Transaction?

You are probably familiar with transactions in the real world. Most classic examples involve money. Consider a credit card transaction. When you make a purchase on your credit card, several things must happen:

- You receive a product or service.
- The credit card company charges your account.
- The credit card company pays the vendor providing the service.

If one of these things fails to happen, the transaction should be *rolled back*. For example, if you ordered a book through the mail and that book never arrived, but the charge appeared on your credit card, you would call the credit card company and ask that the charge be taken off. The credit card company would, in turn, demand that the book publisher either send you the book or refund the payment. One way or another, all aspects of the transaction would either be *committed* or *rolled back*.

The same theory applies to *transactions* that occur on a Web site, particularly if they modify data in a database. Let's look at a quick example.

Suppose you have a retail site. When a customer orders a product, your Web site must receive customer information and order information. Enter the customer information in the Customer table. Verify that the credit card is valid. Verify that the product is in stock. Enter the order information in the Orders table. Send the order to the person who handles shipping. If one of these things fails, the transaction should be rolled back. Prior to MTS, writing the code to handle all of these conditions would have been pretty complex, particularly if there were a lot of user connections involved. Fortunately, MTS can be used to simplify the task.

Microsoft Transaction Server Benefits

In addition to handling transaction commitment and rollback, MTS handles several other issues that arise in a multiple-user environment. These are:

- Thread pooling

  An application with a single thread can only handle a single user. However, writing multithreaded applications is difficult and time-consuming. MTS provides thread management through the use of thread pooling. This simplifies the development process and lets you easily control the number of threads that are running instances of a component.

- Application isolation

  Normally an Active Server Pages application runs in the same process as Internet Information Server. This means that a misbehaving in-process component (DLL) could potentially crash IIS 4.0. To guard against this, MTS allows you to run a Web application inside its own package. If a component in the package misbehaves, only that package will crash. IIS 4.0 will continue to run.

- Integration with Active Server Pages

  It is now easy to build an Active Server Pages application that can take advantage of transactions.

- Integration with Microsoft Message Queue Server (MSMQ)

  The Microsoft Message Queue Server is another server that ships with Windows NT 4.0 Option Pack. This server allows you to queue processes that do not have to occur immediately.

Building transactional Web applications is beyond the scope of this course.

Transaction Server Explorer Snap-in

Microsoft Transaction Server can be managed in the Microsoft Management Console by adding the MTS Explorer Snap-in. This snap-in is added by default when Windows NT 4.0 Option Pack is installed.

A Package is the object that contains the components of an application. Each Package contains two folders: one that contains components and the other that contains roles. A role describes security information and is often associated with User and Group accounts. In addition, there are three objects that can be used to view particular types of information about transactions. These are:

- Trace Messages

  This object allows you to view errors, warnings, and informational messages. You can configure the level of messages that are displayed on the Advanced property page of the Computer object.

- Transaction List

    This object allows you to view a list of transactions that are currently running. This is a good place to start troubleshooting if you suspect a transaction is being blocked.

- Transaction Statistics

    This object allows you to retrieve detailed information about a particular transaction.

Microsoft Index Server 2.0

Microsoft Index Server 2.0 (MIS 2.0) provides you with the ability to provide indexed searches for information contained on your IIS. Indexing is a valuable feature and proper implementation can produce very professional results. Microsoft Index Server 2.0 is easy to administer and requires relatively low maintenance.

Some features of Microsoft Index Server 2.0 are:

- The ability to index multiple Web Servers, including files on a NetWare server or files in a FAT partition.

- Support for full-text and property-value indexing for the following formats:

    Text files (.txt)

    HTML 3.0 and earlier (.htm)

    MS Word 95 and 97 (.doc)

    MS Excel 95 and 97 (.xls)

    MS PowerPoint 95 and 97 (.ppt)

    Binary files (properties only)

    Additional file formats can be indexed, provided you install the appropriate content features.

- The ability to support multiple languages by storing index information in Unicode. Supported languages include:

    Dutch

    French

    German

    Italian

    Japanese

    Spanish

    Swedish

    U.K. English

    U.S. English

    Traditional and Simplified Chinese

- Index Server can index your news messages.

- As the site's file structure changes, indexes are automatically updated.

- Index server includes an automatic error detection and recovery system.

System Requirements

Microsoft Index Server 2.0 can be installed on any existing IIS 4.0 Server. The following are suggested memory requirements for Microsoft Index Server 2.0. These requirements are in addition to the those of the Windows NT 4.0 Server operating system and IIS 4.0.

- Fewer than 100,000 Web pages, 32 MB of additional RAM

- 100,000-250,000 Web pages, 64-128 MB of additional RAM

- 250,000-500,000 Web pages, 128-256 MB of additional RAM

- Over 500,000 Web pages, 256 MB or more

Disk space requirements are dependent on the number of files to be indexed. The index *catalog* will be approximately 40% of the total size of the indexed files. Therefore, if you have 1 gigabyte of Web content, you will need about 400 megabytes of disk space to store the catalog.

Performance is based on the number of documents indexed, the size of the *corpus* (a Latin word meaning *body*), search *scope*, processor speed, and other server-related performance issues.

Installing Microsoft Index Server 2.0

The Microsoft Index Server 2.0 is a component of the Windows NT 4.0 Option Pack and is installed by default. It consists of four sub-components:

- Index Server System Files
- Language resources
- Online documentation
- Sample files

NOTE: Refer to Chapter 4 for more information on IIS 4.0 and Windows NT 4.0 Option Pack installation.

During the installation process, a *Catalog* directory (catalog.wci) is created below the C:\InetPub directory. The index and property cache files are stored in this directory.

Microsoft Index Server 2.0 is configured and managed with the Microsoft Management Console via the Index Server 2.0 snap-in module.

NOTE: You may achieve enhanced system performance by installing the Index Server 2.0 component on a different disk drive than the one containing your Web documents.

Index Server files are copied to the following directories:

\Inetpub\Iissamples\Iissamples
                    Sample HTML files

\Inetpub\Iisadmin\Iisadmin
                    Administration files

\Inetpub\Iishelp\Ix   Document Files

Once the Microsoft Index Server 2.0 component is installed, it begins to index all of the files contained in the virtual directories of the Default Web Site.

The Index Server is a Windows NT Service named *Content Index* (cisvc.exe). Launch the Services utility to view information on installed, running, and stopped Services. The Content Index Service runs continuously and automatically updates changes made to your Web site directories and files, even when the WWW Service is not running.

Understanding the Indexing Process

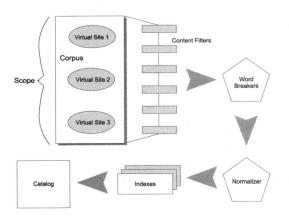

The term *corpus* is used to refer to all the documents that are indexed by a particular catalog. This corpus of documents may be located on the local server or a combination of servers.

A process called CiDaemon is responsible for generating the index. It runs in the background. It creates the index by loading and running the appropriate dynamic link libraries. These DLLs depend on the type of document being indexed, as well as the language in which it was written. Two types of DLLs will be used for each document: Content Filters and Word Breakers.

Content Filters are used to allow the indexing of formatted documents. For example, Microsoft Word uses a different file format than Excel. Microsoft Index Server 2.0 indexes documents based on available Content Filters. It ignores those document formats that it does not recognize.

In addition to text extraction, Content Filters allow Microsoft Index Server 2.0 to recognize language shifts and handle embedded objects. For example, if Microsoft Index Server 2.0 encounters an Excel spreadsheet embedded in a Word document, the server is able to index the text in the Word document as well as text contained in the Excel document.

> *NOTE: Content Filters can be developed by independent software vendors (ISVs) to provide support for additional file formats.*

Once a Content Filter has finished with the document, Index Server uses Word breakers to parse the character stream into individual words. Since different languages separate words differently, language-specific word breakers can be installed.

The Normalizer removes punctuation, capitalization, and words such as *the, of, a, an, and, or,* and other words that have been designated as *noise words.* The pre-identified noise words are stored in a file named noise.dat (for the English language). You can modify the list of noise words or provide your own file. Language-specific noise word files are identified in the Registry under the key: HKEY_LOCAL_MACHINE\SYSTEM\SYSTEM \CurrentControlSet\Control \ContentIndex\Language\<*language*>\NoiseFile.

Once the noise words have been removed, a word list is created in memory. When there are a certain number of word lists in memory, they are merged into a persistent index. The persistent index is stored in the catalog, along with a list of properties.

A *catalog* is associated with a single site. During installation, the Index Server creates a catalog named Web. By default, this catalog is associated with the Default Web Site. you can create multiple catalogs. However, Index Server performs a query on an individual catalog. Therefore, queries cannot be performed across sites.

Microsoft Index Server 2.0 Management

Microsoft Index Server 2.0 Manager is a snap-in to Microsoft Management Console (MMC). The MMC is launched automatically when you start the Index Server Manager. However, you can also add it to any other console, using the procedures described earlier in the course. The following eight parameters are displayed when you select an Index Server:

- Catalog

  The name for the catalogs associated with this Index Server. Separate statistics are maintained for every catalog.

- Location

    The root path for the catalog.

- Size (Mb)

    The amount of space required to hold an index for the cataloged documents.

- Total Docs

    The total number of documents in the catalog directory.

- Docs to Filter

    The number of documents to be filtered.

- Wordlists

    The number of temporary word lists that Index Server has created for the Catalog. When there are 14 to 20 such lists they are merged into a persistent index.

- Persistent Indexes

    The number of permanent indexes for the catalog. Index Server may create additional persistent indexes, which will eventually be merged.

- Status

    The status of the catalog, such as up-to-date or malfunctioning. This parameter is only present when the Index Server is performing an operation on the catalog. If the Status field displays a scan message, you should re-scan the directories in the catalog.

Configuring Global Properties

To view the Properties of your server, right-click on the Index Server folder, then select **Properties**.

Generation Properties

- Filter Files with unknown extensions

    Enable this option to prevent certain files (.exe, .gif, etc.) that do not contain text from being posted to the results view.

- Generate characterizations

    Enable this option to have the Index Server create a summary for every file in a search result. A summary provides users with an idea of what to expect when they select a particular link. The summary does consume additional CPU cycles and may not produce more usable information than the document title.

- Maximum size

    This option is used to determine the maximum number of characters that are returned in a summary.

NOTE: *You make global property changes by configuring the Index Server Properties.*

Configuring Catalog Properties

To view the Properties of a catalog, open the Index Server folder, right-click on the Catalog directory and select **Properties**.

Location Properties

- Name

    The name of the catalog as it appears in the Management Console,

- Location

    The physical location for the catalog.

- Size

    The size of the catalog in megabytes.

NOTE: *The Property values for a catalog override those of the Index Server.*

Web Properties

Click on the **Web** tab to view tracking options.

- Track Virtual Roots

    Enable this option to identify the virtual Web server for which the catalog holds information.

- Track NNTP Roots

    Enable this option to index message content from the News server as part of the overall index.

Generation Properties

Click on the **Web** tab to view tracking options.

- Filter Files with unknown extensions

    Enable this option to prevent certain files (exe, gif, etc.) that do not contain text from being posted to the results view.

- Generate characterizations

    Enable this option to have the Index Server create a summary for every file in a search result. A summary provides users with an idea of what to expect when they select a particular link. The summary does consume additional CPU cycles and may not produce more usable information than the document title.

- Maximum size

    This option is used to determine the maximum number of characters that are returned in a summary.

NOTE: *Characterizations for catalogs can be disabled. This would result in no summaries or abstracts being displayed for files listed on the Results page of a search.*

Microsoft Index Server 2.0 Performance Issues

Index Server performance issues include:

- Property Cache
- Number of Indexed Directories

Adjusting the Property Cache

For values that are frequently queried you can cache the properties on your server. Adding the tag META="AutoProduct" VALUE="*Product name*" to your HTML document allows you to create queries that will look for items that match a specific name.

Adding and Removing Directories

You should not index your entire server. The Index Server therefore needs to know exactly what directories to incorporate. You can add and remove physical directories from a catalog's scope.

When you create a new content directory that you wish to be indexed, you should add the directory to the Index Server's scope. To do so, right-click on either the Catalog or the Directory folder inside it and run **New/ Directory**. Browse to locate the physical directory you wish to index.

To remove a physical directory from the catalog, right-click on the directory and run **Delete**. This does not actually delete the directory from the hard drive. It only prevents the documents inside it from being indexed.

NOTE: *Indexing and searching in Index Server is based on virtual roots. You exclude Virtual Directories from being indexed through the Internet Service Manager. Select the Home Directory Properties page and clear the check from the* ***Index this Directory box.***

Forcing a Scan

You need to force Index Server to scan directories when you make global changes such as:

- Adding or removing a filter.

- Enabling or disabling filtering documents with unknown extensions.

- Adding a new word breaker.

- Changing the size of the characterization summary.

Forcing a Merge

When server response time slows down for queries, it may be necessary to free resources by combining indexes. Combining smaller indexes into larger ones frees up server memory and disk space.

Microsoft Index Server 2.0 Query Features

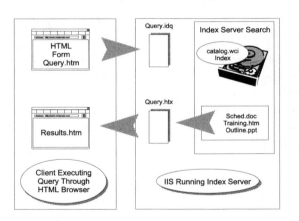

If you have used the Web to search for information, you have probably used a query form. These forms allow users to search your site.

The *Query Scope* defines which documents should be included in the search.

Content query restrictions specify the file properties that should be included in the search. This can include size, modification dates, file names, and authors, among others.

Hit Highlights identifies which parts of each document contain the words defined by the search.

Query Logging can be performed by Internet Information Server, just as any other access logging. Logging will be discussed later in the course.

Query Elements

Let's examine the way that Microsoft Index Server 2.0 handles queries.

A sample HTML query form included with the Index Server can be used to search the indexed files. To view this file, run **Start/Programs/Windows NT 4.0 Option Pack/Microsoft Index Server/Index Server Sample Query Form**.

This will launch Internet Explorer and display the query form.

If you receive an error message indicating that the location cannot be found, enter the following in the Address field:

```
C:\InetPub\iissamples\ISSamples\
   default.htm
```

A Microsoft Index Server 2.0 query is comprised of four components:

- HTML Query form

  Displays a Web page in which the user can enter the query parameters. It will also display the query results.

- Internet Data Query File (IDQ)

  This is the intermediate form that the Index Server will run to search the index for the user's request.

- The HTML Extension File (HTX)

  This is an HTML file containing the result of the search.

- Hit Highlighting information

  This information is contained in a file with the extension .htw. It is combined with the .htx file and formatted appropriately. The resulting HTML is downloaded to the browser.

Query Forms

When using a Web browser, queries are generated by completing the fields in an HTML form. Sample forms are provided with Index Server and can be copied and tailored for your individual needs. Microsoft Index Server 2.0 allows:

- Users to search for words and phrases.

- Users to search by author, subject, file size, and date.

- Users to search with wildcard characters * and ?.

- Users to search by using Boolean operators (AND, OR, NOT).

- Automatic updates when documents are changed.

- User restrictions for document security, ensuring users view only the documents they have permission to view.

Active Server Pages Queries

You can also build query pages with ASP. Use SQL extensions to build the query and ADO to retrieve the data. Then use VBScript or another ActiveX scripting language to format the data. Send the information to the browser using the standard ASP syntax.

Microsoft Index Server 2.0 Security Issues

When the default catalog is created by the Index Server, its Access Control List (ACL) grants access only to Administrators and system services. If you create an additional catalog, make sure to assign the appropriate permissions to guard against unauthorized access.

When filtering documents, Index Server 2.0 also saves the associated Access Control properties created in the NTFS file system. This Access Control information is used by the Index Server to determine if a user is allowed to access a file. If a user has not been granted the necessary permissions to access the file, the file will not appear in the results set.

It is usually a good idea to authenticate users prior to initiating the query. One way to do this is to establish NTFS permissions for the query form (.htm) that initiates the query.

If anonymous logon is allowed, the anonymous user will be used by default as long as all files accessed by the client can be accessed by the anonymous user. Whenever an attempt is made to access a document for which access is denied, an authentication dialog box will be displayed.

SMTP Defined

As its name suggests, Simple Mail Transfer Protocol (SMTP) was designed to handle the transfer of messages from one host to another. One of the most widely used protocols on the Internet, it is described by RFCs 821 and 822. Keep in mind that SMTP is a mail transfer protocol, not a mail system. It does not provide for individual mailboxes for users or other mail features provided by mail systems like Microsoft Exchange. It simply provides a mechanism for transferring messages between hosts, for queuing messages until a message can be forwarded (store and forward), and for notifying the sender when mail cannot be delivered.

Sending Messages

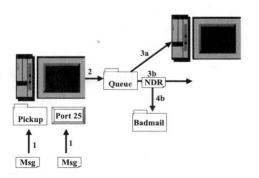

A message can be sent either by saving a text file in the directory named Pickup on the Internet Information Server that is running SMTP or by sending it to the port that has been configured for outgoing mail. By default, this port is Port 25. When the server receives a message, it places it in the Queue folder until it is able to make the necessary connection to deliver it. If it cannot be delivered within the specified amount of time, a non-delivery report (NDR) is sent to the sender. If the NDR cannot be delivered, the message is copied to the Badmail directory.

Receiving Messages

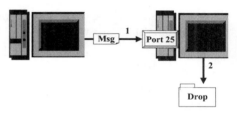

When a message is received in the port designated as the incoming port (port 25 by default), SMTP determines if the final destination of the message is on one of its domains and if it is, deposits that message in the Drop directory. As you can see, this is not a very efficient way to handle mail for a number of recipients. Without a mail system to retrieve those messages and route them to the appropriate users, SMTP is not an appropriate solution for handling incoming mail for multiple users.

Some Appropriate Uses

The SMTP Service is primarily designed for the following purposes:

- To allow users to send a message from your Web site.

   You can configure SMTP and your Web site to allow users to send an e-mail message to the Web administrator. This is appropriate for general-purpose comments or even for technical support questions. Keep in mind that all incoming messages for your domain will be copied to the Drop directory, not to an actual mailbox.

- To allow mail-enabled applications to send outgoing mail.

   Mail-enabled applications can send Internet mail through your SMTP service. The SMTP service can be configured to route the mail to the appropriate domain.

Installing SMTP

The SMTP service can be installed either during Internet Information Server installation or after. To add it after, insert the Windows NT 4.0 Option Pack CD-ROM and allow it to launch **AutoPlay**. Click on **Install**. Click on **Install Windows NT 4.0 Option Pack**. After Setup loads, click on **Next** then click on **Add/Remove**. Select Internet Information Server. Click on **Show Subcomponents**.

Select SMTP Service and click on **OK**. Click on **Next**.

You will be prompted to enter the location where you'd like to install your *mailroot* directory. This is the directory that will contain the Queue, Drop, and Badmail directories. By default, this directory is created at *systemdrive:*\InetPub\Mailroot. It is recommended that you select an NTFS partition for this directory. Click on **Next** to begin reconfiguration and file copy. After the files have been copied, click on **Finish**. Click on **Yes** to restart the computer.

The Microsoft SMTP Service will be started automatically when the computer starts.

The SMTP Management Extension

SMTP can be managed through the SMTP Extension of the Internet Service Manager snap-in. This means that like the FTP and WWW services, SMTP can be managed through the Microsoft Management Console.

SMTP Objects

When the SMTP service is installed, three objects are created. These are:

- Default SMTP Site

   This is the Site object in which you will create domains. The SMTP service can handle only one site. You cannot add additional sites or delete sites.

- Domains

   This object will contain the local and remote domains you create. By default, a local domain is created with the same name as your machine. This is the default domain for your SMTP site.

- Current Sessions

   This object will allow you to view information about current SMTP connections.

Site Properties

The Site object has five property sheets. They allow you to configure a variety of settings that affect how your SMTP site operates. Some of these are similar to the types of settings you can make to WWW and FTP sites. Some are unique to SMTP sites. Let's look first at the properties you can set on the SMTP Site property page.

SMTP Site Properties

The **SMTP Site** tab allows you to set properties that identify the site and limit the connections. These properties are:

- Description

    This is the name of the site. You can keep it at default or change it to something more descriptive.

- IP Address

    This is set to All Unassigned by default. However, you can specify a particular IP address if more than one is configured for the computer. As with WWW and FTP sites, you can configure multiple identities for this site.

- Incoming Connections

    You can specify the port number, the number of simultaneous connections, and the connection timeout value for incoming connections. By default, the number of simultaneous connections is limited to 1000 and the timeout value is set to 600. The default port number is 25.

- Outgoing Connections

    You can specify the port number, the number of simultaneous connections, the number of simultaneous connections per domain, and the connection timeout value for incoming connections. By default, the number of simultaneous connections is limited to 1000 (100 per domain) and the timeout value is set to 600. The default port number is 25. Incoming and outgoing connections can use the same port or different ports.

- Enable Logging

    This setting works the same as for the FTP and WWW services. Logging will be discussed later in the course.

Operators

This property page is similar to that for FTP and WWW sites. You can grant specific Windows NT users and groups the ability to perform some administrative activities on the site.

Messages

This property page allows you to configure settings related to how messages are handled by the site. Settings include:

- Limit message size

    This value sets the recommended limit for a message. A client can send a message larger than this amount without closing the connection, as long as the maximum session size is not exceeded.

- Limit session size

    This setting is the actual limit for the size of a session. If a client sends a message that is larger than this amount, the connection will be closed.

- Maximum number of outbound messages per connection

    This setting determines the maximum number of outbound messages that can be sent before a connection to a receiving server is closed. By setting this number lower than the usual number of messages transmitted during a connection, you can actually improve performance. This is because multiple connections can be used to deliver messages simultaneously.

- Maximum number of recipients per message

  This is set to 100 by default in order to comply with RFC 821. In some implementations of SMTP, sending a message to more than 100 recipients would result in the 101st recipient (and all others after) being dropped from the list and the sender being sent an NDR. In Microsoft's implementation, a new connection is opened to handle the remaining recipients.

- Send a copy of non-delivery report to

  This allows you to specify an e-mail address that should receive copies of each NDR. It might be useful to provide a mail administrator's e-mail address here.

- Badmail directory

  If a message cannot be delivered to a recipient and its NDR cannot be sent to the sender, the message will be copied to the directory specified here. By default, this is set to *systemdrive:*\InetPub\Mailroot\Badmail.

Delivery Properties

The settings on the **Delivery** property page can affect how reliable your SMTP service is. They include:

- Maximum retries

  This is the number of times the SMTP service will attempt to send a particular message before issuing an NDR. This is 48 by default. This can be set separately for messages destined for a remote domain than for those destined for a local domain.

- Retry interval

  This is the number of minutes that should elapse between attempts to send a particular domain's messages. It is set to 1 hour by default. When taken together, the maximum retries and the retry interval determine how soon an NDR will be sent if a message is undeliverable. By default, the NDR would not be sent until 2 days after the message had originally been sent.

- Maximum hop count

  This is the number of SMTP servers through which an outgoing message can pass before reaching its destination. If the number is exceeded along the message route, an NDR will be returned.

- Masquerade domain

  This setting replaces the sender's domain with the name specified here. This is useful because it guarantees that replies to the message will come back to the SMTP server. This setting is only used when this SMTP server is the first hop on the message's journey.

- Fully qualified domain name

  This is usually the name set in the Domain field of the TCP/IP property sheet's **DNS** tab. However, you can override that value here. Keep in mind that if you do, you should also change the MX record on the DNS server. Specifying a fully qualified domain name will speed name resolution.

- Smart host

    You can specify that all outgoing mail be sent to a particular host instead of directly to the domain. This allows another computer to take care of choosing the best route for a particular domain. You can use either a host name or an IP address for this value. However, if you use an IP address, enclosing it in square brackets will optimize performance.

- Perform reverse DNS lookup on incoming messages

    This option allows you to ensure that the host name on an incoming message actually matches the IP address from which the message originated. While this can help authenticate the identity of the sender, it can also decrease performance.

- Outbound Security

    Some servers may require that authentication credentials be passed with the message. If the majority of the domains to which you send messages require a particular type of authentication or encryption, set it here. Otherwise, you will probably want to set these options on a domain-specific basis.

    You have already been introduced to Basic Authentication and Windows NT Challenge/Response. TLS encryption is Transport Layer Security encryption. In order to use this type of encryption, you will need to ensure that the recipient server also supports TLS encryption.

Directory Security

This property page allows you to set security restrictions on the messages that are received or relayed by the site.

Anonymous Access and Authentication Control

This allows you to determine whether or not to accept incoming messages from the anonymous user account and whether to validate a message originator based on Basic Authentication and/or Windows NT Challenge/Response authentication.

Secure Communications

This option allows you to specify that communication can only take place over SSL. Your SMTP site and the remote domain must each have the appropriate keys. If you are in the United States or Canada, you can also specify that you wish to use 128-bit encryption, instead of the 40-bit default.

IP Address and Domain Name Restrictions

This option can be used to limit or grant access based on IP address, subnet mask, or domain name. As with the WWW and FTP services, restricting or granting access by domain name will diminish performance.

Relay Restrictions

This property page allows you to configure which computers, if any, are allowed to use your SMTP site for message relay. Allowing all computers to relay messages through your site will leave you open to those who wish to distribute Unsolicited Commercial E-mail (UCE). However, you may wish to grant certain computers the ability to use your site for message relay. To do so, specify the IP address for those sites here.

Domains

Local Domains

As previously mentioned, a single local domain is created when you install SMTP. This domain is known as the default domain. The property page for the default domain provides the path to the Drop directory.

You can create local alias domains as well. These domains provide an alternate name for the default domain. However, mail for all local domains is stored in the Drop directory. If you change an alias domain to the default domain, the current default domain will be changed to an alias domain. You can only have one default domain for any site.

Remote Domains

You can also create remote domains. A remote domain allows you to override certain site settings when a message is delivered to a particular domain. You can:

- Specify a route

    Any route specified here will override the default route. If a smart host is configured for the site, it will be ignored when mail is sent to this domain.

- Allow incoming mail to be relayed to this domain

    This will enable your SMTP site to serve as a relay host for mail destined to this particular domain.

- Configure outbound security

    This button will display a dialog where you can configure specific security settings for mail that is destined for this domain. These settings will override those set for the site.

Installing NNTP

The NNTP Service can be installed either during Internet Information Server installation or after. To add it after, insert the Windows NT 4.0 Option Pack CD-ROM and allow it to launch **AutoPlay**. Click on **Install**. Click on **Install Windows NT 4.0 Option Pack**. After Setup loads, click on **Next** then click on **Add/Remove**. Select Internet Information Server. Click on **Show Subcomponents**.

Select the Internet NNTP Service and click on **OK**. Click on **Next**.

You will be prompted for the directory that should store the news articles. By default, this file is *systemdrive*:\InetPub\nntpfile. It is recommended that you use a directory that is on an NTFS partition. Click on **Next** to begin configuring Internet Information Server and installing the files. After the files have copied, click on **Finish**. You will be prompted to restart your computer. When the computer reboots, the Microsoft NNTP Service will be started automatically.

News Site Properties

The **News Site** tab allows you to:

- Enter a Description for your site. This is the site name that is displayed by the Microsoft Management Console utility.

- Enter a value for the Path Header option. This is the string that is displayed in the **Path** line in each news posting.

- Enter the server's IP Address. This is the IP address of the NNTP server.

- Configure **Advanced** IP addressing. Select this option to assign multiple IP addresses for this news site

- Select the TCP Port number for the NNTP Service. The default port value is 119.

- Select the SSL Port number for the NNTP Service. The default port value is 563.

- Specify a value for the Connections option. You set a limit on the number of simultaneous NNTP client connections and a time limit on active connections.

- Specify a value for the Connection timeout option. This parameter is used to set time a limit for an inactive news client. The default value is 600 seconds.

- Configure the **Enable Logging** option.

- Configure the Active log format option.

Security Accounts Properties

The **Security Accounts** tab allows you to:

- Enable Anonymous User access.

    Use this option to select the account used for anonymous access. The default is IUSR_*Computername*. The permissions granted the account determine which newsgroups are available to anonymous users.

- Assign News Site Operators.

    Use this option to assign one or more operators to the NNTP Service.

NNTP Settings Properties

The **NNTP Settings** tab allows you to:

- Enable the **Allow client posting** option.

    Enable this option to allow clients to post articles to the news site.

- Configure the **Limit post size** option.

    This option allows you to define the maximum size of news articles that clients can post to the news site.

- Configure the **Limit connection size** option.

    This option determines the maximum size of all the news articles that a client can post in a single session.

- Enable the **Allow servers to pull news articles from this server** option.

    Enable this option to allow other news servers to pull articles from your new site.

- Enable the **Allow control messages** option.

    A control message is one that adds, or deletes an article or newsgroup. You can prevent control messages from being processed by the site or filter who can issue control messages by granting and restricting access to the control.cancel, control.rmgroup, and control.newgroup newsgroups.

    The directories associated with these control newsgroups are created beneath the nntpfile directory under \root\control. Everyone is granted Full Control permission by default. You can use NTFS permissions to grant or revoke access to individual users and groups. As an alternative, you can select to have these groups moderated.

- Configure the SMTP server for moderated groups option.

    Use this option to specify the SMTP mail server where all postings to moderated groups are forwarded. This must be either a valid computer name registered in DNS with a valid IP or a directory on the local hard drive.

- Configure the Default moderator domain option.

    Use this option to specify the default domain for all moderated postings. Articles posted to a moderated newsgroup that does not have a specified moderator are sent to *news_group_name@default_moderator domain,* where the *news_group_name* is the name of the newsgroup to which the article is sent and the *default_moderator_domain* is the value you specified for this domain.

- Configure the Administrator Email Account option.

   Use this option to specify the e-mail address for the recipient of NDRs for moderated newsgroup articles that cannot be delivered to the designated moderator.

You can also moderate newsgroups from a news client. When configured for moderated articles, the NNTP Service sends articles automatically to a specified SMTP server for delivery to the moderator.

If an article cannot be delivered to the moderator, a non-delivery report (NDR) is returned to the Administrator E-mail account address. For these messages to be processed by SMTP, an account must exist on the SMTP server.

Home Directory Properties

The **Home Directory** tab allows you to:

- Configure the home directory to be **A directory located on this computer** or **A share located on another computer**.

   Remote shares should be entered using a UNC name as shown below:

   *Servername**sharename*

- Configure the Local Path option.

   This is the local directory for the NNTP Service. The default value is C:\Inetpub\nntpfile\root.

- Configure the Network directory option.

   This allows you to specify the network directory where news articles are located. The default value is *Servername**directory**subdirectory*\\.

- Enable the **Allow posting** option.

   Enable this option to allow clients to post articles to the home directory.

- Enable the **Log access** option.

   Enable this option to generate a log of news client activity.

- Enable the **Restrict newsgroup visibility** option.

   Enable this option to restrict the viewing of newsgroup lists in this directory to users who have access permission for the newsgroup. (This option adds processing overhead and should not be used for newsgroups that allow anonymous access.)

- Enable the **Index news content** option.

   Enable this option to index newsgroups in this directory with Microsoft Index Server, which allows users to search for specific text.

Secure Communications Settings

This button allows you to configure encryption for outgoing data by requiring the client to use Secure Sockets Layer (SSL) for connections to the NNTP Service. You can:

- Enable the **Require Secure Channel** option.

   This option allows you to ensure that outgoing data is encrypted by requiring the client to use Secure Sockets Layer (SSL) for connections to the NNTP Service.

- Enable the **Require 128-bit Encryption** option.

   This option allows you to limit access to the virtual directory to clients using the 128-bit key strength encryption in SSL. Clients attempting to connect using the 40-bit key strength encryption in SSL are refused. Because of export restrictions, the 128-bit key strength encryption feature is available only in the United States and Canada.

You can create virtual directories to store news articles, which increases the capacity of files that can be stored. Use the Directories option in Internet Service Manager or Internet Service Manager (HTML) to configure virtual directories for specific newsgroups.

The NNTP Service requires approximately 540 bytes per stored article, plus 1 KB for every 128 articles, in addition to the space required for the articles themselves. Select an NNTP home directory location with enough space to accommodate these requirements.

> *NOTE:* *The home directory must reside on a Microsoft Windows NT Server disk partition formatted as Windows NT file system (NTFS).*

Directory Security

The **Directory Security** tab allows you to:

- Select a Password Authentication Method.

    You can choose one or more authentication methods. Click on **Edit** to view the authentication options.

    Enable the **Allow Anonymous** option.

    Enable this option to allow any client access to the contents of this directory.

Enable the **Basic Authentication** option.

Enable this option to select Basic password authentication. NNTP defines an authorization protocol, called AUTHINFO, that is based on clear-text passwords. The NNTP Service supports this clear-text password authorization protocol as Basic password authentication. It also extends the protocol to support delivery of confidential data between the NNTP Service and an NNTP client. The NNTP Service provides these features as extensions to the NNTP AUTHINFO protocol.

Enable the **Windows NT Challenge/Response** option.

Enable this option to select the standard challenge/response security mechanism that is provided with the Microsoft Windows NT Server 4.0 operating system. This security feature makes it possible for businesses to provide secure logon services for their customers. Sites that already use Windows NT Challenge/Response in an internal system can benefit by using a single, common security mechanism.

Enable the **Enable SSL Client Authentication** option.

By selecting this option you enable secure client authentication using SSL encryption and certificates. This option requires a server certificate from a valid certificate authority (CA).

Enable the **Require SSL Client Authentication** option.

Enable this option to require that clients provide SSL-encrypted user names and passwords.

Enable the **Enable Client Certificate Mappings to Windows NT User Accounts** option.

If the client software has an SSL client certificate installed, the NNTP Service will use the Microsoft Windows NT account that is mapped to that certificate to authenticate users. Choose **Client Mappings** to enter certificates and the Windows NT account names.

- Configure IP Address and Domain Name Restrictions (IP Filtering).

   You have several options for restricting access to newsgroups. Choose **Edit** to view restriction options.

   By default, the news site is accessible from all IP addresses. However, you can grant or deny access to specific IP addresses, while allowing or denying access for a larger group. You can do this by specifying a single IP address, a group of addresses using a subnet mask, or a domain name.

NOTE: *Using Windows NT Challenge/Response authentication requires a news client that supports this authentication method. Microsoft Internet Mail and News supports Windows NT Challenge/Response authentication.*

Groups

The **Groups** tab allows you to:

- Create newsgroups using the **Create new newsgroup** option.

   Select this option to create a new newsgroup. You can specify whether a newsgroup is to be moderated. When a newsgroup is moderated, articles are sent to the newsgroup moderator for review before they are posted to the newsgroup.

- Use the Newsgroup name option.

   This option allows you to search for a newsgroup by full or partial name.

- Configure the Limit results to option.

   Use this option to limit the number of newsgroups displayed by the **Find** option.

- View the Matching newsgroups list.

  This list displays the newsgroups that were located by the **Find** option.

NNTP Newsgroup Expiration Policy

Create NNTP Service Expiration Policies to enforce an expiration policy for any number of newsgroups managed by the NNTP Service. You can define an expiration policy to delete all news articles older than a specified number of days, or to delete the oldest articles when newsgroups reach a specified size, or both.

To create NNTP Expiration Policies, run **Start/ Programs/Windows NT 4.0 Option Pack/Microsoft Internet Server/Internet Service Manager** to launch the Internet Service Manager. Open the Internet Information Server folder, then open the webserver computer icon.

Open the Default NNTP Site folder and right-click on **Expiration Policies**. Select **New,** then **Expiration Policy.**

Enter a name for the new expiration policy, then click on **Next.**

Select the appropriate option to apply the expiration policy to all newsgroups on this NNTP site or to a selected subset of newsgroups.

If you selected to apply the expiration policy to a subset of newsgroups, you are prompted to enter the names of the newsgroups to which you wish to apply the policy. Click on **Next** to continue.

You can enable message expiration by selecting the **When articles become older than** option. This option is enabled by default and the time limit value is set to 7 days. You can also enable a disk space limit on the selected (or all) newsgroups. This option is disabled by default. Click on **Finish.**

When you are finished, the new expiration policy will appear in the Microsoft Management Console window.

Internet Service Manager (HTML)

During the installation of the Windows NT 4.0 Option Pack you installed the Internet Service manager (HTML). This option installs the necessary HTML and dynamic link (DLL) files to administer your Web site using a browser.

To launch the HTML version of Internet Service Manager, run **Start/Programs/Windows NT 4.0 Option Pack/Microsoft Internet Information Server/ Internet Service Manager** (HTML).

The first time you launch the utility you are prompted to select an appropriate font size to suit your display resolution.

After selecting the font size you are presented with the HTML version of Internet Service Manager.

If you are administering your Web site using any browser except IE, the browser will prompt you for a username and password before the contents of the HTML files in the directory are returned. If you are using IE, it will try to use the current username and password, that is, the username and password used when logging on at the client. If those values aren't valid on the server, you will be prompted for a username and password.

You can also access the HTML version of ISM by launching a browser and entering the following URL:

```
http://computername:<port>/iisadmin/
    default.htm.
```

The port is the one configured for the Administrative Web Site. This is set to 4867 by default. If you omit the port number from the URL, IIS 4.0 will attempt to identify you as an operator. If you are identified as an operator, you will be able to perform those activities operators are permitted to perform, but will not have all of the permissions of an administrator.

If you have not changed the Directory Security settings on the Administration Web Site and you are running a browser from any computer other than your IIS 4.0, you will receive the following message when attempting to access the Web site:

By default, all computers except the localhost (identified by its loopback address 127.0.0.1), are denied access to the administrative site. You must be working at an authorized workstation to use the HTML ISM utility.

Remote Site Administration

To authorize a remote workstation to use the HTML ISM utility, perform the following:

- Launch the Internet Service Manager on your IIS 4.0.
- Locate the Web site you wish to remotely administer.
- Right-click on the Web site and select **Properties**.
- Click on the **Directory Security** tab.
- Click on the **Edit** button for IP Address and Domain Name Restrictions.
- Add the IP address or DNS host name for the remote system you wish to authorize.

Using the HTML ISM Utility

You can perform many site administration tasks using a browser and the HTML ISM utility. From the opening page, you can:

- Create a new directory.
- Delete an existing directory.
- Rename an existing directory.
- View the properties of a Web site.

Creating a Directory

To create a directory, click on the Create link. Enter a name for the directory and click on **OK**.

Deleting a Directory

To delete a directory, click on the Delete link. Select the directory to delete, then click on **OK**.

Renaming a Directory

To rename a directory, select the directory to rename and click on the Rename link. Enter the new name for the directory, then click on **OK**.

Viewing and Modifying Site Properties

To view and modify the properties of a Web site, select the site and click on the Properties link.

Click on the Operators link to view the Web Site Operators list.

Click on the Performance link to view IIS 4.0 Performance properties.

Click on the ISAPI Filters link to view installed ISAPI Filters.

Click on the Home Directory link to manage the site's Directory Properties.

Click on the Documents link to manage the site's Documents properties.

Click on the Security link to manage the site's Security properties.

Click on the HTTP Headers link to manage the site's HTTP Headers properties.

Click on the Error Messages link to view the site's Custom Errors properties.

Three important warnings to remember when using the HTML ISM utility:

1. If you are using a non-IE browser, do not turn off Basic Authentication while you are administering IIS 4.0. You will be disconnected and will not be able to log in to remote administration.

2. If you stop the WWW service, you will be disconnected and will not be able to restart it using HTML ISM.

3. If you delete the iisadmin virtual directory on the server you are administering, you will be unable to use HTML-ISM to administer that computer.

Remote management makes it easier to manage multiple servers. Any IIS 4.0 that has HTML ISM installed on it can be managed over the Internet, if you have the proper username and password and the appropriate permissions are configured on the Administrative Web Site.

Scripting Overview

Prior to the release of Windows NT 4.0 Option Pack, administrators were limited to writing DOS batch files when they wanted to automate administrative tasks. Part of Microsoft's strategy for future versions of the Windows and Windows NT operating systems is the Zero-Administration Initiative. An important element of this is to provide administrators and developers with powerful scripting abilities and a standard object model they can use to manipulate operating system objects and system services.

You are already somewhat familiar with the ability of Internet Explorer and Internet Information Server to run scripts. This is how they execute VBScript and JScript either on the client or on the server. Windows NT 4.0 Option Pack includes two tools, the Windows Scripting Host and the Command Line Scripting Host, that allow you to run scripts without displaying them in a browser. Let's look at both of these utilities.

Windows Scripting Host

If you select to install the Windows Scripting Host (wscript.exe), it will be installed in the *systemroot*\System32\ directory. It will also be registered as the default application to run when a VBScript (.vbs) or JScript (.js) file is run. You will see a little later how you can change the default scripting host to the Command-Line Scripting Host (cscript.exe).

To run a script that does not require command-line parameters, simply double-click on the icon for the script. If the script requires command-line parameters, you will have to use the **Run** command and type the following:

```
scriptname parameters
```

    or

```
wscript scriptname parameters
```

The Windows Scripting Host has several properties you can set to influence how it runs all scripts on the system. To set the Windows Scripting Host's properties, double-click on wscript.exe.

You can set the number of seconds scripts will execute before being terminated, as well as whether or not to display a logo when a script is executed from the command prompt. These properties can also be set on individual scripts by right-clicking on the script and running **Properties**. Click on the **Script** tab. When you close the dialog, a .wsh file with the same name as the script is created. Use this file instead of the .vbs or .js file to run the script using these individualized properties.

Command-Line Scripting Host

The Command-Line Scripting Host can be run from a command prompt. It uses the syntax:

```
CScript scriptname.extension
    [//option...]  [/arguments...]
```

Each *option* should be preceded by two slashes. Each argument should be preceded by a single slash. The arguments are command-line parameters that are passed to the script. The following options are supported:

//?	Show the options available for the command. Executing CScript with no script name will provide the same result.
//B	Batch Mode: Do not display script errors and user prompts.
//I	Interactive Mode: Display script errors and user prompts.
//H:CScript or **WScript**	Use this option to change the default scripting host to either CScript or WScript.
//S	This option will save the command options used. The next time the current user executes a script, those options will be used by default. This is set on a per-user basis.
//T:*nn*	Timeout: This option sets the maximum number of seconds the script should be allowed to run. This is the same as setting the property for the script.
//logo	Display a banner when the script is executed. This is the option by default.
//nologo	Do not display a banner when the script is executed.

Some Sample Scripts

When the Windows Scripting Host is installed, some sample administrative scripts are installed at *systemroot*\inetsrv\adminsamples. They are not simple scripts for the non-programmer to understand. However, they may prove useful for your day-to-day administrative needs. Information about the arguments they require can be discovered by double-clicking on them.

Installing Microsoft Site Server Express

Microsoft Site Server Express can be installed when you install Internet Information Server or you can add it later. To add it after installation, insert the Windows NT 4.0 Option Pack CD-ROM and let it run **AutoPlay**. Click on **Install**. Click on **Install Windows NT 4.0 Option Pack**. Select to open the file from its current location and click on **OK**. After the Setup program launches, click on **Next**. Click on **Add/ Remove**.

You can select to install all of the components of Microsoft Site Server Express 2.0 or you can view the available subcomponents by clicking on **Show Subcomponents**. The available subcomponents are shown below.

You can select to install the Content Analyzer, the Usage Analyzer, the Posting Acceptor, or the Web Publishing Wizard. The purpose of each of these will be discussed a little later in the chapter. After you have selected the components you wish to install, click on **OK**. Click on **Next**. Your Internet Information Server will be reconfigured and the files will be copied to your disk.

Site Server Express Components

These components are:

- Content Analyzer

    This component provides a visual representation of a Web site. It can be used to analyze the documents on your Web site to locate broken hypertext links. You can also generate reports in HTML format to view details on Web site content.

- Usage Import and Report Writer

    Use these components to analyze IIS 4.0 log files.

- Posting Acceptor 1.01

    This component provides RFC 1867-compliant Web document posting over HTTP.

You can also upgrade to the full version of Microsoft Site Server 3.0 or Microsoft Site Server 3.0 Commerce Edition.

To view the Site Server Express 2.0 components, run **Start/Programs/Windows NT 4.0 Option Pack/ Microsoft Site Server Express 2.0**.

Select the **Upgrade to Microsoft Site Server** option to view information on added functionality provided by version 3.0. Your browser will launch and you will be taken to the appropriate location on the Microsoft Web Site.

Using the Posting Acceptor

The Microsoft Posting Acceptor is an add-on tool for IIS 4.0 that allows Web content developers to upload files to your site using HTTP.

IIS 4.0, Microsoft Peer Web Services, and Microsoft Personal Web Server can use the Posting Acceptor to allow the posting of content from a number of sources including:

- Microsoft Web Publishing Wizard/API
- Microsoft Internet Explorer
- Netscape Navigator 2.02 or later

The Posting Acceptor utility can use the Microsoft Content Replication System (CRS) to simultaneously distribute content to multiple servers.

The Content Analyzer

The Content Analyzer can be used to analyze the objects on your Web site or on other Web sites. This section will look at the following topics:

- Running the Content Analyzer
- Using WebMaps
- Tree View WebMap
- Cyberbolic View WebMap
- Using Site Summary Reports
- Site Summary Report Statistics
- Using the Quick Search Feature
- Displaying Pages

Let's start by looking at how to launch the Content Analyzer.

Running the Content Analyzer

To launch the Content Analyzer, run **Start/Programs/ Windows NT 4.0 Option Pack/Microsoft Site Server Express 2.0/Content Analyzer**.

When you launch the Content Analyzer you are presented with the following options:

- View User's Guide
- New WebMap
- Open WebMap

You can also elect to bypass the opening dialog by selecting the **Don't show this dialog box at startup anymore** option.

Using WebMaps

WebMaps allow you to visualize your Web site's directory structure in two different viewing modes. These are:

- Tree View WebMap
- Cyberbolic View WebMap

To create a new WebMap, launch **Content Analyzer** and select **New** from the **File** menu. You are presented with the option of creating the new WebMap from a URL or from a file.

Select the **Map from URL** option.

Enter the URL of the site you would like to map. To create a map of the Default Web Site on the local computer, you can use http://localhost for the Home Page Address (URL) value, then click on **OK**. The **Options** button lets you customize several important settings.

The options you can set include:

- Ignore Case of URLs

  Internet Information Server treats URLs as case-insensitive. This means that the same object might be referred to by uppercase in one document and lowercase in another. If you do not ignore case when creating your WebMap, these will be considered separate objects. If you are creating a WebMap of a UNIX server, you should not ignore case.

- Verify Offsite Links

  It is likely that you provide links to other Web sites. If you select this option, the existence of those objects will be verified. This may be necessary sometimes, but it will increase the amount of time it takes to create the map.

- Honor Robot Protocol

  By default, the Content Analyzer will ignore sites that restrict spiders. To map sites that restrict spiders, turn this option off. Keep in mind, however, that while this might be appropriate when analyzing your own Web site, it is not appropriate when creating a WebMap of a Web site that belongs to some other company.

- User Agent

  This is set to the Microsoft Content Analyzer by default. However, if you provide special handling for certain browsers on your Web site, you will probably want to create a WebMap using various User Agents.

After you have typed the URL of the Web site you would like to analyze, you will be prompted for a destination.

You can view the status of the Content Analyzer as it reads directories and documents.

A progress indicator is displayed as the analyzer generates the Site Summary Report.

Internet Explorer launches automatically to display the Site Summary Report.

Click on the WebMap for localhost link. This option allows you to save the WebMap to a file.

After you have specified a path, click on **Save**.

When the WebMap has been saved, click on **OK**.

Scroll down to view the contents of the report. Minimize your browser.

Maximize the Content Analyzer utility.

The Tree View WebMap is displayed in the left window pane while the Cyberbolic View WebMap is displayed in the right window pane.

Tree View WebMap

The Tree View WebMap is similar in appearance to the Windows NT Explorer. Icons are assigned to each object. The home page is shown at the top of the window pane. Icons are represented in levels with the home page representing Level 1, similar to a book outline.

Control icons (small gray squares) can contain a plus sign (+), minus sign (-), or question mark (?). By clicking various control icons you can alter the view of the Cyberbolic View WebMap. Click on the plus sign to expand and the minus sign to contract an object. Question marks in control icons indicate that a page has not yet been examined by Content Analyzer.

Cyberbolic View WebMap

The Cyberbolic View WebMap provides a dynamic visualization of a Web site. This view displays relationships between Web objects. By clicking on different control icons you can change the starting point of the Cyberbolic View WebMap. As you click on objects in the Cyberbolic View, the object will move left or right of center. Two toolbar buttons can be used to modify the view's orientation.

You can select the **Display Options** command from the **View** menu to determine which objects to display and other display-related parameters.

Full-length descriptions are displayed as you move the mouse cursor over an object in the Cyberbolic View.

You cannot collapse or expand levels in the Cyberbolic View.

Using Site Summary Reports

Site Summary Reports are designed to aid your understanding of your Web site's structure and the content types used. Reports include:

- Page, image, and application object counts and sizes.
- The number of objects and links that are broken, missing, or functional.
- Number of levels, starting at the home page.
- Average links per page.

You can generate a Site Summary Report in one of three ways:

- Create a new WebMap and select the **Generate Site Reports** option.
- Click on the **Generate Site Reports** button in the toolbar.

- Select **Generate Site Reports** from the **Tools** menu.

Site Summary Report Statistics

The Site Summary report provides three categories of statistics. These are Object Statistics, Status Summary (Onsite and Offsite), and Map Statistics.

Object Statistics

The following is a description of Site Summary Report Object statistics:

- Pages

  The number pages and their total size

- Images

  The number of images and their total size

- Gateways

  The number of links associated with Common Gateway Interface (CGI) scripts using GET or POST commands

- Internet

  The number of links pointing to Internet services objects

- Java

  The number of links to Java applications and their total size

- Applications

  The number of links to applications and their total size

- Audio

  The number of links to audio objects and their total size

- Video

  The number of links to video objects and their total size

- Text

  The number of links to text objects and their total size

- WebMaps

  The number of links to WebMap objects and their total size

- Other Media

  The number of links to other media objects and their total size

- Totals

  Web site total objects and their total size

Status Summary—Onsite & Offsite

The Status Summary statistics are used to determine the condition of your Web site's links, both Onsite and Offsite. Onsite statistics provide information on local links while Offsite statistics provide information on remote links.

The following is a list of Status Summary Onsite and Offsite statistics:

- OK
- Not found (code 404)
- Other Errors
- Unverified

Map Statistics

Map statistics provide additional information about your Web site including:

- Map Date

  The creation date of the report

- Levels

  The number of Levels of the analyzed site

- Average Links per Page

  The average number of links per page

Using the Quick Search Feature

The Content Analyzer utility includes eight pre-configured Quick Search options to help you detect errors or possible problems on your Web site. To start a Quick Search, select **Quick Search** from the **Tools** menu.

The eight pre-configured Quick Searches are:

- Broken Links

    Locates links whose target is unavailable.

- Home Site Objects

    Displays objects that are in your home page's domain. Determines if damaged objects can be accessed and repaired through the local security structure.

- Images without ALT

    Locates images that do not include the optional ALT text string.

- Load Size Over 32 KB

    Locates resources that are larger than 32 kilobytes in size.

- Non-Home Site Objects

    Displays objects that are not in your home page's domain.

- Not Found Objects (404)

    Locates objects that could not be located when the WebMap was generated.

- Unavailable Objects

    Displays objects that could not be located or were not available when the WebMap was created.

- Unverified Objects

    Displays objects that have not been checked for accessibility.

Displaying Pages

You can load a particular Web page by double-clicking on it in the Cyberbolic View. This is helpful because it allows you to view the page as users will view it. If you click on hyperlinks while in the browser, the current location in the WebMap will also be adjusted.

Generating Log Files

Site Usage reports are generated by creating and analyzing log files. You must enable logging for your Web site or FTP site in order to generate log files.

To enable logging, view the Properties of your Web or FTP site. Click on the **Web Site** or **FTP Site** tab and select the **Enable Logging** option. You can select a format for your log file. If you plan to analyze the log file using the Usage Analyzer, you should create the file using W3C Extended Log File Format. The W3C Extended Log File Format is an ASCII file that can be customized to contain various types of information. Selecting ODBC Logging will let you store the logged information in a relational database, but it requires you to create the database and a DSN. Logging to a database will also use more processor time and could impact performance. Choosing NCSA logging creates an ASCII file, but the information is preconfigured and more limited than that provided by the W3C extended format.

Log File Management

The Extended Logging properties sheet allows you to tailor the tracking and logging of server activity. For most installations the default logging options are acceptable. Log file management is an important component of IIS 4.0 management.

Log files track users who've visited your site, time of visit, documents requested, and downloaded/uploaded files.

The **Extended Properties** page allows you to select from twenty different events that may be logged.

Log File Contents

IIS 4.0 log files are comma-delimited ASCII files that contain hyphens in fields where there is no valid value (empty fields). The order of fields in the file is:

> Client IP Address
>
> Client Username
>
> Date
>
> Time
>
> Service
>
> Computer Name
>
> IP Address of Server
>
> Processing Time
>
> Bytes Received
>
> Bytes Sent
>
> Service Status Code
>
> Windows NT Status Code
>
> Name of Operation
>
> Target of Operation

Because every single Web and FTP access generates a logging entry, log files can grow to be very large. No facility is provided to limit log file size.

Log File Analysis

A tool such as Webtrends (www.webtrends.com) is useful for analyzing log file data.

Generating a Report From a Log File

To generate a report from a log file, you need to import the file into the Content Analyzer database. This is done with the Usage Import utility. To launch the Usage Import utility, click on **Start/Programs/Windows NT 4.0 Option Pack/Microsoft Site Server Express 2.0/Usage Import**.

The first time you launch the Usage Import utility you will be informed that no sites have been configured. Click on **OK**.

Select the log file format you specified for the Web or FTP site, then click on **OK**.

Enter the name of your DNS domain in the Local domain field, then click on **OK**.

Enter the URL for your home page, such as http://localhost.

Click on the **Excludes** tab. Select any hosts or image types that you wish to exclude from the report, then click on **OK**.

The Usage Import utility will now finish loading.

Report Writer

The Report Writer utility is used to analyze and produce reports from your Web or FTP site log files.

To launch the Report Writer utility, click on **Start/Programs/Windows NT 4.0 Option Pack/Microsoft Site Server Express 2.0/Report Writer**.

Click on **OK** to create a report from the Report Writer catalog.

Click on the plus sign (+) next to Detail Reports to expand the list. Scroll down to view the various options.

Click on the minus sign (-) next to Detail Reports to contract the list. Click on the plus sign (+) next to Summary Reports to expand the list. Scroll down to view the various options.

Click on the minus sign (-) next to Detail Reports to contract the list. Re-open the Detail Reports folder and select one of the options, then click on **Next**. We've selected the Browser and operating system detail report.

Determine the date scope of the report, then click on **Next**.

Select any filters you wish to employ to limit the amount of information contained in the report, then click on **Finish**.

The results of the report are displayed.

Detail Reports

The Report Writer utility includes nine pre-configured Detail Reports. These are:

- Bandwidth

  This report displays byte transfers in hourly, daily, and weekly increments. You can determine server trends and use the data to create a baseline for your server.

- Browser and Operating System

  This report provides information on client browser market share, versions, security, and local operating system. You can determine the types of browsers and operating systems being used to access your site.

- Geography

  This report displays the cities, states, provinces, and countries of users who have visited your site.

- Hit

  This report displays the number of hits on your server. This report is useful for site expansion and capacity planning.

- Organization

  This report displays the names of the companies of users who have visited your site.

- Referrer

  This report displays the names of sites that have referred users to your site through a hypertext link.

- Request

  This report displays the least/most requested documents on your site.

- User

  This report displays the number of visitors to your site, as well as first-time visitors, users per organization, document requests, and length of stay.

- Visits

  This report displays the requests per visit, average length of stay, pages most likely to be accessed first and last, and visit trends.

Summary Reports

The Report Writer utility includes twelve pre-configured Summary Reports. These are:

- Bandwidth

  This report displays bandwidth used by the site by day of week, hour of day, and work hours vs. non-work hours. This report can be used to determine bandwidth problems, such as abnormal usage or saturation.

- Browser and Operating System

    This report provides information on client browsers and local operating system.

- Executive

    This report provides a summary of Detail Reports information.

- Executive Summary for Extended Logs

    This report provides a summary of extended Log File Detail reports.

- Geography

    This report provides a summary of the Geography Detail report.

- Hit

    This report displays a summary of the Hit Detail report.

- Organization

    This report displays a summary of the Organization Detail report.

- Path

    This report displays the sequence of user page requests over a client session.

- Referrer

    This report displays a summary of the Referrer Detail report.

- Request

    This report displays a summary of the Request Detail report.

- User

    This report displays a summary of the User Detail report.

- Visits

    This report displays a summary of the Visit Detail report.

Summary Reports

The Report Writer utility includes twelve pre-configured Summary Reports. These are:

- Bandwidth

    This report displays bandwidth used by the site by day of week, hour of day, and work hours vs. non-work hours. This report can be used to determine bandwidth problems, such as abnormal usage or saturation.

- Browser and Operating system

    This report provides information on client browsers and local operating system.

- Executive

    This report provides a summary of Detail Reports information.

- Executive Summary for Extended Logs

    This report provides a summary of extended Log File Detail reports.

- Geography

    This report provides a summary of the Geography Detail report.

- Hit

    This report displays a summary of the Hit Detail report.

- Organization

    This report displays a summary of the Organization Detail report.

- Path

    This report displays a summary of the Organization Detail report.

- Referrer

    This report displays a summary of the Referrer Detail report.

- Request

    This report displays a summary of the Request Detail report.

- User

    This report displays a summary of the User Detail report.

- Visits

    This report displays a summary of the Visit Detail report.

Hardware Performance Issues

The Windows NT 4.0 Server operating system requires significant resources to provide satisfactory performance for applications such as the Internet Information Server. You must provide a server hardware platform that is sufficient to service the clients that connect to your Web site.

Specific hardware and software requirements for IIS 4.0 were provided earlier in the course. These should be considered sufficient for lightly accessed servers only. A few important components to consider for high-performance server selection are:

- Server Central Processing Unit (CPU) Type and Speed

    The server CPU type and speed determine the maximum number of instructions per second that the Windows NT Server 4.0 computer can perform. The Windows NT 4.0 Server operating system is available for both Intel and DEC Alpha series CPUs.

    Currently, the highest performance CPU available from Intel is the Pentium II running at 400 MHz. The highest performance Alpha processor available at this time offers a 533-MHz clock speed.

    You should evaluate your overall Web site requirements and select the appropriate processor platform for your needs.

- Server Motherboard Cache RAM

    Cache RAM is high-speed (typically 10 nanoseconds or less), static memory used to buffer data transfers between the server's CPU and main memory. A minimum of 512 KB of cache RAM should be installed. Pentium II-based systems do not use motherboard cache RAM. Instead, Intel has packaged the CPU and cache RAM together in a single package for enhanced performance.

- Server Expansion Bus Type and Speed

    Expansion cards such as network adapters and disk controller boards also play a key role in determining overall system performance. The speed at which data can be transmitted through the server's expansion bus is determined by the bus type, bus width, and bus throughput.

    The most common expansion bus type in use today is the Peripheral Component Interconnect (PCI) bus introduced by Intel. The PCI bus has a maximum data throughput speed of 528 MBps. All Intel Pentium and Pentium II-based motherboards utilize the PCI bus. PCI technology has also been adapted by other manufacturers, including DEC and Apple Computer.

- Server Disk Channel

    The server disk channel is a critical component that has a profound effect on Internet Information Server performance. The primary responsibility of a Web server is to listen for client requests, read documents from a disk storage device, and transmit the document contents to the requesting client through a network interface.

    A slow disk channel will become a significant bottleneck in a Web server. For this reason, you should only install the highest performance disk drives and controllers in your server.

At the low-end of the performance scale are Ultra DMA Integrated Drive Electronics (IDE) and narrow Small Computer Systems Interface (SCSI) disk drives and controllers. Wide, Ultra SCSI drive/controller combinations offer good to moderate performance. You can utilize Redundant Arrays of Inexpensive (or Independent) Devices (RAID) technology for the best possible performance and reliability.

RAID arrays can be configured in several *Levels,* which provide several configuration options. The highest RAID level is Level 5, which offers the highest degree of performance and fault tolerance. Most high-quality disk arrays offer hot-swap capabilities that allow you to replace defective devices without needing to power the system down.

- Server RAM

    A very important factor in maximizing performance is the number of times IIS 4.0 locates the contents of a requested document in server cache memory. The bigger the cache, the better the performance. Adding RAM to your NT server can significantly improve its performance.

Critical Peripheral Components

- Tape Backup System

    A high-performance tape backup system is an absolute requirement for maintaining your Windows NT Server computer. Regular file system backups are an important part of system administration. You should purchase a DAT, DLT, or other high-performance tape backup unit and institute a backup schedule that only performs backups during off-peak hours.

- Uninterruptible Power Supply (UPS)

   All computers running the Windows NT Server 4.0 operating system should be connected to an uninterruptible power supply (UPS). A UPS provides protection against low-voltage conditions (brownouts) and power outages (blackouts). Most units also provide surge suppression to prevent equipment damage due to lightning strikes or other electrical problems.

Enhancing IIS 4.0 Performance

Internet Information Server 4.0 performance is also affected by software parameters that can be adjusted to accommodate various application requirements. To optimize the performance of your Web server, perform the following tasks.

- Use the Performance Tuning option to balance Windows NT Server memory requirements.

- Use the Bandwidth Throttling option to limit the total network bandwidth that can be consumed by the Web Service or by particular Web sites.

- Enable the HTTP Keep-Alives option so that client connections to the Web Service can remain open without timing out.

- Use the Windows NT Performance Monitor to determine overall server usage and create a baseline to assist in troubleshooting and future system expansion planning.

The Internet Service Manager utility is used to configure tuning parameters for Web Services.

Performance Tuning

The first step in optimizing your Web server is to verify that you are not under- or over-allocating server memory resources to IIS 4.0. This is controlled by the Performance Tuning option.

To view the current Performance Tuning configuration for your server, run **Start/Programs/Windows NT 4.0 Option Pack/Microsoft Internet Server/Internet Service Manager**.

Open the Internet Information Server folder, then open the webserver computer icon.

Right-click on Default Web Site and select **Properties**. Click on the **Performance** tab.

You should adjust the Performance Tuning slider based on the number of anticipated daily Web server document requests (connections). If you set the value slightly higher than the actual number of connections, performance will improve. If you set the value significantly higher than the actual number of connections you will waste server memory and other Services will not achieve peak performance.

Bandwidth Throttling

The allocation and management of network bandwidth is an ongoing issue in the administration of IIS 4.0. World Wide Web, video, audio, and other applications have boomed in popularity, significantly increasing bandwidth requirements on both large and small networks.

The cost of bandwidth varies. Bandwidth on a Local Area Network is relatively inexpensive. The cost of network adapters and hubs that transmit data at 100 Mbps has fallen tremendously. In addition, advanced switching products allow network designers to achieve maximum performance even on busy networks.

On the other hand, the cost of Wide Area Network bandwidth is relatively high and is likely to remain so for some time to come. Internet connectivity options range from 14.4-Kbps dial-up connections through DS-3 (45 Mbps) or faster service.

IIS 4.0 provides the Bandwidth Throttling feature to help you manage network bandwidth. Bandwidth Throttling affects only Web documents containing static information. Active content such as Active Server Pages (ASP), ISAPI Filters, and ISAPI Extensions are not affected.

The Bandwidth Throttling feature offers two forms of bandwidth control:

- Overall Web Site Bandwidth Throttling

    Use this option to reserve a portion of the total bandwidth of your Internet connection for internal network users.

- Individual Site Bandwidth Throttling

    Use this option to limit the maximum bandwidth used by a given Web site.

You must adjust these two options carefully as under- or over-allocating bandwidth to the server or to a particular site could have a negative impact on system performance.

Overall Web Server Bandwidth

You configure overall Web server bandwidth through the Web Server properties. You enable bandwidth throttling by selecting the **Enable Bandwidth Throttling** option. The default value (when enabled) is 1,024 Kbps. If your Internet connection has enough available bandwidth you may wish to increase this value. If you are using IIS 4.0 to host an Internet Web site, you will probably need to increase this value unless it will have an adverse affect on internal Internet users.

Individual Site Bandwidth Throttling

To configure the individual site bandwidth throttling option, right-click on the site's icon and select **Properties**. Click on the **Performance** tab.

You enable bandwidth throttling by selecting the **Enable Bandwidth Throttling** option. The default value (when enabled) is 1,024 Kbps and is likely to be too small for most applications.

HTTP Keep-Alives

When requesting documents from an HTTP server, clients connect to and disconnect from the server many times. This is not necessarily the most efficient method of communicating.

The **HTTP Keep-Alives** option allows client connections to the Web server to remain active rather than establishing a new connection with each additional request. This option is enabled by default and should remain enabled under normal circumstances.

The Effects of CGI and ISAPI on Server Performance

When 100 people access your Web site and request to execute the same ISAPI program, only a single copy of the program is kept in memory. In contrast, when 100 people access your Web site and request to execute the same CGI program, 100 copies of the program may be loaded into memory.

Whenever possible, use ISAPI programs instead of CGI programs.

Performance Monitor Overview

Performance Monitor can be used to:

- Check performance of system objects.
- Compare the performance of different systems.
- Gather data for more detailed analysis.
- Set alerts to occur when selected object parameters hit specified levels.

- Run executable commands or batch files when alerts occur.

- Create report screens displaying exact values in a timely manner.

Windows NT Server includes a standard set of performance counters for objects such as the memory cache, disk usage, processor, processes, and threads. Network counters are installed according to the network software running at the system. Some applications, such as SQL Server for Windows NT or Microsoft Systems Management Server (SMS), also install their own counters.

Performance Monitor Views

The Performance Monitor supports four view options so that you can display information in a format that best suits your needs. The available views are:

- Chart

  In this view, the values of selected counters are displayed as either a line graph or a histogram. The graphical representation makes it easy to monitor available resources or to see performance bottlenecks. This view can become confusing, however, if you try to track too many simultaneous counters.

- Alert

  The Alert view allows you to select counters and instances to be monitored, each with an alert threshold value that you specify. When a counter reaches the threshold, an alert is generated.

- Log

  Creating a log file lets you gather data from selected counters over a period of time and perform offline analysis later. This gives you a way of doing detailed analysis of performance data. Because you can track multiple machines in a single file, you can also perform detailed comparative analysis.

- Report

  The Report view displays the current values for selected counters in a report format. This view allows you to compare exact values, and makes it relatively easy to simultaneously display a larger number of counters and still make sense of them all.

Performance Monitor defaults to the Chart view, displaying data in a line graph format. As you switch between foreground views, those in the background remain active.

Charts

The Add to Chart dialog lets you set the values to be displayed in a chart.

Computer	This is the system from which data is collected.
Object	The object identifies a set of related counters, such as logical disk, physical disk, NetBEUI, and so on.
Counter	This is a list of individual counters available for the selected object.
Instance	If there is more than one instance of an object running, each instance is listed and may be selected separately.

The Color, Scale, Width, and Style selections let you control the appearance of the chart.

Alerts

The Alert view lets you monitor system activity and generate an alert when the alert criteria are met or exceeded. Alerts use the same object, counter, and instance selections as charts. You set the value at which an alert is generated. You can also specify a program to run, either an executable or a batch file, when the alert occurs. This can be set to run only on the first occurrence, or on every occurrence of the alert.

Logs

When selecting log contents, you only make object selections. All of the counters for that object are recorded at the interval you set.

After making your object selections, you must choose **Log** from the **Options** menu, give the log file a name, and click on the **Start Log** button to start recording data.

Report

Reports use the same object, counter, and instance selections as charts. The difference is that reports provide you with exact numerical values. You can set the update period, which defaults to updating the report every five seconds.

This is helpful when you need accurate data regarding system activity or want to make exact comparisons between systems.

IIS 4.0 Counters

The following categories contain counters that can be monitored by Performance Monitor:

- Active Server Pages
- Browser
- Cache
- Content Index

- Content Index Filter
- FTP Service
- HTTP Content Index
- Internet Information Services Global
- Logical Disk
- Memory
- NBT Connection
- NNTP Commands
- NNTP Server
- NWLink IPX
- NWLink NetBIOS
- NWLink SPX
- Objects
- Paging File
- Physical Disk
- Process
- Processor
- Redirector
- Server
- Server Work Queues
- SMTP Server
- System
- Telephony
- Thread
- Web Service

Many IIS 4.0-related counters are repeated for the various objects. This is because you will want to track many of the same values for different services.

Using Performance Monitor

To launch the Performance Monitor utility, run **Start/ Programs/Administrative Tools (Common)/ Performance Monitor**.

Before any information is displayed, you need to select counters for the parameters you wish to monitor. Click on the **Edit** menu and select **Add to Chart**.

Click on the Object field and select the Web Service object.

If you are not sure what a particular counter is used for, select the counter and click on **Explain** to view a description.

Click on **Add** to add the Bytes Total/sec counter to the chart. Scroll down to select the Current Anonymous Users counter, then click on **Add**. Scroll down to select the Maximum Connections counter, then click on **Add**. Click on **Done** to begin viewing the chart.

You should not see much activity unless there are clients accessing your Web server.

Performance Report

You can use the Performance Monitor utility to produce a performance report and then export it to a spreadsheet or other application for further analysis. To generate a performance report, select the Report view.

Select **Add to Report** from the **Edit** menu. Add the desired counters, then click on **Done**. To update displayed counters, select **Update Now** from the **Options** menu.

To export report data for use in another application, select **Export Report** from the **File** menu. Reports may be exported in TSV or CSV format.

Index